Women Pilgrims in Late Medieval England

Women Pilgrims in Late Medieval England explores the important phenomenon of women and pilgrimage in the late Middle Ages. This interdisciplinary and thoughtful book examines the medieval perceptions of pilgrimage, gender and space. It studies real life examples of women pilgrims such as Margery Kempe and Elizabeth de Burgh as evidence as well as literary texts and women pilgrims represented in the visual arts.

Women Pilgrims in Late Medieval England investigates how widespread women pilgrims were, their motivation, the social and familial dynamics of medieval pilgrimage and the representation of women pilgrims in literature, art and historical documents. This stimulating study will herald the way for further discussion and research into medieval women pilgrims.

Susan Signe Morrison is Associate Professor of English at Southwest Texas State University.

D0421649

Routledge Research in Medieval Studies

Leabharlanna Poibli Chathair Baile Átha Cliath

Dublin City Public Libraries

Women Pilgrims in Late Medieval England

Private piety as public performance

Susan Signe Morrison

London and New York

First published 2000
by Routledge
2 Park Square, Milton Park, Abingdon, Oxfordshire OX14 4RN

Simultaneously published in the USA and Canada
by Routledge
711 Third Avenue, New York, NY 10017
First issued in paperback 2014

Routledge is an imprint of the Taylor and Francis Group, an informa company

Transferred to Digital Printing 2006

© 2000 Susan Signe Morrison

Typeset in Garamond by
HWA Text and Data Management Ltd

All rights reserved. No part of this book may be reprinted or reproduced or
utilized in any form or by any electronic, mechanical, or other means, now
known or hereafter invented, including photocopying and recording, or in
any information storage or retrieval system, without permission in writing
from the publishers.

British Library Cataloguing in Publication Data
A catalogue record for this book is available from the British Library

Library of Congress Cataloging in Publication Data
Morrison, Susan Signe, 1959–
    Women pilgrims in late medieval England: private piety and public
    performance /
Susan Signe Morrison.
      p. cm. – (Routledge research in medieval studies)
    Includes bibliographical references and index.
    1. Christian pilgrims and pilgrimages–England–History. 2. Christian
    women–Religious life–England–History. 3. Church history–Middle
    Ages, 600–1500. I. Title. II. Series.

    BX2320.5.G7 M67 2000
    263'.04242'082–dc21   99-087891

ISBN 978-0-415-22180-1 (hbk)
ISBN 978-1-138-00746-8 (pbk)

Contents

Figures

Acknowledgements

I am grateful to numerous people who have shown support over the years in my efforts to pursue this project, particularly Michel-André Bossy, Geoffrey Russom, and Elizabeth Kirk. I would also like the thank the National Endowment for the Humanities (NEH), without whose support in the form of a Fellowship this book could never have been finished. The NEH is also to be thanked for a Summer Institute on Chaucer and Langland which it supported and which inspired me to continue in pursuing this research. I would like to thank Elizabeth Robertson, James Simpson, Sarah Beckwith and, most especially, David Benson, for their wonderful knowledge and joy in purveying it. The other participants on the NEH Institute were delightful and stimulating scholars whose comments provoked and challenged, particularly Joan Baker and Kathy Hewett-Smith. I would also like to thank the anonymous reader whose many good suggestions helped me revise this book.

Southwest Texas State University also supported this project with numerous summer research grants. For their support and advice, I would also like to thank Jack Gravitt, Lydia Blanchard, Tom Grimes and Paul Kens. Mimi Tangum of the Office for Research and Sponsored Programs was a wonderful leader with demanding standards. At the same office I would like to express my appreciation to Marilyn Douglas and June Hankins for their willingness always to help. For his knowledge, suggestions and comments over the past few years, my gratitude goes to Edgar Laird and, for his loyal support, Daniel Lochman. Many thanks as well to Laufey V. Bustany and Einar Petursson of the Arni Magnusson Institute, Reykjavik, for the information about Icelandic pilgrims. Mark Hansen is also to be thanked for his many suggestions in what theorists to pursue. Various students have also provided much stimulation and in particular I would like to acknowledge Susan Lucas and Jason King. Both Laura Sewell and Jessica Green were invaluable in allowing me to work on this book.

I am also grateful to those who helped me at the British Library, Bodleian Library, the Museum of London, the Huntington Library and the Royal Commission on the Historical Monuments of England in Swindon. At Southwest Texas State University, Melvia Randle and her staff were always good-humoured about the many interlibrary loan requests I made.

My parents first took me on a pilgrimage when I was seven, and so they introduced me to this wonderful topic and experience. Additionally, they have supported and sustained my interest over the years and provided leads to new sources. My mother,

Joan, in particular is to be thanked for accompanying me on a pilgrimage to Walsingham and having a terrific sense of adventure and humour.

I especially would like to thank my husband, Jim Kilfoyle, for his painstaking reading of numerous drafts. He was also willing to see every church on the Pilgrims' Way and offered unflagging support, even when yet another rood screen loomed before us. His unfailing humour and inventive imagination, rivalled only by Chaucer's, enabled me to finish the pilgrimage to Canterbury. I look forward to many other pilgrimages, both secular and religious, accompanied by him. I would also like to thank my daughter, Sarah, for not deleting everything when she banged on the computer keys. She and Jim are my inspiration always.

Introduction

As a professor in an English department, I regularly teach Chaucer and *The Book of Margery Kempe*. A number of years ago I went to the library to find a book on women pilgrims. I wanted to compare the fictional Wife of Bath and the historical Margery Kempe to other women pilgrims who actually existed in the late Middle Ages so I could see how the figures I dealt with in the classroom adhered to or deviated from the norm. After a long search I realized there was no such book. That is how this study came to be written.

Evidence exists that many women went on pilgrimage. Using historical sources, Jonathan Sumption speculates that '[i]t is possible that at the close of the middle ages women formed the majority of visitors at many shrines'.[1] Archeological finds have uncovered remains indicating pilgrimage undertaken by women. For example, both men's and women's graves have been found to contain scallop shells, the symbol of the pilgrimage to St James in Compostela.[2] But historical women pilgrims have generally been ignored as a category worthy of study, lumped in with generic pilgrims. Women pilgrims need to be addressed as a separate category since they could experience pilgrimage differently from men.

Ronald C. Finucane's suggestion in his study of miracle stories[3] that women constituted a large percentage of English pilgrims has not yet been adequately recognized in discussions of medieval pilgrimage. Both the historical condition and the literary output of medieval women have been extensively researched over the past two decades, but no work has yet attempted to compile and interpret references to female pilgrims, who constituted an important group in terms of numbers and in terms of their impact on artistic works produced in late medieval English society. Specific instances of women pilgrims illustrate the vital state of religion in late medieval England. For example, in the miracle stories of St William of Norwich by Thomas of Monmouth, numerous women's names come up as pilgrims. These include Claricia, wife of Gaufridus de Marc, who was probably the Lord of Markshall near Norwich. Muriel, wife of Alan de Setchy, both related to the sub-prior of Norwich, was a pilgrim as well. Also mentioned is Lady Mabel de Bec, daughter of Sir Bartholomew de Creak of North Creak in Norfolk. Other names included are Alditha, Hildebrand, Emma de Wighton, Agnes, Matilda, Godiva, the wife of Roger of North Tudenham, and a little girl from Mulbarton, a town five miles southwest of Norwich. A large proportion of the pilgrims in these stories was female.[4]

But miracle stories provide problematic evidence for women pilgrims' activities. As Eleonora C. Gordon has pointed out in her study of accidents among medieval children in the miracle stories of six English saints and martyrs, there are

> limitations to the historical validity of an analysis of miraculous recoveries. The subjects are self-selected ... We do not know how many petitioners failed to receive help. Parents who appear in accounts of miraculous recoveries among children, who prayed for help, made a vow, and undertook a pilgrimage, obviously cared deeply about their offspring. Indifferent or abusive parents ... do not appear ... The ending is always happy ... Nevertheless, even with these limitations, accounts of children's miraculous recoveries from accidental injuries provide valuable material about medieval children and about the response to those about them to life-threatening catastrophe.[5]

Finucane's recent volume *The Rescue of the Innocents: Endangered Children in Medieval Miracles*, mandatory reading for those interested in issues concerning medieval childhood, also acknowledges the problems with using miracle stories as historical evidence.[6] He explores two genres of documentation as sources for information about childhood in the late Middle Ages: canonization proceedings and books or registers of miracles (informal records of pilgrims' tales recorded by clerics at various shrines) concerning childbirth, accidents, illnesses, and purported deaths of children. These sources give detailed information about children's lives and their parents' interactions with them; however, the genres are restricted to incidences of illness or accidents which are happily resolved through a saint's intervention, leaving us to only guess at unsuccessful vows to saints. Additionally, witnesses may have exaggerated. The exact meaning of the witnesses, who spoke in the vernacular, may have been altered when their words were translated into church Latin, since translation inevitably commits interpretation. Clerical attitudes about sex, pregnancy, and childbirth could enter the records in the form of sermonizing.

Despite these limitations, Finucane convincingly shows how these sources supplement imaginative literature generally devoted to depicting the lives of the nobility as well as scientific, medical, legal, and ecclesiastical texts.[7] In his study of various shrines in England, *Miracles and Pilgrims: Popular Beliefs in Medieval England*, Finucane has shown a corrolation in the recorded English miracle stories which suggests that the majority of pilgrims who attended a local shrine were women (and lower class) while the majority of pilgrims attending a distant shrine were male (and upper class).[8] However, we will see how noble and rich women travel quite far and frequently on pilgrimage. André Vauchez, in his monumental study *Sainthood in the Later Middle Ages*, has shown that overall in the later Middle Ages, there was an increasing preference for recent and local saints over saints from the early centuries of Christianity.[9] Generally, popular cults were followed more by those less powerful in society, servants and apprentices, the small merchant class or craftsmen, while local cults were supported by the local gentry. Vauchez divides medieval Western Europe into two areas with differing characteristics concerning saints. England belongs to the non-Mediterranean west, along with France and the Low Countries, where the suffering leader, frequently the holy bishop-martyr, was venerated in a clerically constructed cult through the early fourteenth century.[10] Local devotions became increasingly popular in the later Middle Ages.

The proportion of male to female pilgrims varied from shrine to shrine, often due to the type of miracle promised by the mythology of the saint worshipped there.[11] The types of miracles recorded corresponded accordingly. Relief from crippling diseases and blindness were to be associated with the lower class and more commonly women, while non-healing miracles were most often for upper-class men.[12] Among the types of miracles recorded for Becket include those dealing with pregnancy, childbirth and sterility.[13] Godric of Finchale, a Norfolk man whose shrine was near Durham, was a saint who attracted more local, female and lower-class pilgrims. Of 244 recorded miracles, two-thirds were for women.[14] Similar miracle proportions in terms of gender are true for St Frideswide of Oxford. Of 108 posthumous miracles, two-thirds were for women. Finucane argues that Godric and Frideswide are unusual since most other English shrines catered to a majority of male pilgrims,[15] though I will show how Walsingham was another shrine which catered to women.

In a parallel study analysing the miracles recorded for the upper Bavarian pilgrimage site of Hohenpeißenberg, Rebekka Habermas discovered that women pilgrims constituted at least half of the pilgrims headed for this site.[16] In the stories a quarter of the miracles experienced by women concern gender-specific illnesses, often dealing with pregnancy, delivery and its aftermath. Three-quarters of the miracles women experienced, however, dealt with non-gender-specific illnesses, which Habermas uses as material for her argument that the pilgrimage experience with the direct access to Marian pictures and the ensuing miracle was essentially non-sexist, despite a patriarchal church structure. The class represented by these women pilgrims was, for the most part, the peasant class.[17] Habermas's work, with its focus on gender elements, is a model for the kind of future scholarship which needs to be undertaken for all pilgrimage sites. Unlike Habermas, however, I will be arguing that gender-specific illnesses, mainly having to do with fertility and childbirth, are fundamental to understanding women's relationship to pilgrimage. As I will argue, a gender-specific illness is never the private business of the woman suffering it. This, in turn, affects the act of pilgrimage the sufferer undertakes.

This book investigates the social and familial dynamics of medieval pilgrimage with particular focus on women pilgrims and how they were represented in literature, art, and historical documents. Many women travelled for the sake of the family, which was often centred on the woman's body, the body which could have sex, reproduce, carry a child, give birth and lactate. But if this body could not function properly – if it were sterile, if the child it carried miscarried, if the child it carried died or was sickly, if the body could not heal after birth, if the body could not produce milk to feed the child – then the body, a metonymy for a healthy functioning family, needed to be cured. The woman's body, then, stands for the family. If the woman's body is healed, so is the family. The woman's body is not private. It symbolizes the state of her family's health.

The family is not a private entity, discrete from society. While acts may have taken place within the household which we would call 'private', they were conditioned by and affected social interaction. As Daphne Spain has pointed out, '[t]he space outside the home becomes the arena in which social relations (i.e., status) are produced, while the space inside the home becomes that in which social relations are reproduced. Gender-status distinctions therefore are played out within the home as well as outside of it.'[18] Home and outside, private and public, are integrally linked to one another. The family reflects social structures, particularly in terms of gender relationships.

Georges Duby has shown how in the feudal period the line between the private and public spheres was fluid. Privacy is not a matter of space, but of power: 'Paradoxically, as society became increasingly feudal, there was less and less private life because power in all its forms had become more and more private.'[19] Private life was found in family life. But family was a fluid notion as well. Family or collective could be a voluntary group, such as *juvenis*, or young aristocratic males who travelled together.

> Thus, in feudal society, private space was divided, composed of two distinct areas: one fixed, enclosed, attached to the hearth; the other mobile, free to move through public space, yet embodying the same hierarchies and held together by the same controls. Within this mobile cell peace and order were maintained by a power whose mission was to organize a defense against the intrusion of the public authorities.[20]

As the Middle Ages wore on, personal privacy and piety increased. The twelfth century bore witness to the shift to more and more personal autonomy, as we can see in the rise of the genre of biography and the increase in anchoritic life style. The establishment by the Fourth Lateran Council in 1215 of annual confession, which was to be private, regular and compulsory, is a watershed event for interior spirituality. This internalization of piety was encouraged in thirteenth-century sermons.[21]

But where does the act of pilgrimage lie in terms of personal piety? The act of pilgrimage, an act of personal devotion, is a deeply social act. It is performed – often – for social reasons which, in the case of women pilgrims, are often family reasons. Pilgrimage is a religious activity, socially sanctioned, for healing the woman's body or the offspring of that body. If the pilgrimage succeeds, if the body is healed (gives birth when it could not before, lactates while it could not before, and so on), this, in turn, endorses the religious authorities who deemed a shrine a sacred space. If the family is well, so is the society which spins the family into its web. The distinctions between the woman's body and family, between family and society, between society and religious hegemony, are blurry. Any personal act of devotion becomes a public and political one during its performance by anyone, whether illustrious or obscure. Pilgrimage is a social construct and is viewed by society, represented by that society, and interpreted by that society. It becomes a legal enterprise in judicial pilgrimage (not discussed in this book) and is the site of contesting religious beliefs, as in the Lollard critique of pilgrimage. Pilgrimage is never 'naturally' undertaken. It is conditioned by and conditions society.

Pilgrimage breaks down the distinctions between seemingly discrete 'texts' – the sacred and profane, the body and society, the performer and the audience, even, ultimately, male and female. Pilgrimage exposes the porousness between boundaries, those between traditional binaries such as the sacred and profane, public and private, and audience and actor. Pilgrimage is penetrable, just as the woman's body can be sexually penetrated and, in secular literature, is sexualized and made open to public discourse. The woman's body, confined by flesh, represents the family which is a building block of the social order. This body is open to literary interpretation and is appropriated by the family, society, and public discourse. The sacred appropriates the profane, just as the secular realm utilizes sacred symbols. The performer, conditioned by society, can manipulate the audience in her performance of pilgrimage, at the same time empowering that audience into its own performance.

Art constitutes one element in the performance of pilgrimage. Determining how women pilgrims were represented visually and what visual art they themselves encountered will help us to understand how pilgrimage functioned spiritually for late medieval English women. This argument of the book continues recent discussions investigating the ways art – stained glass, statuary, rood screens, etc. – reflected and shaped female piety, as carried on in the work of Eamon Duffy, Roberta Gilchrist and in the Courtauld Institute conference, 'Art, Architecture, and Spirituality in the Later Middle Ages' (October 1994). I reconstruct how women pilgrims travelled spatially to Walsingham, which claimed to possess a few drops of the Virgin's milk. This was an enormously popular shrine in the wake of an intensified Marian cult. By understanding the pilgrimage experience using material culture, such as church art, we can better see how women pilgrims interacted in churches along pilgrimage routes. Church art gives us clues as to which pilgrims travelled along particular pilgrimage routes and what kinds of audience were expected. For example, mother saints were depicted on the north side (the traditionally 'female' side) of pilgrimage churches to Walsingham. Thus the women pilgrims would find these mother saints reflected opposite them spatially. The symbolism of the Walsingham shrine, the depiction of many saints whose legends involve milk, and the fact that the Milky Way was referred to as the Walsingham Way in late medieval England because it pointed north to the shrine, have led me to name this opening chapter of my book 'The Milky Way: women pilgrims and visual art'.

Chapter 2 provides a look at historical documents dealing with women and pilgrimage. Again, family plays a large part in pilgrimage activity, if only implicitly. Many widows undertook a pilgrimage after their husbands' deaths, presumably to pray for the dead spouse's soul. This personal act of piety is thus familial, to aid a spouse, and, by being familial, social, since this act is recorded in the social space of legal documents, wills, and papal letters.[22] Husbands and wives accompanied each other on pilgrimage, often for reasons of family (for example, a child's health). Spouses wrote to each other of pilgrimage. We also see women who were noble or well known undertaking pilgrimage with one another or with family. Historical documents render the personal act of piety a legal one. Economic interests propelled the need for extensive control and documentation of pilgrimage activity. The women designate power of attorney while they go abroad, which is a financial act. The women need a letter of protection, and, while under the king's protection, the monies they carry in and out of the realm are controlled. Papal letters dispensing commutation of vows often specify financial compensation for shrines. Inquisitions Post Mortem need to establish deaths to distribute property.

The official response to pilgrimage activity, primarily in the post-plague period, includes restrictions on movement. There were fears of false pilgrims, fuelling anxiety about social disorder. Pilgrims were often accused of abandoning their families. Henry VIII picks up on this convention in his justification for dissolving the monasteries. Concerning the pilgrim, he says,

> This man loketh for a new worlde. That man compasseth some depe drifte in his head. Some one hath an especiall devocion to goe to Ierusalem, to Rome, or to sainct Iames in Galice, leuyng his wife and children succourlesse in the meane while at home.[23]

I hope this book will show this criticism not to be universally accurate, since, paradoxically, so many pilgrims, both men and women, left the family for the sake of the family. Documents record women pilgrims who have become prey to danger and crime, yet pilgrims become the site of attempted control in legal documents. Pilgrimage is suspect by both the state and by the state's enemies, the heretical Lollards. The attempt by the state and Lollards to paint pilgrimage activities as liminal and potentially threatening shows how central such activity was to defining late medieval society. Three women – Margery Kempe (who will be discussed at greater length in a later chapter), Elizabeth de Burgh and Elizabeth of York – illustrate how women from two different classes had their pilgrimage activities recorded. Pilgrimage defies an easy division between control and lack of control. The very attempt to record and document pilgrims' activities indicates how certain aspects of the pilgrimage experience, such as spirituality, are unrecordable and only controlled with difficulty by an official body.

Chapter 3 continues the discussion of this movement through space by a never-private body by exploring medieval theories of space and perceptions of space. Space is a crucial arena for study since spatial processes and social processes are inseparably intertwined. After looking at various views of pilgrimage in terms of space and place, we can conclude spatial practice of pilgrimage is a gender-specific phenomenon. Further, pilgrimage breaks down the traditionally easy distinctions of sacred and secular or profane space. This ambiguity or breakdown can be seen in the pilgrimage window of stained glass at York Cathedral, which includes both parodic and normalized depictions of women.

Representation is a form of power. In literature, women pilgrims were often singled out for criticism and concern. Two letters from the Anglo-Saxon period foreshadow concerns which become topoi in the literature and official documents in the late medieval period in England, wherein the woman pilgrim was translated into an icon of transgressive mobility and social disorder. In a letter of 747, St Boniface suggests to Cuthbert, Archbishop of Canterbury, that his synod and princes

> … forbid matrons and veiled women to make these frequent journeys back and forth to Rome. A great part of them perish and few keep their virtue. There are

very few towns in Lombardy or Frankland or Gaul where there is not a courtesan or a harlot of English stock. It is a scandal and disgrace to your whole church.[24]

St Boniface's letter ushers in a topos of English women pilgrims, whose unmonitored movement on pilgrimage in the late medieval period becomes figured as and displaced into sexual activity in secular literature, as we see in Chapter 4. In a letter from 796, the Frankish king Charlemagne writes to King Offa of Mercia, 'Concerning pilgrims who desire to reach the thresholds of the blessed Apostles, they may go in peace. But we have discovered that certain persons fraudulently mingle with them for the sake of commerce: they are to pay the established toll at the proper places.[25] This concern over false pilgrims, particularly ones who have economic motives disguised by the garb of religion, becomes a heightened concern, almost an obsession, after the plague in mid-fourteenth-century England. Women pilgrims are images – real or camouflage – of the society of late medieval England. The topos of the sexual woman pilgrim is intimately related to medieval perceptions and representations of space. The fleshly body of the woman pilgrim taints sacred space. The women pilgrim figures, as we will see, reflect an anxiety on the part of post-plague English society of movement and hierarchical disruption, witnessed in documents which control the movements of pilgrims and assume the presence of false pilgrims. Further, we can see how gender constructs the pilgrimage experience. Duby has argued that the woman's body required constant surveillance. 'Anatomically she is destined to remain secluded in a supplementary enclosure, never to leave home without an escort … Before woman's body a wall is to be erected: the wall of private life.'[26] But the woman on pilgrimage cannot be private, even if she is experiencing personal devotion. A woman in public space makes herself open to interpretation. The woman pilgrim in secular literary works becomes the symbol of a disorderly public body, while the woman pilgrim in religious texts remains under the control of religious and political ideology, appropriated by the generic conventions of saints' legends.

This bifurcated image of women pilgrims in literature, the sexual, suspect woman in secular works and the valorized one in religious texts, can be seen in Margery Kempe's *Book*, which is explored in Chapter 5. Kempe utilizes the topoi present in literature to transform herself from the secular transgressive woman, to the appropriated, orthodox one of sacred literature. An examination of another binary follows. The ambiguity or breakdown between performer and audience can be seen in Kempe's recorded life, which illustrates the performative nature of pilgrimage. Kempe's visions catapult her into performance – she assists at Christ's birth or interacts and speaks with saints. Kempe becomes a spectacle which we spectators find we must interpret, thereby rendering us actors and spectacles ourselves.

The last chapter opens up questions for future research into women pilgrims, looking at the family in pilgrimage literature, where it is present and where it is absent. Chaucer, Kempe, and Langland all use family conjoined with pilgrimage in differing ways. I would argue that Langland's use of family and pilgrimage records the importance of family for pilgrimage activities of both men and women. Ultimately we perform Kempe's life and text.

By examining literary and historical documents, as well as material cultural artifacts, this exploration of woman and pilgrimage attempts an interdisciplinary study of an important phenomenon of the later Middle Ages. One of the challenges in this project was the detective work of finding real women pilgrims and, secondly, seeing how they fit in with the better known examples in literature, such as the Wife of Bath, or the figure of Margery Kempe, who has received much attention in recent years. My hope is that the theoretical issues I raise open up space for further discussion into aspects of gender and pilgrimage.

Notes

1 Jonathan Sumption, *Pilgrimage: An Image of Mediaeval Religion*, Totowa, NJ, Rowman and Littlefield, 1975, p. 262. See also Kurt Köster, *Ausgrabungen in Schleswig, Pilgerzeichen und Pilgermuscheln von Mittelalterlichen Santiagostraßen*, Neumünster, Karl Wachholtz Verlag, 1983, pp. 151–2.
2 Köster, op. cit., pp. 151–2.
3 *Miracles and Pilgrims: Popular Beliefs in Medieval England*, London, Dent, 1977.
4 See *The Life and Miracles of St William of Norwich by Thomas of Monmouth*, A. Jessopp and M. R. James, eds, Cambridge, Cambridge University Press,1896.
5 Eleanora C. Gordon, 'Accidents Among Medieval Children As Seen From the Miracles of Six English Saints and Martyrs,' *Medical History* 35, 1991, pp. 145–63, here p. 146. Also on the topic of using saints' lives as historical source material see Ronald C. Finucane, 'The Use and Abuse of Medieval Miracles,' *History* 60, 1975, pp. 1–10 and Christian Krötzl, 'Parent-Child Relations in Medieval Scandinavia According to Scandinavian Miracle Collections,' *Scandinavian Journal of History* 14, 1989, pp. 21–37.
6 New York, St Martin's Press, 1997, p. 51. Quoting from Pierre-André Sigal, 'La grossesse, l'accouchement et l'attitude envers l'enfant mort-né à la fin du moyen âge d'après les récits de miracles,' in *Santé, médecine et assistance au Moyen-âge: 110e Congrès national des Sociétés savantes*, Montpellier, 1985, pp. 23–41, Paris, 1987, here p. 34.
7 Finucane 1997, op. cit., pp. 2–3, 36–7.
8 Finucane, 1977, op. cit., p. 186.
9 *Sainthood in the Later Middle Ages*, Jean Birrell, trans., Cambridge, Cambridge University Press, 1997, pp. 133, 139. Though Aviad M. Kleinberg, *Prophets in Their Own Country: Living Saints and the Making of Sainthood in the Later Middle Ages*, Chicago, The University of Chicago Press, 1992, p. 10 ff., takes issue with some of Vauchez's quantification.
10 Vauchez, op. cit., pp. 157–8, 222.
11 Finucane 1977, op. cit., p. 59.
12 Ibid., p. 148.
13 Ibid., p. 105.
14 Ibid., p. 127.
15 Ibid., p. 129.
16 Rebekka Habermas, 'Weibliche Erfahrungswelten: Frauen in der Welt des Wunders,' in *Auf der Such nach der Frau im Mittelalter: Fragen, Quellen, Antworten*, Bea Lundt, ed., München, Wilhelm Fink Verlag, 1991, pp. 65–80, here p. 68.
17 Habermas, op. cit., pp. 71, 73, 75, 77.
18 Daphne Spain, *Gendered Spaces*, Chapel Hill, The University of North Carolina Press, 1992, p. 7.
19 Georges Duby, ed., *A History of Private Life*, Vol. II, *Revelations of the Medieval World*, Arthur Goldhammer, trans., Cambridge, MA, Belknap Press, 1988, p. 25 (see also pp. 7, 8, 29).
20 Ibid., pp. 509–10.

21 Ibid., pp. 511, 531–2, 530.

22 'Law does no more than symbolically consecrate – by *recording* it in a form which renders it both eternal and universal – the structure of the power relation between groups and classes which it produced and guaranteed practically by the functioning of these mechanisms.' Pierre Bourdieu, *Outline of a Theory of Practice*, Richard Nice, trans., Cambridge, Cambridge University Press, 1977, p. 188.

23 Christian K. Zacher, *Curiosity and Pilgrimage: The Literature of Discovery in Fourteenth-Century England*, Baltimore, The Johns Hopkins Press, 1976, pp. 54–5. See also Vauchez, op. cit., p. 334.

24 *The Letters of Saint Boniface*, trans. Ephraim Emerton, New York, Octagon Books, 1973, p. 140.

25 Quoted in James Campbell, ed., *The Anglo-Saxons*, London, Penguin Books, 1991, p. 101.

26 Duby, op. cit., p. 524.

1 The Milky Way

Women pilgrims and visual art

[Matilda of St Hilary] found the infant ... cold and stiff ... She seized him in her arms and said, 'St Thomas, restore my son to me. When he had a hernia previously you restored him to health. Now he is dead restore him to life, holy martyr.' Moreover she ran and took the relics of the saint which she had brought from Canterbury out of a chest. She put the blood of the saint on the mouth of the dead infant and thrust a piece of the cloth into his throat, continuously crying and saying, 'Holy martyr Thomas, give me back my son. He will be brought to your tomb if he revives. I will visit you on bare feet. Hear me' ... After she had cried out in this way for about two hours, the martyr had mercy and restored her infant to life ... The countess, mother of the restored boy, took on unaccustomed toil, and setting out to Canterbury on bare feet with the boy performed her promised pilgrimage.[1]

In the above example, Matilda indicates how she has twice called on St Thomas to help her son. This mother goes on pilgrimage in thanks for the saint's happy intervention, accompanied by her child who was cured. The saint's relics are crucial to this story, functioning as medicine does today, the catalyst for good health. The vow, a contract between Matilda and St Thomas, seals the healing process. Clearly, women and children, fashioned by miraculous relics, went on pilgrimage. But how did unrecorded women pilgrims travel? What were their experiences?

By reconstructing the pilgrimage experience using material culture, sermon literature, and personal testament, we can better understand how pilgrimage functioned spiritually for women pilgrims. The works of such women mystic-pilgrims as Margery Kempe and St Birgitta of Sweden, whose *Revelations* were translated into Middle English, suggest that depictions of saints along pilgrimage routes could provoke intense mystical and visionary responses. Using these narratives along with sermon literature, we can see that illiterate women, taught saints' legends through church art and sermons, would be encouraged to identify with certain saints. Women pilgrims were a specifically addressed audience at shrines. I will argue that the route to Walsingham catered for women pilgrims. By concentrating on the depiction of saints along two pilgrimage routes to the Walsingham shrine, I will suggest that women pilgrims would identify with specific saints due to their association with milk, and be encouraged by the church's official endorsement of such saints.

Identification with saints and images

Women pilgrims, many, no doubt, illiterate, would learn details of beloved saints' lives from sermons, which would be reinforced by paintings and statuary, the so-called 'books of the illiterate'.[2] The pulpit evoked the saints for two purposes: to stimulate worship and to promote imitation of the holy lives of the saints.[3] Sermons also commented on the use of images of the saints depicted in churches. Paintings and statues were explained in homilies and endorsed as aids to proper devotion for illiterate laymen and women. Walter Hilton wrote, 'What Scripture conveys to clerks, that a picture is wont to exhibit to layfolk.'[4] Master Rypon of Durham quotes Pope Gregory the Great: 'Therefore pictures should be had in churches, in order that those who are ignorant of letters, should at least read with their eyes upon the walls what they are not able to read in books.'[5] Images were good because they stimulated the memory in recalling Christ's passion. John Myrc in his example for the sermon *De Solempnitate Corporis Cristi* writes,

> ... [Þ]e roode is þe Kyngis sele of Heuen, and oþyr ymages þat ben made of holy sayntes þat ben in Heuen wyth hym: and þerfore men worschipen ymages. For, as Ion Bellet tellet, ymages and payntours ben lewde menys bokys, and I say boldyly þat þer ben mony þousaund of pepul þat couþ not ymagen in her hert how Crist was don on þe rood, but as þai lerne hit by syȝt of ymages and payntours.[6]

An anonymous treatise suggests

> And thus by images and peynture y-maked by mannes honde thou mayste y-se and knowe how holy seyntes of hevene lovede almyȝty god, and how grete and dyverse passiouns they suffrede for love that they hadde to him – as by the ymage of seynte Laurence that is y-peynte or y-grave holdynge a gredel in his honde bytoknyng and shewyng how Laurence was y-rosted upon a gredel, and also by ymage of seynte Kateryne that ys ypeynt holdyng in here hond a whel and a swerd, schewyng what passioun the holy virgyne Katryne suffrede; and so by ymages of other seyntes thou myst somdel y-knowe what passioun they suffrede for love that they hadde to almyȝty god.[7]

Nicholas Love's early fifteenth-century translation from the Latin *Meditationes Vitae Christi*, entitled *Mirror of the Blessed Life of Jesus Christ*, addresses a lay audience with particular attention to women.[8] He prescribes images for the laity who are illiterate and need to learn about Christ's life:

> ande þerfore to hem is pryncipally to be sette in mynde þe ymage of crystes Incarnacion passioun & Resurreccion so that a symple soule þat kannot þenke bot bodyes or bodily þinges mowe haue somwhat accordynge vnto is affecion where wiþ he may fede & stire his deuocion.[9]

Illiterate Christians, male or female, could learn or reactivate their memories of holy stories by viewing religious images.[10]

We have abundant evidence from *The Book of Margery Kempe* for the relationship between church images and the spiritual reaction by a viewer. While we cannot read Margery's text as an objective historical account,[11] it does provide evidence for us concerning one woman's reception of images. Her account accords with prescriptive homiletic texts which promote images as an aid to worship. In a sense, her work provides a *praxis* of sermon literature's theoretical recounting of how images can help nurture devotional states. Margery frequently enters a visionary state upon viewing an image in a church. For example, while on a trip to Norwich

> sche went to þe cherch ... wher þis creatur sey a fayr ymage of owr Lady clepyd a pyte. And thorw þe beholdyng of þat pete hir mende was al holy ocupyed in þe Passyon of owr Lord Ihesu Crist & in þe compassyon of owr Lady, Seynt Mary, be whech sche was compellyd to cryyn ful lowde & wepyn ful sor, as þei sche xulde a deyd.[12]

Margery modelled her life on the lives of saints and mystics, such as Bridget of Sweden and Margaret of Oingt, whom Richard Kieckhefer discusses in *Unquiet Souls: Fourteenth-Century Saints and Their Religious Milieu*. Kieckhefer points out that the saints he studied 'would have had access to the works of art that were on public display in churches and chapels everywhere they went, and often in homes and along roadsides as well'.[13]

Kieckhefer concludes that the art saints saw would have influenced their visions. But people other than the recorded saints would have seen the same art. How might they have received such images?

The Virgin Mary was particularly venerated in the late Middle Ages and her images consequently accorded much prestige. Images of the Virgin Mary dominate women's visionary writings. Renate Blumenfeld-Kosinski points out concerning Margaret of Oingt that

> [m]any of the images she uses have their direct origin in the art and literature of the time. There are many examples of visionaries who saw the Virgin Mary just as she could be seen as a statue of their church, or the infant Jesus just as He was depicted in an illuminated manuscript the nun had been perusing.[14]

In one homily, John Myrc explains the iconography of the Annunciation as shown in church art, 'Þen ben þer summe þat asken why þer stondyth a wyne-potte and a lyly bytwyx our lady and Gabyrell at hur salutacyon.' Myrc goes on to explicate the miracle of a lily springing forth from a pot which converted a Jew.[15]

Frequent sermons were given on the Virgin Mary and female saints. Clarissa W. Atkinson goes so far as to suggest that as stories of Mary's miracles became more widely accessible and loved, a heterogeneous audience in terms of estate and gender constructed 'the new "Mary"'[16], who was increasingly powerful in aiding helpless men, women and children. Miracles associated with images of the Virgin appear repeatedly in sermon literature. John Myrc, in a sermon *De Natiuitate Beate Marie*, tells of a widow who prays to the Virgin to help her son in prison. When nothing happens, the widow goes to the Virgin's image in her church and takes it. She commits her act of extortion with the intention of keeping the image until her son returns home. Thereafter the Virgin frees the son. 'Then was þys womon wondyr glad of þe comyng of hur sonne, and anon scho ʒode to þe ymage, and bar hit aʒeyne to þe chyrch, and set hit aʒeyne' and thanks the Virgin.[17] The miraculous nature of the image of the virgin recurs in women's visionary works. In her *Life of the Virgin Saint Beatrice of Ornacieux*, Margaret of Oingt describes just such a miraculous event taking place with an image of the Virgin. Beatrice has fallen asleep in her cell and her guardian slips away to join the service of matins, locking the door behind her. Beatrice awakens and prays to the Virgin to let her go to the church to pray.

> Then she took an image of Our Lady that was painted on a piece of wood and put it through the hole in the door and said: 'Now I will see, sweetest Lady, if you want me to stay here all alone.' At these words she found herself on the other side of the door, without the door having opened, and it remained locked as before. Then she replaced the image of Our Lady in the opening and went to matins at her proper place (in church). When the prioress and the others saw her there, they were stupefied and some of them ran to see whether she had broken the door; but they found it well locked and the image in the opening inside.[18]

Birgitta of Sweden also strongly identified with the Virgin and her mother. After her death, her order at Vadstena placed three statues of Anne, the mother of Mary, in its mother house.[19] In a vision, the Virgin even turns up to attend to Birgitta at the birth of one of her children. After Birgitta experiences the mystical pregnancy of carrying the Christ child, Mary even 'adopts' Birgitta as her daughter-in-law.[20]

The visions that we are told were inspired by church art, as recorded in the above examples, are generically close and could be viewed merely as conventional attempts to justify the piety of the visionary to the audience. Carolyn Walker Bynum and Blumenfeld-Kosinski, for instance, both suggest how women could utilize visions, of the Eucharist in particular, to create a kind of priestly authority denied them by the church.[21] But, while ordinary women may or may not have had visions in response to art and images (which remain unrecorded or undiscovered), they certainly heard the same sermons and received the same art works as recorded by known mystics. Furthermore, wills provide extensive evidence for the devotion lay and religious medieval women had to images. Waterton's *Pietas Mariana Britannica* points out various images which existed and which in many cases were venerated and left legacies in Suffolk and Norfolk. Many pilgrimages were made to Horstead's Our Lady of Pity and legacies were occasionally left for the sanctuary. In Ipswich the image of Our Lady of Grace in St Mary's Chapel was a great pilgrimage site. Sir Thomas More tells of a miracle connected with this image concerning a knight, Sir Roger Wentworth, one of whose daughters was twelve years old and who was apparently possessed by the devil. She goes on pilgrimage to Our Lady of Ipswich. Ultimately, 'the maiden her self in the presence of all the companye restored to theyr good state perfectly cured, and sodeinly.' In King's Lynn, the image of Our Lady on the Mount received numerous offerings by pilgrims on their way to Walsingham. In 1504, Agnes Est left a 'pair of beads of silver' to 'Our Lady in the Steeple' of St Andrew's in Norwich. Many women left money to St Peter, Mancroft, which had a chapel of St Nicholas and one of the Virgin. Reepham had a celebrated image of the Virgin which was frequented by pilgrims. Margery Kempe, on her way to the continent for her pilgrimage to the Holy Land, went to Norwich 'and offeryd at þe Trinite, & sythen sche went to ʒermowth, & offeryd at an ymage of owyr Lady, & þer sche toke hir schyp'.[22] The Countess of Warwick, Isabel, in her last will and testament from 1439, clearly perceived the importance of images and of imaging herself with various saints.[23]

> And my Image to be made all naked, and no thyng on my hede but myn here cast bakwardys, and of the gretnes and of the fascyon lyke the mesure that Thomas Porchalyn hath yn a lyst, and at my hede Mary Mawdelen leyng my handes a-crosse, And seynt Iohn the Evangelyst on the ryght syde of my hede; and on the left syde, Seynt Anton, and at my fete a Skochen of myn Armes departyd with my lordys, and ij Greffons to bere hit vppe; And all a-bowt my tumbe, to be made pore men a[n]d wemen In theire pore Array, with their bedys In theire handes ... All so I woll the tabelet with the Image of oure lady with a glasse to-fore hit, be offred to our lady of Walsyngham, and my gowne of grene Alyr cloth of gold with wyde sleves, And a tabernacle all-so of syluer, lyke as the tymbur is In maner ouer oure lady of Cauersham/ All-so I woll the grete Image of wex that is at London be offred to our lady of Worcestre ...[24]

Her will, which describes the tomb to be built after her death depicting her surrounded by various saints for all eternity, concretely realizes Margery Kempe's vision wherein she interacts with various saints. Vauchez explains how in the later Middle Ages veneration of the saints became increasingly distanced from the cult of relics, thanks in part to the rise in the importance of the image. Saints became more universal, since they were not linked only to where their relics lay, but also to where their images were. Images were even supposed to be capable of healing in the way in which relics were reputed to.[25]

While visionary works and wills indicate the strong veneration of images by women, sermons also warned against their misuse. One sermon celebrating the feast of St Nicholas, tells of a miracle concerning an image of St Nicholas. It was kept by a Jew who displayed the image, telling it to protect his shop from robbery. One day while he was absent, thieves steal his goods. In his anger, the Jew 'toke and schowrget and bete þus image of Saynt Nycholas, as hyt had ben Seynt Nycholas hymselfe, and þus spake to hym ...' The Jew tells the image how foully served he has been by the image. Then St Nicholas goes to the thieves, 'and schowet hom hys sydys all blody ...' He tells the thieves to return the goods to the Jew, which they dutifully do, at which the Jew converts.[26] While one could read the moral of the tale as it is good to beat your image of a saint to get back your goods, in fact the lesson reveals the perception of images in the late Middle Ages. The beaten image translates into the literally beaten body of the saint himself. The image does not stand in for the holy person depicted.

It is that holy person. Hence the many examples of women's veneration of images indicate women's connection not with an inanimate painted object but with the saint him or herself. This sermon indicates that, whether or not men and women did identify with saints, layfolk were clearly perceived as identifying with saints, and were officially encouraged to imitate their holy lives and seek their aid.

The image as 'stand-in' for saint recurs numerous times, often in the context of a miraculous event involving Jews. One of Myrc's sermons, *In Inuencione Sancte Crucis*, tells of Jews coming upon a crucifix, which incites them to violence.

> Þys ys an ymage of þat Ihesu þat our fadyrs dydden to deth; wherfor, as þay dydden to hys body, do we now to hys ymage! Then þay token þys ymage and blyndwaruet hit, and boffeton hit, and bobbyd hyt, and aftyr beton hit wyth scorgys, and crownet hit wyth þornys, and aftyr dydden hit on þe cros, and naylet hyt fote and hond to þe cros. And soo, at þe last, þay maden þe strengest man of hom take a sper, and wyth all his myght þrost hit to þe hert. And anon when he dyd soo, blod and watyr ran out down by þe syde.[27]

The image of Christ bleeds which they attack as their fathers attacked the body of Christ. The blood heals the sick and gets put into crystal vials, some of which eventually ends up in England as the relic known as the Blood of Hailes. In another sermon, *De Exaltacione Sancte Crucis*, Myrc uses an example from the *Legenda Aurea*. A Jew comes to a church:

> And for he sygh no man þeryn, he ȝeode to a rode, and for gret envy þat he had to Crist, wyth his swerde, he kytte þe þrote, and anon þerwyth þe blode sporrut out, þat hyt besprong al his cloþys.[28]

The crucified image of Christ bleeds just as the man Christ. The bleeding image causes the Jew to convert, of course, but also shows once again how interchangeable the image and the imaged were perceived to be. In a final example from Myrc, *De Mirac[u]lis Beate Marie*, a Jew who cannot believe that a virgin could bear a child, asks a monk to paint an image of her on a board. 'And so he purtrayed a wondur fayre ymage of our lady, and hur chylde in hur arme, and a lytel feyre pappe on hur brest …' The monk admits the actual Mary is twenty times fairer than his image of her.

> And so, as þe Iew stode and loked on hur, þe chylde þat was on hur arme, toke his heed awey fro þe borde, and toke his modyr pap in his honde, and mylked oute mylke, and sowked þerof. And when þe Iew sye þat, he kneled adown and þonked God, and cryed our lady mercy, and seyde he wyst wel þat hit was lasse wonder a mayde to ber a chylde, þen that ymage þat was purtrayed on þat borde, forto take his heed fro þe borde, and also þat pap to yeve mylke.[29]

Whereupon the Jew converts. Using linguistic theory, one could refer to Christ or Mary as the signified and his or her image the signifier. In medieval orthodox Christian views on religious images, the signified and the signifier functioned almost interchangeably. Both could bleed, suck or give suck. Both could precipitate conversion.

Walsingham and women pilgrims: family matters

How could a pilgrimage experience be gender-specific? Carolyn Walker Bynum has suggested that women's central images or symbols are continuities of their everyday experiences.

> ... [Women] continue or enhance in image (for example, bride, sick person) what the woman's ordinary experience is, so that one either has to see the woman's religious stance as permanently liminal or as never quite becoming so ... Told by the theological and exegetical tradition that they represented the material, the physical, the appetitive and lustful whereas men represented soul or mind, women elaborated images of self that underlined natural processes. And in these images, the woman's physical 'humanness' was 'saved,' given meaning by joining with the human-divine Christ.[30]

As Bynum points out, '[A]ll women's central images turn out to be continuities.'[31] However, elsewhere Bynum has discussed the multivalent quality of such images which function as 'not merely reflecting and shaping but also inverting, questioning, rejecting and transcending gender as it is constructed in the individual's psychological development and sociological setting.' Such symbols 'are never merely a model of the cultural fact of gender.'[32] Believers were meant to believe in and identify with martyrs of either sex.[33]

While it is important to remember how symbols, images, and saints can work similarly for both men and women, we will see how the attraction of Walsingham for women was underscored iconographically through the depictions of specific saints, both male and female. After all, Bynum has pointed out how women and men did not necessarily have a relationship with saints of their own sex.[34] But for women on pilgrimage, familial concerns were an overwhelmingly crucial motivation for heading to a shrine. Fertility, childbirth, and the health of surviving children constitute a dominant feature in women pilgrims' recorded motivations for setting out on pilgrimage. Women pilgrims, many on pilgrimage due to their experiences as mothers, would have seen and identified with the saints depicted in churches on the way to Walsingham whose legends refer to milk and/or motherhood.

Walsingham was one of the two most popular English shrines, receiving the most donations after Canterbury, possibly even exceeding its donations in the fifteenth century.[35] Almost every English monarch visited the shrine, beginning with Henry III. For example, Richard II and his queen went on pilgrimage in May and June 1383 to Walsingham and Bury St Edmund.[36] In 1460 Warwick, the so-called 'Kingmaker', went on pilgrimage with his wife to Walsingham.[37] Letters are a wonderfully vivid source of information concerning pilgrimage. One Paston letter gives us information about royalty travelling to Walsingham. James Hawte in 1469 writes to Sir John Paston, '... [A]nd as for the King, as I understand, he departyt to Walsingham upon Friday come seven-night, and the Queen also, if God send her hele.'[38] Then in 1471 Sir John Paston writes, 'I heard yesterday that a Worsted man of Norfolk that sold worsteds at Winchester said that my Lord of Norfolk and my Lady were on pilgrimage at our Ladye [of Walsingham] on foot; and so they went to Caistor.'[39] The pilgrimage activities of the nobility and well-known was greeted as important information to pass on. Henry VII frequently visited the shrines at Walsingham and Canterbury. Interestingly, after a triumphant battle in 1487 against the Irish, the 'banner used in the battle was presented to the shrine at Walsingham',[40] suggesting the political importance and public nature of that particular shrine. The pilgrimage activity of his wife, Elizabeth of York, daughter to Edward IV, we will examine more closely in Chapter 2.

The association of Walsingham with women originates with the establishment of the shrine. The story of the founding of the shrine at Walsingham tells of Richeldis de Faveraches, who in 1061 had a thrice-repeated vision of Our Lady. Richeldis begged to be allowed to honor the Virgin somehow. The Virgin Mary led Richeldis 'in spirit' to Nazareth where Gabriel greeted her in the House of the Annunciation. Richeldis then rebuilt the house she encountered in this vision. Walsingham became known as England's Nazareth, England increasingly thought of itself as 'Mary's Dowry',[41] and Walsingham's connection with the Annunciation is crucial. The Galaxy or Milky Way was called the 'Walsingham Way',[42] pointing across the heavens to 'England's Nazareth'.[43]

While no statistics exist on how many women came to Walsingham, circumstantial evidence suggests that such a pilgrimage site would have provided a big draw for women. Women's devotion specifically to Walsingham can be seen in wills in which women leave various monies and goods to the shrine or goods bought at or inspired by the shrine. Eamon Duffy has suggested that late medieval wills stipulating pilgrimages to local shrines emphasized statues or paintings more than relics. Images or items connected in some way with saints and their pilgrimage shrines are frequently cited in wills. In 1383 Mabel Maloysel bequeathed a gold ring 'with a stone called a diamond with an image of Saint Mary of Walsingham'.[44] Lady Elizabeth Andrew left a ring with diamonds to Walsingham in 1474 and in 1498 Lady Ann Scrope left 'X of my grete beedes lassed with sylke crymanesyn and goold with a grete botton of goold and tasselyd with the same'.[45] In a list of expenses in 1502–3 for Elizabeth of York, wife of Henry VII, were numerous small donations to shrines including one of half a mark to Walsingham and Our Lady of Sudbury.[46] In 1505 Lady Catherine, widow of Sir John Hastings, bequeathed to Walsingham her velvet gown.[47] Fourteen bequests to Our Lady of Walsingham appear in Lincoln wills for 1516–32, including one from Catherine Barton for 'a corse gyrdell with a pendyll and a bukkyl of sylver'.[48] Anne Barett from Bury St Edmund's bequeathed to Walsingham 'corall bedys of thrys fyfty and my maryeng ryng with all thyngys hangyng theron'.[49] Women also wanted proxy pilgrimages made after their deaths. In 1448, Alice Winter stipulated that she wanted a man to be hired to make a pilgrimage, for her soul 'and the souls of the people to whom she was bound, to the cross at Newton [three such places in Norfolk alone], the cross at Reydon, the cross at Terrington and St John's Chapel at Terrington, the Holy Trinity and All Saints of Lynn and St Margaret of Lynn, St Felix of Babingley, St Leonard of Norwich and Our Lady of Walsingham, as well as to the cross 'of the north door, London,' [possibly the preaching-cross in the cemetery of St Paul's Cathedral] and to St Thomas of Canterbury'.[50] Queen Catherine, the wife of Henry VIII, in her will of 1536, requested that a pilgrimage should be made to Our

Lady at Walsingham, and that the pilgrim undertaking this journey should distribute '200 nobles in charity upon the road'.[51] One of the richest sets of medieval letters, the famous Paston letters, contain a number of references to pilgrims or pilgrimage activity. In 1443 Margaret Paston writes to her husband John who has been sick:

> My mother promised another image of wax of the weight of yourself to Our Lady of Walsingham and she sent 4 nobles to the 4 orders of friars at Norwich to pray for you; and I have promised pilgrimages to be made for you to Walsingham and to St Leonard's [Priory, Norwich]. By my troth, I never had so heavy a season from the time that I knew of your sickness until I knew of your amending, and still my heart is not at great ease, nor shall be until I know that you are truly well.[52]

Clearly both women feel that Walsingham has the power to aid in cases of illness.

While none of the few extant miracle stories associated with Walsingham concern women, we can deduce that there were undoubtedly some by looking at miracle stories from other shrines. The nearby shrine in Thetford was much frequented by pilgrims and its image of the Virgin was said to bring miraculous cures, including one for a woman who overlaid her child and killed it. The mother ran up to the image of the Virgin, who intervened and revived the dead child. Canterbury was also visited in cases involving fertility, childbirth and children. Benedict of Peterborough 'reported that female pilgrims to St Thomas's shrine were occasionally suffering from an incautious choice of diet during pregnancy or lactation'.[53] The miracles of St Thomas include transmuting water into milk.[54] Among the miracles accredited to Thomas by William of Canterbury include that of Margaret of Hamilton, who vowed during the agony of childbirth to go on pilgrimage, and a woman of Liseux who was relieved of her pregnancy when the time of childbirth was past. The wife of William, a knight of Fulletby in Lincoln, was enabled to bear a child.[55] Rome was another site travelled to in these sexual and reproductive cases, as with the Norman couple in 1063 who travelled there to cure 'their sterility'.[56] As for evidence of Walsingham being visited by women with childbearing plights, one can look to Elizabeth of York, who, after losing both her four-year-old daughter Elizabeth and an infant son, made a pilgrimage to Walsingham.[57]

In his famous colloquy, *A Pilgrimage for Religion's Sake*, Erasmus extensively discusses Walsingham, which he visited in the summer of 1512 and perhaps again in 1514. It is a satirical work and, as such, cannot be relied upon as fact. But in their dialogue, Ogygius tells Menedemus much about his travels to the shrines in Walsingham and Canterbury. Ogygius even quotes a letter supposedly written by Mary, Mother of Jesus, to Glaucoplutus in which she complains about the requests people make when praying to her. 'Some people's prayers are not so irreverent as absurd. An unmarried girl cries, "Mary, give me a rich and handsome bridegroom." A married one, "Give me fine children." A pregnant woman, "Give me an easy delivery."'[58] Ogygius describes so extensively and comically the Virgin's milk which the shrine claimed to possess that Menedemus is forced to comment, 'O Mother most like her Son! He left us so much of his blood on earth; she left so much of her milk that it's scarcely credible a woman with only one child could have so much, even if the child had drunk none of it.'[59] While Erasmus is clearly poking fun at shrine fever, in doing so he also exposes what were undoubtedly motivations for pilgrims such as infertility and childbirth anxieties.[60]

In *Childhood in the Middle Ages*, Shulamith Shahar refutes Phillipe Ariès' famous contention that parents in the Middle Ages did not value their small childen by citing the numerous saints' legends in which parents go on pilgrimage to save the life of a child.[61] She relates that pregnant women, apprehensive about their deliveries, would go on pilgrimages. Childless couples, midwives, pregnant women and their families would fulfill vows of pilgrimage if a woman conceived or if the mother and child were saved.[62] In one saint's legend, a woman who had given birth to several dead infants vows to go on pilgrimage should she give birth to a live child.[63] Parents would vow to go on pilgrimage to a particular saint's shrine if a dead child could be revived.[64] Shahar cites Finucane's work which quantified miracles of some nine popular saints. About one-third or more of the cases in which people appealed to a saint for help dealt with the healing of infants, toddlers and small children of both sexes. If a child became sick, the parents would take a vow to go on pilgrimage if the child were healed. In cases of chronically sick or handicapped children, they would often be taken by one or both parents to a shrine, possibly staying there for days or weeks until a cure was enacted. Various shrines advertised their successful miracles, showing that cures for children were of vital importance for parents. The propaganda of children's recoveries would be made known, thus enhancing the reputation of a saint and the popularity of a shrine.[65] Eleonora C. Gordon's study looks at shrine records for Becket, Wulfstan, Simon de Montfort, Thomas Cantilupe, Edmund the Martyr, and Henry VI. Here she found recorded 134 children or adolescents (eighty-one boys and forty-six girls and seven of unknown sex) in 135 accidents or freak occurrences. Almost all of these incidents record parents or close relatives. Typically in the case of accidents, the victims or their parents would vow to go on pilgrimage in return for recovery. Mother pilgrims were involved in many of these cases.[66]

Finucane's entire book *The Rescue of the Innocents: Endangered Children in Medieval Miracles* examines canonization proceedings and registers of miracle stories which exclusively concern parental vows and/or pilgrimages to cure their sick, injured, or apparently lifeless child. In his examination of over 600 such stories, Finucane's work shows that both parents grieved at their child's misfortune, though societal expectations differed for mothers and fathers concerning overtly emotional responses; that illness claimed more children than accidental injuries and drowning; that sons seemed to have been treated with more care and effort than daughters in cases of illness, though the numbers indicate the possibility that girls became increasingly valued in the later medieval period. These materials offer glimpses into the everyday lives of people of all classes of medieval society. Finucane presents dozens of examples to show how women went on pilgrimage, vowed to go on pilgrimage, or had someone else go on pilgrimage in order: to get pregnant, to have a safe delivery, to help an apparently damaged or sick foetus, to avoid childbirth pain, to expel a dead foetus, to help with postpartum pain, to help with failed milk supply, to help have a live birth after numerous stillbirths, and to help after overlaying an infant in bed. Finucane points out that in many of these stories saints were called upon to help not neonates but mothers, who may have been injured and not have healed from pregnancy or childbirth.[67] The rest of his book concerns dozens of examples of parents making vows, undertaking curative rites, and vowing to go on pilgrimage and/or going on pilgrimage to help ill or injured children. Clearly motherhood, even prior to the conception of a child, could be a vital motivation for female pilgrimage activity. Contemporary work on shrines visited mainly by women shows that the female pilgrims also seek assistance in matters related to the female life cycle. Rachel's Tomb on the road to Bethlehem is visited by women seeking aid in matters of marriage, pregnancy and birth. Women trying to get pregnant believe that physical contact with the tomb will aid them. A ritual involving tying a red string seven times around the tomb and then wearing the string as an aid in achieving fertility is practised even today.[68]

Vauchez records the type of miracles recorded in canonization processes from 1201–1417. In the fourteenth century, with the rise of the importance of the image and its thaumaturgical power, a saint could intercede at increasing distances. This change correlates with the increase in the number of children cured. Women undergoing a difficult delivery could vow to visit an image or shrine if helped. Children stillborn, accidentally smothered, or somehow injured, such as by drowning, were frequently the protagonists in miracle stories. The fourteenth and fifteenth centuries witnessed 'an increase in the protective and liberating role of the saints and the extension of their power of intercession to all areas of human life.'[69]

Documents indicate how women pilgrims were accommodated for in ways that men did not need to be. The Hospitallers' *Riwle* 'prescribes the mode of conduct and way of life for all members of the Order of the Hospital' and is written by Blessed Raymond de Puy, second Master of the Hospital of St John in Jerusalem starting in 1120. His instructions carry the most explicit directives concerning the care of babies born to women pilgrims.

> Si femme i veint ke seit enceinte
> E de meseise seit ateinte,
> Si ele quert la charité
> Pur amur Deu de maiesteé,
> L'en li trove la [tut] sun vivre
> Treske la k'e[le]seit delivre
> De l'enfant e seit ben garie,
> Pur amur Deu, le fiz Marie.
> Dunc l'en [le] fasce cristien
> Ke pus n'eit le diable rien.
> Si dunc nel poet la mere pestre,
> Si comandera dun[c] li mestre
> Ki il seit livré a nurir, [to whom the child is to be handed over for feeding]
> Pur Deu ke vout pur nus murir,
> Treske il seit de tel [e]age
> De sei garir, curteis et sage.
> [E] pus [ceo] seit a sun pleisir
> De remeindre u de loec partir.

The work continues to suggest marrying off foundlings to protect them from poverty and moral degeneration.[70] Later Statutes instituted by Roger des Moulins (1177–87), in The Chapter-General of 1181, state:

> It is also decreed that little cradles should be made for the babies of women pilgrims born in the House, so that they may lie separate, and that the baby in its own bed may be in no danger from the restlessness of its mother.
> And all the children abandoned by their fathers and mothers the Hospital is accustomed to receive and to nourish. To a man and a woman who desire to enter into matrimony, and who possess nothing with which to celebrate their marrige, the House of the Hospital is accustomed to give two bowls (*escueles*) or the rathions [sic] of 2 brethren.[71]

This indicates that not only did women undergo such pilgrimages, but often enough with children so that certain provisions had to be made for them. The possibility also exists that some women pilgrims were pregnant and gave birth while on pilgrimage and therefore needed the cradles thus provided. The priest John of Würzburg wrote around 1170 about a hospital next to the church of John the Baptist adjacent to the Church of the Holy Sepulchre. He writes that in the hospital

> in various houses a great crowd of sick people is collected, some of them women and some men. They are cared for, and every day fed at vast expense. The total of persons at the time when I was present I learned from the servitors talking about it, and it was two thousand sick persons. Between night and day there were sometimes more than fifty corpses carried out, but again and again there were new people admitted.[72]

Among the children born in Jerusalem include Margaret from Beverley in Yorkshire. Conceived in England, she was born there while her parents were on pilgrimage around 1155. A Latin verse text by her brother Thomas of Froidmont [or Froimont] praises her life, which includes such highlights as her return to Jerusalem in 1187 where she fought in a siege of the city by Saladin with a cooking pot on her head as a kind of helmet. During the siege she helped the tired soldiers by bringing them something to drink. After being wounded, captured and ransomed, imprisoned again, tortured and set to hard labour, a time she refers to as a kind of 'slavery', and ransomed a second time, she travelled to Antioch. This trip across the desert she makes dressed in sackcloth and accompanied only by her psalter. In a forest a miraculous event occurs. A Turk, who has stolen her precious psalter, returns it and renounces his violent ways. Once in Antioch, she is arrested by Muslims besieging the city. Upon uttering the Virgin's name she is released by the head infidel. After her release she again makes her way to Jerusalem, makes pilgrimages to Compostela and Rome and retires to a French nunnery.[73]

Medieval hospitals would assist pilgrims as well as others in need. Hospital charity generally stated its intention to aid women in need as in the

Petition and Statute of 1414...The foundation deed of Holy Trinity, Salisbury, sets forth that 'lying-in women are cared for until they are delivered, recovered and churched.' The Spital near Blyth was newly constructed in 1446 for the lodging of strangers and distressed women ... It is recorded that the two London infirmaries of St Mary without Bishopsgate and St Bartholomew undertook this work; in both institutions the touching provision was made that if the mother died, her child should be brought up there until the age of seven.[74]

In 1363 a papal letter allows a

[r]elaxation, during ten years, of a year and forty days of enjoined penance to penitents who on the principal feasts of the year visit the chapel of St Mary the Virgin, in the poor hospital of Canterbury, commonly called 'Estbruge', founded by St Thomas the Martyr, for the poor, for persons going to Rome, for others coming to Canterbury and needing shelter, and for lying-in women.[75]

Clearly pregnant women went to this chapel and hospital while on pilgrimage to Canterbury.

The Hospital of the English, the Hospice of the Blessed Trinity and St Thomas, was founded in 1362 in Rome to protect English pilgrims, especially poor ones, who had been exploited by Roman landlords at the Jubilees in 1300 and 1350.[76] The Hospice contained seven altars; four were dedicated to St Thomas, one each to Our Lady, St Nicholas, and St Catherine. There were several images of Our Lady and the Our Lady on the altar wore a silver crown given by 'Katryn Inglish woman', wife of Hankyn [Haukyn?] Stonspall.[77] In Stow's description of the hospitality available, he writes,

And if any woman happen to be nigh hir time of deliverance, so that she dare not take hir journey, she is to be honestly kept till she be purified: and if she be of power, to take hir childe with hir: if not, to be kept there untill it were seaven yeeres olde.[78]

The link between a saint and a specific population, such as women of child-bearing age, can be seen in literature. One of story from *Mirk's Festial* tells about how Mary was the midwife for Elizabeth;[79] an ordinary woman undergoing the potentially life-threatening anguish of childbirth might very well call on this experienced midwife to help her in her hour of need. Such an example appears in the late fourteenth-century *Life of St Bride* (Birgitta or Bridget of Sweden), the pilgrim-mystic. After Birgitta's death, a woman gave birth to a dead infant.

[W]hen she came to herself she prayed to God humbly that through the merits of the so-celebrated widow [Birgitta], the child might come to life. She prayed that if the baby would revive, she would visit the tomb of the holy widow with a wax image, and immediately the baby became warm and began to breathe, becoming full of life. The woman, full of devotion and joy, went to implement her vow.[80]

Wax images of miraculously cured diseased limbs or individuals adorned many a pilgrimage site. In this case, the mother would set out to bring an image of the revived child as a sign of Birgitta's efficacy as a saint. At Walsingham, wax images representing miraculous cures decorated the shrine where a statue of Mary with the infant Jesus was the focus of meditation. This motherly image would appeal to women like the one mentioned above who needed help for a specifically motherly problem.

Why would women be so concerned with venerating saints' images? Recent scholarship has argued for the appreciation of and possible identification with female saints by medieval women. Roberta Gilchrist and Marilyn Oliva point out in their work on religious women in medieval East Anglia that

> Several aspects of the various female religious lifestyles suggest specific symbolic associations between women and female saints. The saints' dedications of some of the diocese's convents, to St Barbara and St Catherine in particular, show an abiding affiliation between women and female saints.[81]

The association between lay person and saint can be seen, for example, in folk medical practice. Various relics were believed to purvey sympathetic magic, particularly in aiding women in childbed or infertility.[82] The danger of childbirth for women, both physically and spiritually (unchurched women dying after childbirth could not be buried in holy ground) yoked to an increasingly personal piety heightened the 'medieval affective piety for the maternity of Mary'.[83] Gail McMurray Gibson elaborates on the use of relics which women would look to when pregnant, using a kind of sympathetic magic to help them in childbirth, which suggests the resonance of divine or saintly images or associated items for pious medieval women. For example, on her pilgrimage in Italy, Margery Kempe visits a woman who has an image of the Lord in a chest which she and other women dress up and kiss as though it were Christ Himself.

> And þe woman the which had þe ymage in þe chist, whan þei comyn in good citeys, sche toke owt þe ymage owt of hir chist & sett it in worshepful wyfys lappys. & þei wold puttyn schirtys þerup-on & kyssyn it as þei it had ben God hym-selfe.[84]

Gibson comments,

> The gesture of placing the statue of the infant Christ in the laps of pious women suggests ritual blessing of the womb to ensure fruitfulness and protection from the dangers of childbirth as much as opportunity for visual contemplation of the Nativity of Christ.[85]

Art, in this case a Christ doll, is perceived as having actual and concrete effects on people's lives.

The performative quality of art is implicit in the 'sympathetic magic' of pilgrimage ampullae. For example, a vial of Mary's milk was said to be at Walsingham and pilgrims could buy ampullae filled with holy water and a drop of this milk, presumably to aid in fertility, childbirth, or lactation. One of the most frequently uncovered pieces of pilgrim artistic debris are ampullae and pilgrim badges, produced for the masses of pilgrims popularizing various pilgrimage sites. In fact, by 1200 a new word *ampuller* had come into existence to describe the craft which produced cheap mementoes for Canterbury pilgrims. Cheap pewter or lead ampullae were mass-produced in various shapes and were reputed to contain miraculous water mingled with Becket's blood, collected at his death and then repeatedly diluted. These ampullae could take different shapes: rectangular, scallop-shaped or pouch-like, even one in the shape of a boat, depicting Becket on his return from exile in France. Inscriptions also appeared on the ampullae with such slogans as 'Thomas is the best doctor of the worthy sick.' Starting in the early fourteenth century, pilgrims' badges proliferated, not just at Canterbury but other pilgrimage sites as well, such as Bromholm, St Albans, Bury St Edmunds, Pontefract, Westminster and, especially, Walsingham.

While written sources confirm that precious metal ampullae existed, few survive, probably melted down for money or to be recast. While some ampullae were hung around the neck, others were badges which one sewed onto clothing. One ampulla shows Becket's murder, another shows him preaching. One ampulla depicts St Thomas's burial; on the reverse Henry II's penance. One shows Thomas's martyrdom and the Crucifixion. The typical size of such ampullae is under 10 centimetres by 8 centimetres, some measuring much smaller. Pilgrims could also buy souvenirs of the sword which killed Becket or the Canterbury bell, a sign of the pilgrimage. Walsingham badges depicted the Holy House of Walsingham with the Annunciation and the Coronation or the Virgin. There also was a Walsingham ampulla cast, embossed with 'W' and depicting the two wells there with their reputedly miraculous healing powers. Some signs would be manufactured on church precincts. In Walsingham, for example, badges were made both by townspeople and at a workshop at the priory, both groups hoping to cash in on a very profitable business. While there is no evidence who owned the badges thrown away, it is clear that purchasers of badges provided money for those who manufactured them. Pilgrims were a vital source of income for monastic houses. Some of these pilgrim and badge buyers were women, acting out an important economic role in the pilgrimage industry.[86]

The badges or ampullae functioned as everyday proof or credentials for the pilgrim's journey to a pilgrimage site. However, they were not legal entities.

> As visible proofs of the pilgrim's status, these badges entitled the wearer to the benefits of the Corporal Works of Mercy (food, drink, shelter, etc.) and offered a certain protection in times of warfare and unsafe roads. They were never recognized as legal evidence of the performance of penitential or penal pilgrimages which had been imposed by a court of law.[87]

But the relics did function as socially recognized evidence that the pilgrim did indeed make his or her intended pilgrimage. Perhaps, too, they signed the bearer as a soul whose sanctity was to be respected. Badges were perceived as possessing miraculous powers. They functioned almost like secondary relics. Some were brought back for sick friends and relatives to aid in their recovery.[88] Elizabeth Newhouse, in a letter to

Figure 1 Pewter pilgrim badge portraying the Annunciation from the Shrine of Our Lady of Walsingham

her son Roger Wright approximately 1525–6, mentions that she has been to Walsingham. She calls herself a 'poor widow', as she has four children to raise. Clearly her husband has recently died and she tells Roger of the settlement.

> And your father hath left me the new house that I dwell in, unto me and my children for ever, and two closes or fileds. Also I have no good token to send you at this time but a Walsingham broach [sic], and your sister Margaret recommendeth her unto you. No more at this time, and Jesu preserve you.[89]

This letter suggests that the Walsingham brooch she sends her son functions as a good luck talisman.

Gary Vikan discusses the importance of mimesis in pilgrimage art, focusing on the early Byzantine period. Pilgrims wanted to see and touch holy places where they could 'reenact the sacred events that had rendered the sites holy in the first place'.[90] The early pilgrims to Palestine reenacted biblical events in a ritual which was a topos of the pilgrimage experience. The power of these services drew on 'significant *place*, significant *time*, and significant, mimetic *action*'.[91] Art was created to serve the pilgrim whose beliefs and behaviour would interact with the art.

The ampullae are vital repositories of both popular art and as reproductions in miniature of no longer extant artworks at popular pilgrimage sites, many of which were lost or destroyed during the Reformation. Cynthia Hahn analyses the role of imagery in these souvenirs. The spiritual journey of pilgrimage is a form of the rebirth the soul undergoes through baptism. The imprint of the blessing on the ampullae or badges can be read as a 'spiritual seal'. The pilgrim's experience transformed the ampullae.

They were incomplete until the pilgrim 'filled' them with his or her experiences – specifically, used them in a ritual blessing in which they were filled with holy oil or water and then sealed. They became, as it were, a personalized representation of the rebirth and sealing of the pilgrim.[92]

The ampullae were thus a 'holy simulacrum of that experience … ampullae and certain other tokens were – in their essence, substance, and appearance – efficacious simulacra of the potent spiritual experience of the pilgrim.'[93] The ampullae function as portable signs of the pilgrim herself, validating her pilgrimage experience.

The Milky Way: the shrine at Walsingham

How does the above evidence – for women's involvement in pilgrimage, their veneration of images and identification with saints – help us to understand women pilgrims in late medieval England? We need to focus on one particular shrine, Walsingham, and the images encountered on its major routes, to see how women received art on pilgrimage and, thus, how pilgrimage was in part experienced. In this way we can understand what Jamie S. Scott and Paul Simpson-Housley have dubbed the 'geographics of religion', in other words, the symbolic function of the geographical in the shaping of religious self-understanding.[94] Gail McMurray Gibson argues that childbirth and its related imagery dominated fifteenth-century East Anglian art and ceremony.[95] Gibson, whose focus of interest is on the N-Town plays, attempts to understand the 'visual imagination and habits of mind' of a fifteenth-century audience.[96] The visual art of East Anglian churches is 'useful … for reconstructing something of the iconographic experience and expectations of the patrons and audiences who performed and watched the plays on East Anglian streets and stages.'[97] In East Anglia the Marian cult is characterized by Walsingham with its

> mimetic representation of the indwelling of God. Indeed, no better example exists of the image theology of the late Middle Ages than the Walsingham shrine, a replica or stage setting that pilgrims saw as proof of the Virgin's accessibility, the place where Mary – particularized, localized, in bodily likeness – had made her home, and had heard the angel's message.[98]

In arguing for the intensity of Marian piety in East Anglia and the personal identification with saints, Gibson concludes that '[t]he images of sculpture, painted glass, altarpiece, the actors in the theatres of public or private devotion likewise *in imitatio Mariae* created their own Creator, invoked Christ's birth and redemptive suffering from the salvation drama of the Incarnation.'[99] In this way, Margery Kempe's visions and reenactments of Christ's life are exemplary of the iconographic experience and expectations of fifteenth-century East Anglian audiences.

Art is not merely descriptive, but directive, affecting the emotions and actions of pilgrims. Alphonse Dupront argues that the sacred place in pilgrimage becomes the place of the cult of an image.[100] Sacred images render presences visible and provide access to the sacred.[101] An image nourishes belief and provides proof of the immediate truth of the saints. Images make the eternal immediate. There can be no sacred space nor development of a cult without an image.[102] This image is placed within the space of a shrine, church or cathedral. In her study of early medieval saints' shrines in both the east and the west, [Cynthia] Hahn has shown how there was a

> visual rhetoric of sanctity – a rhetoric that condenses the holy past and the sacred present within the particularities of a given space…The first characteristic of visual rhetoric, the purposeful creation of the miraculous or the unique, means that all elements of a shrine, including location and spatial organization, were carefully orchestrated for their effect upon the viewer.[103]

In her specific discussion of the Church of St Martin in Tours, Hahn comments on the 'calculation and staging of the pilgrim's experience of the shrine'.[104] This is also true to the pilgrim's experience of Walsingham.

There are about eighty rood screens in Norfolk, which divide the chancel from the nave, most of them dating from 1450–1530, and generally made of wood and adorned with painted saints. A saint may be depicted on a screen for a number of reasons, including the dedication of the church, the Christian name of the donor and patron saints.[105] While Clifford Flanigan argues that English vernacular drama had become a kind of popular liturgy for a lay society separated from the altar by rood screens and 'philosophical abstractions',[106] painted rood screens in East Anglia are low to the ground, rarely rising about four feet, not obstructing the vision of the altar. Rood screens were perceived as aids to devotional meditation. I'll focus on two routes approaching Walsingham and try to imagine a medieval woman pilgrim making the journey and viewing the rood screens and other art in the churches she enters.[107]

One route would take our woman pilgrim through Sporle and its church of St Mary. Recently uncovered there is a late fourteenth-century wall cartoon of the life of St Katherine. Katherine, the patron saint of nurses, was beheaded and her wounds ran with milk rather than blood.[108] In Litcham, the next town on the route, our female pilgrim would encounter a rood screen from 1436 in the church of All Saints. Depicted are the following figures [some disputed]: a nun, Cecilia or Margaret of Scotland, Dorothy, Juliana, Agnes with Lamb, Petronilla (with book and key), Helena (with the true cross), Ursula (with a sheaf of arrows). Helena was a mother – of Constantine – and a pilgrim herself. Ursula reputedly went on pilgrimage to Rome.[109] The nun represents one type of female religious life in late medieval England.

But the majority of female saints depicted on that screen, and, indeed, on Norfolk rood screens in general, aside from the Blessed Virgin, were Roman virgin martyrs as they occur in *The Golden Legend* (*Legenda Aurea*).[110] Eamon Duffy argues patrons would want to contribute to such screens as 'a guaranteed way to enlist the help of uniquely powerful intercessors'.[111] But Thomas J. Heffernan in *Sacred Biography: Saints and Their Biographers in the Middle Ages* reads the characteristic structures and symbols of some of the sacred biographies of virgin martyrs, like Agnes, Agatha, Christina, Dorothy and Katherine, as reflecting the transformation of the heroine from virgin to bride of Christ to mother.[112] Most scenes of physical abuse in these legends are centred on the 'symbol of woman's maternity and sexuality, the breasts'.[113] 'Her breasts as the symbol of her maternity are mutilated and finally severed, to underscore the miraculous metamorphosis of the virgin into a nurturing mother, virtually a deity in her own right.'[114]

He continues to talk about the reception of such stories:

> For those in the convent or contemplating a monastic vocation, [this type of virgin martyr biography] legitimized a type of spiritual betrothal and maternity. For the unmarried woman in the village, whether a widow or not yet of marriageable age, it may have provided a model conferring some degree of status on females who remained single ... Lastly ... married women with children would have seen their [own] importance in [Christian salvation].[115]

Even the virgin martyrs depicted on the screens would evoke for the careful sermon listener images of milk and motherhood. Some of the saints were patron saints of various aspects of women's sexuality. Margaret was the patron saint of childbirth and Dorothy would be invoked to prevent miscarriage.[116]

If the woman pilgrim took an alternate route via East Dereham, she would have encountered Withburga on the screen. An eighth-century East Anglian religious, she is depicted on six rood screens in Norfolk. A tame deer is the emblem she is typically shown with. According to William of Malmesbury, it provided Withburga with milk. Also in East Dereham is Etheldreda or Audrey, who had two chaste marriages and is usually depicted as an abbess with two does, who were said to have supplied the Ely community she founded with milk during a famine.[117] After East Dereham, our pilgrim would arrive in North Elmham. The saints depicted on the now reconstructed rood screen from the early fifteenth century are Barbara, Cecilia, Dorothy, Zita, Juliana, Petronella, Agnes, Christina (of Tuscany), in other words, the usual cast of virgin martyrs with the addition of Zita, the patron saint of domestic arts. She is depicted with her apron and keys. As the Lollard homilist suggests, this would have been a particularly appealing saint for a lay woman who could identify with the symbolic importance of Zita's keys. Think of the first chapter of *The Book of Margery Kempe*, where sanity and power for Margery are signified by the return of the buttery keys. Also, Barbara and Katherine would be invoked in childbirth.[118]

These two routes meet up in Fakenham/Hempton and head north. Just before Walsingham is the church of Houghton St Giles. Depicted on the rood screen are, from left to right, Emeria, said to be the sister of Anne, mother of Elizabeth [she is also the ancestress of St Servatius of Maestricht, probably the boy depicted with her here], Mary Salome with her sons (James and John), the Virgin Mary and Christ, Mary Cleophas with her four sons, Elizabeth with her son (John the Baptist) and Anne teaching the Virgin to read. Of all mothers, Anne is especially important, representing maternity and miraculous fertility, since after years of childlessness she finally gave birth to Mary.[119] Devotion to her and the Holy Kindred grew in the later Middle Ages. Women who needed to become fertile would find hope in the depictions of Anne and Elizabeth. Heffernan connects the virgin martyrs with these motherly figures.

Figure 2 The rood screen at Houghton St Giles showing, from left to right, Emeria with St Servatius, Mary Salome with her sons (James and John), The Virgin Mary and Christ, Mary Cleophas with her four sons, Elizabeth with her son John the Baptist and Anne teaching the Virgin to read

> ... both Christian virgins and mothers beget children, albeit the one spiritual and the other biological ... Such 'play' between the paradoxical relatedness in the opposition of virgin and mother, in the ability of barren women to conceive, was a deep and abiding aspect of medieval Christianity's spiritual legacy and exemplified in both the Old and New Testaments in the figures of such 'saintly' women as Sarah, Samson's mother, Ruth, Hannah, Elizabeth, and Mary.[120]

As Atkinson points out, '[i]n almost all early medieval lives of female saints, monastic authors presented 'real' or significant motherhood as a spiritual rather than a biological relationship ... A woman could emulate Mary by remaining a virgin and acquiring spiritual offspring'.[121]

This screen at Houghton St Giles has a complete image of abundant maternal fruitfulness, appropriate just before Walsingham.[122] As Victor and Edith Turner have suggested, pilgrims become vulnerable to images on pilgrimage and see them in a new way. The central shrine is preceded by others 'so that the final ingress to the holiest shrine of all will be for each pilgrim a momentous matter'.[123] This church itself is dedicated to Giles who is the patron saint of nursing mothers. Giles appears on numerous Norfolk rood screens, usually with the deer who supposedly supplied him with milk while living as a hermit. It has been suggested that Giles is a saint women especially identified with. His association with milk is crucial to that relationship and provides continuity with the women saints associated with milk and motherhood.[124]

Figure 3 Detail from the rood screen at Houghton St Giles showing, from left, Emeria and her descendant St Servatius and Mary Salome with her sons James and John

Figure 4 Detail from the rood screen at Houghton St Giles showing, from left, the Virgin Mary with Christ and Mary Cleophas with her four sons

Figure 5 Detail from the rood screen at Houghton St Giles showing, from left, Elizabeth with John the Baptist and Anne teaching the Virgin to read

The association of the north side of the church with women has been discussed by Margaret Aston[125] and Roberta Gilchrist in *Gender and Material Culture: The Archaeology of Religious Women*.[126] Aston discusses the segregation of the sexes in medieval churches, where women were usually placed on the north side of the church with a distinct hierarchy among the female sex. A third-century text, for example, lists hierarchically deaconesses, virgins, widows and finally young women with children.[127] The Lady Chapel or Altar would likewise usually be on the north side of the church.

> Other Marian imagery might also be located on this side, as is the case at Wiggenhall St Mary in Norfolk, where the carvings on the benchends are segregated like their occupants. Male saints were carved on the south side; the virgin was on the north. The Virgin was specially at home on this side of the church – and so were women believers … Altars or chapels belonging to the 'women's side' of the church seem often to have become the special preserve of female parishioners, virtually lending the building itself a male/female orientation.[128]

This orientation informs marriage ceremonies today, where the bride's party typically sits on the left (north), and the groom's on the right (south).

Gilchrist uses Aston's point that, when a crucifix faces a congregation, at Christ's right hand are the women. For the female audience facing this crucifix and situated on the north or left side of the church, then, the Virgin Mary and Mary Magdalene would be reflected back to them as in a mirror image, while John the Baptist would be reflected back towards the male portion. Iconography and images, Gilchrist argues, reflect and cement hierarchical relations and segregation. She writes that '[s]pace is a medium through which social relationships are negotiated … [space is] primary to the construction of gender identity'.[129]

> It is likely that hierarchical spatial divisions were reinforced by the embellishment of architectural features. In this way space becomes a matrix constructed by the location and forms of images. Iconographic themes are built through sequences of related sculpture, glass, wall-paintings and ceramic tiles. The patterning of such images would help to establish and cement hierarchical relations … A building's iconography signalled overlapping, multiple meanings. The message intended at any time, or directed towards any specific group, can sometimes be better understood in conjunction with other media, such as manuscript illumination, stained glass, wall-painting and sculpture.[130]

The female figures depicted on the Houghton St Giles rood screen are on the north side of the church, while those of male figures are on the south side.[131] Using these ideas of space and gender, we can see that the church of Houghton St Giles constructs a spatial relationship between women pilgrims and 'milky' women saints by the use of images.[132]

What did milk signify in the Middle Ages? In a personal narrative (dated 1553–5) a Spanish Franciscan pilgrim to the Holy Land describes the origin of the Virgin Mary's milk as a relic.

> [W]e saw the cave where the Virgin remained for some time, giving suck to the infant Jesus. This place is an underground cavern and contains an altar. Mothers who have no milk are in the habit of using fragments and earth from this grotto … Outside the church [in Bethlehem] is a cave, entered by a small door, in which the Blessed Virgin Mary gave suck to her son and remained for some time hidden, probably from fear at the time of the massacre of the Innocents. The pilgrims take pieces of the earth of this grotto for the use of women who have no milk.[133]

This quote suggests the significance of this relic of the Virgin Mary for women and helps us to understand the motivations for their pilgrimages both before and after the Reformation. Milk signified not only femaleness, but motherhood and fertility, both symbolic and literal.[134] Even today women visit the Milk Grotto and believe that eating the white powder from the walls will increase their milk supply. Susan Starr Sered speculates that there was once a water supply visited by infertile or pregnant women which was then associated with Christianity and Judaism and appropriated by religious authorities of both religions. She also points out that insufficient milk supply was a terrible tragedy in the Middle Ages, especially for poor women who could not afford a wet nurse.

In making sense of female physiology, medieval medical theories, drawn on ancient ones, directly connected milk, which provided food to the infant, with menstrual blood, which provided food and matter to the fetus. Aristotle believed '[if women] do conceive, the milk dries up, because the nature of the milk is the same as that of the menstrual blood …'[135] Pseudo-Albertus Magnus' *De Secretis Mulierum* explicitly discusses the link between milk and blood.

> Someone might ask why menses do not flow in pregnant women. The answer is that they are converted into something, for [as the text says] two veins lead from the womb to the breasts, and thus the menses are transferred to the breasts, where they are cooked and receive the form of milk, and carried back through these veins to nourish the fetus in the mother's womb. For this reason nursing women, for example wet nurses, do not have as much menses as other women because it is changed into the matter of milk.[136]

Bynum in *Holy Feast and Holy Fast* has painstakingly traced concentric meanings emanating from the symbols of blood and milk in medieval men's and women's lives, explicitly connecting Mary's milk with the blood of Christ. For example, the Virgin Lactans, or suckling virgin, was increasingly a backdrop on the altar for the eucharist.[137] Margaret of Oingt's writings are suggestive of the multivalent meanings of motherhood in visionary literature. In her *Page of Meditations*, Margaret speaks to Christ, 'Oh, beautiful sweet lord, what bitter pain could the sweet mother feel who was present and thus knew you, she who had nourished and breastfed you, when she saw you die such a vile and unjust death.'[138] Mary's breasts parallel Christ's wounds, a Christ who is also lactating mother. Julian of Norwich writes,

> The mother can give her child to suck of her milk, but our precious Mother Jesus can feed us with himself, and does most courteously and most tenderly, with the blessed sacrament, which is the precious food of true life … The mother can lay her child tenderly to her breast, but our tender Mother Jesus can lead us easily into his blessed breast through his sweet open side …[139]

Margaret of Oingt writes of Christ's life and passion as a kind of childbirth or labour. She says to Christ,

> Are you not my mother and more than mother? The mother who bore me laboured at my birth for one day or one night, but you, my sweet and lovely Lord, were in pain for me not just one day, but you were in labour for more than thirty years. Oh, sweet and lovely Lord, how bitterly were you in labour for me all through your life. But when the time approached where you had to give birth, the labour was such that your holy sweat was like drops of blood which poured out of your body onto the ground … Oh, Sweet Lord Jesus Christ, who ever saw any mother suffer such a birth.[140]

That the Virgin's milk is linked to Christ's blood enhances the Virgin's role as co-redemprix, the mother of the eucharist and salvation. Milk, as Atkinson puts it, was a 'vital substance'.[141] The Virgin's milk and breasts represented 'supernatural healing' and was 'a reward for devotion,' as in the case of Bernard of Clairvaux who is rewarded with three drops of her milk.[142] The Virgin cancelled Eve's sin and reclaimed motherhood and suckling from sin. Suckling is not a sign of humility, as Marina Warner argues,[143] but power; integral and crucial for salvation. John Myrc explains why Mary is always depicted with Christ, in other words, in her role as mother:

> [F]or ryght as Cryst fulfylled þe old lawe and þe newe yn all þat lay to a man, ryght so oure lady fulfyllet boþe lawes yn all þat lay to a woman … So oure lady before [God called Christ his son] was callet Iosephs wyfe; but aftyr scho was callet Ihesus modyr, and was þe passyngar nome of worschip to hur and more lykyng to hor alway aftyr. Wherfor ȝet, forto schew all crystyn pepull how moche scho louet hor sonne Ihesu, wher þat any ymage of hur ys, euer scho haþe sonne Ihesu on hur arme wyth hur.[144]

Mary's power comes from her role as mother of Christ. And the entry of a pilgrim into a roadside hospice was 'likened to the incarnation in the womb of the Blessed Virgin'.[145]

It is possible that ordinary women also derived a kind of authority in their lay roles as mothers through the images seen in churches. Resort to a specific saint suggests an empathy and intimacy felt by the Christian for that saint.[146] Images of specific saints were certainly seen as powerful and efficacious in helping true believers in miracle stories.[147] Furthermore, biological motherhood itself in the later Middle Ages was increasingly sanctioned as an appropriate path for women to show their love of God.

> [T]he physical and emotional pains of motherhood could in themselves be a source of divine revelation and an intimate bond with Mary and with Christ. Instead of blocking access to the sacred [as was held through the tenth century], motherhood made it available through sorrow and suffering, permitting women to share the tears of Mary and the pains of Christ.[148]

Ordinary women, many of them mothers themselves, would find the images of mother saints, an empowered virgin mother, and a motherly Christ as endorsements of their own lives as mothers. The paradox of the Virgin Mother and the motherly male God would be reflected in the enhanced status of ordinary women.

Ultimately, of course, these women pilgrims reentered a society in which they were not exalted like the Virgin Mary. Fatima Mernissi's analysis of contemporary Moroccan pilgrimage seeks to understand the phenomenology of pilgrimage; in other words, what practitioners themselves derive from the experience.[149] She reads the pilgrimage sanctuary as an anti-establishment site for women in developing third-world countries, particularly in North Africa. 'The sanctuary offers a dramatic contrast to [women's] subordinate position in bureaucratic, patriarchal society where decision-making positions are held by men.'[150] Just like the medieval woman pilgrims on the way to Walsingham, Islamic women pilgrims tend to look for help for in controlling their reproduction and sexuality through a saint's or saints' mediation. By enacting or attempting to enact their own cure, these mainly illiterate women no longer are passive recipients of educated male doctors' orders, but shape their own lives and 'attempt to mediate [their] place in the material world'.[151] Seeking help from saints, lay women enact shaping their own lives and construct a woman's community among the pilgrims at the shrine. 'Sanctuaries, which are the locus of antiestablishment, antipatriarchal mythical figures, provide women with a space where complaint and verbal vituperations against the system's injustices are allowed and encouraged.'[152]

But Mernissi goes on to point out that the activities which occur in the sanctuary do not affect power structures outside of it. Like Bakhtinian carnival, which is licensed 'disorder' ultimately controlled by the state, pilgrimage finally does not function as a subversive activity.

> The saint in the sanctuary plays the role of the psychiatrist in the capitalist society, channeling discontent into the therapeutic processes and thus depriving it of its potential to combat the formal power structure. Saints, then, help women adjust to the oppression of the system … [S]anctuaries are 'happenings' where women's collective energies and combative forces are invested in alienating institutions which strive to absorb them, lower their explosive effect, neutralize them.[153]

Sered in her analysis of Rachel's Tomb and the Milk Grotto in Bethlehem agrees with Mernissi's analysis. Women worshipping at female-oriented shrines do not ultimately assert their independence of male religious structures, but reaffirm their commitment to those very structures while working within them. While sanctuaries may provide 'women's space', they must also be approved by the male establishment so they won't be shut down.[154] Similarly, medieval pilgrimage may have allowed sites of female empowerment or exaltation, but it did not function as a fundamentally subversive activity outside of the sacred space, even though pilgrimage and its endorsement were increasingly depicted as a subversive activity in the early Reformation period.[155]

Hélène Cixous writes that 'woman is never far from "mother" ... There is always within her at least a little of that good mother's milk. She writes in white ink.'[156] Women on pilgrimage to Walsingham would be encouraged to 'write themselves' as holy mothers due to the images encountered along the routes to the shrine. The motivations for women to go on pilgrimage might be milk-related – lactation difficulties, infertility, and childbirth anxiety. The Lollard critique of images disregards how images enabled women to find their place in religion. Seeing images of 'milky' saints would encourage a mother's identification with the saints since they themselves were milky. Women looking at mother saints in these rood screens would find themselves legitimated in the faith, hence the – doomed – resistance to the Reformation's dismantling of pilgrimage. The depiction of such saints in a public forum, a church on an important pilgrimage route, reinforces the perceived power of such saints and the women who identified with them. For many women pilgrims the route to Walsingham was, symbolically and literally, the Milky Way.

Notes

1 Jennifer C. Ward, *Women of the English Nobility and Gentry 1066–1500*, Manchester, Manchester University Press, 1995, p. 72.

2 G. R. Owst, *Preaching in Medieval England: An Introduction to Sermon Manuscripts of the Period c. 1350–1450*, Cambridge, Cambridge University Press, 1926, pp. 294, 245, 257. As, for example, in John Myrc's *Festial*, a popular sermon book with narrative sermons based on the lives of the saints. See Theodor Erbe, ed., *Mirk's Festial: A Collection of Homilies by Johannes Mirkus*, London, Kegan Paul, EETS, 1905.

3 Owst, *Literature and Pulpit in Medieval England*, Oxford, Basil Blackwell, 1966, p. 134.

4 Owst 1966, op. cit., p. 137.

5 Owst 1966, op. cit., p. 140. Michael Camille comments on a twelfth-century allusion to this comment of Gregory. To justify the lack of text with his pictures of the life of Christ, the artist of the *St Albans Psalter* writes, 'For it is one thing to venerate a picture and another to learn the story it depicts, which is to be venerated. The picture is for simple men what writing is for those who can read, for those who cannot read see and learn from the picture the model which they should follow. Thus pictures are, above all, for the instruction of the people.' Quoted in Camille, 'Seeing and Reading: Some Visual Implications of Medieval Literacy and Illiteracy', *Art History* 8, 1985, pp. 26–49, here p. 26. Camille goes on to point out that Gregory's dictum became a 'common orthodox argument' and 'was embodied in Canon Law,' p. 32.

6 Erbe, op. cit., p. 171/23–9.

7 Owst 1966, op. cit., pp. 142–3.

8 See Lynn Staley, *Margery Kempe's Dissenting Fictions*, University Park, PA, The Pennsylvania State University Press, 1994, p. 119.

9 Michael G. Sargent, ed., *Nicholas Love's 'Mirror of the Blessed Life of Jesus Christ,'* New York, Garland, 1992, p. 10; Staley, op. cit., p. 143. Love also uses milk as a rhetorical

metaphor in his writings in urging English as a medium for religious writings, 'þe whiche as childryn hauen nede to be fedde with mylke of lyȝtte doctryne & not with sadde mete of grete clargye & of [hye contemplacion].' Quoted in Staley, op. cit., p. 144. See also '"The milk of knowledge"': Language, Pedagogy, and the Body in the Middle Ages,' Robin R. Hass, paper delivered at The 1995 Medieval Institute, Western Michigan University; Clarissa W. Atkinson, *The Oldest Vocation: Christian Motherhood in the Middle Ages*, Ithaca, Cornell University Press, 1991, p. 158.

10 See Gail McMurray Gibson's discussion of similar arguments in the fifteenth-century *Dives and Pauper* in her book *The Theater of Devotion: East Anglian Drama and Society in the Late Middle Ages*, Chicago, The University of Chicago Press, 1989, pp. 14–15.

11 Staley, op. cit., pp. 76–7 and p. 169.

12 Sanford Brown Meech and Hope Emily Allen, eds, *The Book of Margery Kempe*, London, Oxford University Press/Early English Text Society, 1961, p. 148.

13 Chicago, The University of Chicago Press, 1984, pp. 112–13.

14 'The Idea of Writing as Authority and Conflict,' in *The Writings of Margaret of Oingt*, Renate Blumenfeld-Kosinski, trans. and ed., Newburyport, MA, Focus Information Group, Incl, 1990, p. 74. Camille points out that visual art also sometimes showed influence of contemporary drama. Camille 1985, op. cit., p. 31.

15 Erbe, op. cit., pp. 108/25–6.

16 Atkinson, op. cit., pp. 132–3.

17 Erbe, op. cit., p. 248/12–15.

18 Blumenfeld-Kosinski, op. cit., p. 62.

19 Atkinson, op. cit., p. 173.

20 Atkinson, op. cit., pp. 181–2.

21 See Carolyn Walker Bynum's *Jesus as Mother: Studies in the Spirituality of the High Middle Ages*, Berkeley, University of California Press, 1982, chapter 5, and Blumenfeld-Kosinski, op. cit., pp. 6, 72.

22 Edmund Waterton, *Pietas Mariana Britannica*, London, St Joseph's Catholic Library, 1879, pp. 55–7, 115; Meech and Allen, op. cit., p. 60.

23 See Frederick J. Furnivall, ed., *The Fifty Earliest English Wills in the Court of Probate, London; A.D. 1387–1439; with a Priest's of 1454*, London, Oxford University Press, 1882/1964, p. 297. Many women wanted images made of themselves in churches out of brass, statues, stained glass. See ibid., p. 116, n.3 for Isabel's illustrious parentage and descendants, among whom are included Edward III and Henry, Duke of Warwick. Also Norman Tanner, *The Church in Late Medieval Norwich*, Toronto, Pontifical Institute of Medieval Studies, 1984, p. 297.

24 Furnivall, 1882/1964, pp. 116–19.

25 Vauchez, op. cit., pp. 448, 452.

26 Erbe, op. cit., pp. 14/28–14/35.

27 Ibid., pp. 145/29–36–146/1.

28 Ibid., p. 252/5–83.

29 Ibid., pp. 302/29–31, 302/34–38–303/1–3.

30 Carolyn Walker Bynum, *Fragmentation and Redemption: Essays on Gender and the Human Body in Medieval Religion*, New York, Zone Books, 1991, pp. 33, 48.

31 Ibid., p. 48. In a similar vein, Joan Bechtold has analysed Bridget of Sweden's visions and points out that 'childhood and motherhood could be very empowering experiences for [her], and they provided her with a visionary knowledge exclusive to women.' From 'St Birgitta: The Disjunction Between Women and Ecclesiastical Male Power' in Julia B. Holloway, Constance C. Wright and Joan Bechtold, eds, *Equally in God's Image: Women in the Middle Ages*, New York, Peter Lang, 1990, pp. 88–102, here p. 94.

32 Carolyn Walker Bynum, 'Introduction: The Complexity of Symbols,' in *Gender and Religion: On the Complexity of Symbols*, eds. Caroline Walker Bynum, Steven Harrell, and Paula Richman, Boston, Beacon Press, 1986, pp. 8, 15, quoted in Sheila Delany,

Impolitic Bodies: Poetry, Saints, and Society in Fifteenth-Century England: The Work of Osbern Bokenham, New York, Oxford University Press, 1998, p. 187.

33 Delany, ibid., p. 189.
34 Bynum, '... and Woman His Humanity: Female Imagery in the Religious Writing of the Later Middle Ages,' in *Gender and Religion*, p. 259, quoted in Delany, ibid., p. 187.
35 Eamon Duffy, *The Stripping of the Altars: Traditional Religion in England c. 1400–c.1580*, New Haven, Yale University Press, 1992, p. 191, suggests that the heyday of the Canterbury shrine was over by the fifteenth century. Patrick J. Geary discusses the fluctuations in a pilgrimage shrine's popularity, often linked to the rate of reported cures due to a relic. 'Sacred commodities: The circulation of medieval relics,' in *The Social Life of Things: Commodities in Cultural Perspective*, Arjun Appadurai, ed., Cambridge, Cambridge University Press, 1986, p. 169–91, here p. 180. Geary also cites the controversial work of Lionel Rothkrug, who has 'argued that pilgrimages to saints' shrines are almost totally nonexistent in such areas as Saxony, which had been the major focus of [8th and 9th century relic] translation. Could it be that despite the official propaganda attesting to the popularity of these relics, the native populations were never really drawn into the system of values within which they had meaning? Since Rothkrug shows, on both micro and macro levels, a startling coincidence between areas lacking pilgrimages and areas where the Reformation succeeded, it is tempting to argue that these regions never accepted the hagiocentric religion that was medieval Catholicism,' ibid., p. 190. See Lionel Rothkrug, 'Popular Religion and Holy Shrines: Their Influence on the Origins of the German Reformation and Their Role in German Cultural Development,' in J. Obelkevich, ed., *Religion and the People*, Chapel Hill, NC, 1979, and *Religious Practices and Collective Perceptions: Hidden Homologies in the Renaissance and Reformation, Historical Reflections* 7:1, 1980.
36 J. C. Dickinson, *The Shrine of Our Lady of Walsingham*, Cambridge, Cambridge University Press, 1956, p. 25.
37 Ibid., p. 34.
38 Edmund Waterton, *Pietas Mariana Britannica*, London, St Joseph's Catholic Library, 1879, p. 175.
39 Ibid., pp. 175–6.
40 See Gladys Temperley, *Henry VII*, Westport, CT, Greenwood Press, 1914/1971 rep., pp. 62, 412, 416; Eric N. Simons, *Henry VII: The First Tudor King*, New York, Barnes & Noble, Inc., 1968, pp. 97, 101, 298.
41 Duffy 1992, op. cit., p. 256. The custodians at the Walsingham shrine, Duffy hastens to add, had a lot to do with promoting the notion of England as 'Mary's Dowry.'
42 Waterton, op. cit., p. 172.
43 The Galaxy was appropriated to other pilgrim roads too. The Turkish name for the road to mecca was called Hadji's Way or Way to Mecca; in Italy, France and Northern Europe the Milky Way was associated with Compostella and was called 'St Iago's Way' or 'Jacobstrasse.' See Leonard E. Whatmore, *Highway to Walsingham*, Walsingham, The Pilgrim Bureau, 1973, p. 21.
44 Tanner 1984, op. cit., p. 90.
45 Dickinson, op. cit., pp. 37–8.
46 Ibid., p. 42. See also Nicholas Harris Nicolas, *Privy Purse Expenses of Elizabeth of York, Wardrobe Accounts of Edward the Fourth*, London, William Pickering, 1830, repr. New York, Barnes & Noble, 1972, p. 3.
47 Dickinson, op. cit., p. 38.
48 Ibid., p. 46.
49 Ibid., p. 47.
50 Tanner 1984, op. cit., pp. 85–6.
51 Richard Taylor, *Index Monasticus*, London, Richard and Arthur Taylor, 1821, p. xviii.
52 *Private Life in the Fifteenth Century: Illustrated Letters of the Paston Family*, ed. Roger Virgoe, New York, Weidenfeld & Nicolson, 1989, p. 44.

53 Sumption, op. cit., p. 74.

54 Ibid., p. 59.

55 See *Materials for the History of Thomas Becket*, ed. James C. Robertson, Vol. I, London, Longman & Co., 1875, pp. 226, 264, 393.

56 Sumption, op. cit., p. 81.

57 Nancy Lenz Harvey, *Elizabeth of York: The Mother of Henry VIII*, New York, Macmillan Publishing Co, Inc., 1973, pp. 169–70. Elizabeth loses no interest in Walsingham – Nicolas, op. cit., p. 3 – where she pays a priest to make a vicarious pilgrimage there for her. See also Chapter 2 of this volume.

58 *The Colloquies of Erasmus*, Craig R. Thompson, trans., Chicago, The University of Chicago Press, 1965, p. 290.

59 Ibid., p. 295.

60 In discussing modern French pilgrimage, Barbara Corrado Pope says that women 'used pilgrimages for their own needs, to provide them with occasions for all-female sociability and to petition the Virgin or the local patron saint for aid with problems of sexuality and reproduction'. See 'Immaculate and Powerful, The Marian Revival in the Nineteenth Century,' in *Immaculate and Powerful: The Female in Sacred Image and Social Reality*, Clarissa W. Atkinson, Constance H. Buchanan and Margaret R. Miles, eds, Boston, Beacon Press, 1985, pp. 173–200, here p. 174.

61 Chaya Galai, trans., London, Routledge, 1990, p. 95.

62 Shahar, op. cit., pp. 36–7.

63 Ibid., p. 44.

64 Ibid., pp. 130, 140.

65 Ibid., pp. 145–9.

66 Eleonora C. Gordon, 'Accidents Among Medieval Children as seen from the Miracle of Six English Saints and Martyrs', *Medical History*, 35, 1991, pp. 145–63, here, pp. 146, 149. For more on Cantilupe and the miracles cited in his canonization process, including child-related ones, see Vauchez, op. cit., pp. 490–5.

67 New York, St Martin's Press, 1997.

68 Susan Starr Sered, 'Rachel's Tomb and the Milk Grotto of the Virgin Mary: Two Women's Shrines in Bethlehem,' *Journal of Feminist Studies in Religion* 2, 1986, pp. 7–22, here pp. 7–8.

69 Vauchez, op. cit., pp. 470, 472.

70 *The Hospitallers' Riwle*, K. V. Sinclair, ed., London, Anglo-Norman Text Society, 1984, pp. 23–4, ll. 779–96, and ll. 797–814.

71 Quotes from *The Rule Statutes and Customs of the Hospitallers 1099–1310*, E. J. King, London, Methuen, 1934, pp. 35, 38. See also *Cartulaire Général de l'ordre des Hospitalliers de S. Jean de Jérusalem (1100–1310)*, J. Delaville Le Roulx, Paris, Ernest Leroux, 1894, pp. 426–28, 627.

72 John Wilkinson, Joyce Hill, and W. F. Ryan, *Jerusalem Pilgrimage 1099–1185*, London, The Hakluyt Society, 1988, p. 166.

73 Text in Joseph F. Michaud, *Bibliothèque des Croisades*, Paris, A. J. Ducollet, 1829, Vol. III, pp. 369–75. See Anthony Luttrell, 'Englishwomen as Pilgrims to Jerusalem: Isolda Parewastell, 1365' in Holloway, *et al.*, pp. 184–97, here pp. 185, 193, fn 12. See also M. de Florival, 'Un Pèlerinage au XIIe Siècle, Marguerite de Jérusalem et Thomas de Froidmont,' *Bulletin de la Société Académique de Laon*, 2, 1887.

74 Rotha Mary Clay, *The Medieval Hospitals of England*, London, Frank Cass & Co. Ltd, 1966, pp. 8–9. In the early sixteenth century there was a prevalent thought that hospitals were being exploited by sham sick and disreputable women. A 1536 poem exists on this topic by Robert Copland, *The hye way to the Spyttell hous.*, Clay, op. cit., p. 1.

75 *Calendar of Entries in the Papal Registers Relating to Great Britain and Ireland 1362–1404*, W. H. Bliss and J. A. Tremlow, eds, London, Eyre and Spottiswoode, 1902, p. 36.

76 References to John Allen, 'The Englishmen in Rome and the Hospice 1362–1474,' *The English Hospice in Rome, The Venerabile* 21, 1962, pp. 43–81, and George Hay, 'Pilgrims

and the Hospice,' *The Venerabile*, 21, 1962, pp. 99–144; here pp. 49, 19, 23.

77 Ibid., p. 106.

78 Ibid., p. 57–8.

79 Erbe, op. cit., p. 184/10.

80 Julia B. Holloway, *Pilgrim and the Book: A Study of Dante, Langland and Chaucer*, 2nd Edn, New York, Peter Lang Publisher, 1992, p. 20.

81 See *Religious Women in Medieval East Anglia*, Norwich, Centre of East Anglian Studies, 1993, p. 82.

82 Gail McMurray Gibson, 'St Margery: *The Book of Margery Kempe*' in Holloway, *et al.*, pp. 144–63, here p. 154. At a talk at the Parents and Children in Medieval Societies Conference, held at King's College, London on December 3, 1994, Sebastian Sutcliffe spoke about 'Religious Aspects of Childbirth in Late Medieval England' and pointed out that birth girdles telling Christ's life were used during labour. However, Atkinson points out that while '[i]t is sometimes asserted that medieval women found strength and support through identification with the maternal status and power of the Virgin ... it cannot be demonstrated from the writings of twelfth-century Cistercians ...', op. cit., p. 123.

83 Gibson 1989, op. cit., p. 61.

84 Meech and Allen, pp. 77–8.

85 Gibson, op. cit., p. 63.

86 See Geary 1986, op. cit., pp. 21–2.

87 Leonie von Wilckens, 'Die Kleidung der Pilger,' in *Wallfahrt Kennt Keine Grenzen*, Lenz Kriss-Rettenbeck and Gerda Möhle, eds, Zürich, Verlag Schnell & Steiner, München, 1984, p. 223.

88 Ampullae information from Jonathan Alexander and Paul Binski, eds, *Age of Chivalry: Art in Plantagenet England 1200–1400*, London, Weidenfeld and Nicolson, 1987, pp. 218–24. Also see B. W. Spencer, 'Medieval Pilgrims' Badges: Some General Observations Illustrated Mainly from English Sources,' in *Rotterdam Papers: A contribution to medieval archaeology*, J. G. N. Renaud, ed., Rotterdam, W. Stempher and Zoon C. V. Deventer, 1968, pp. 137–9, 143–4.

89 Mary Anne Everett Wood, ed., *Letters of Royal and Illustrious Ladies of Great Britain*, London, Henry Colburn, 1846, Vol 2, pp. 3–4.

90 Gary Vikan, 'Pilgrims in Magi's Clothing: The Impact of Mimesis on Early Byzantine Pilgrimage Art,' in Robert Ousterhout, ed., *The Blessings of Pilgrimage*, Urbana, University of Illinois Press, 1990, pp. 97–107, here p. 99.

91 Ibid., p. 100.

92 Cynthia Hahn, 'Loca Sancta Souvenirs: Sealing the Pilgrim's Experience,' in Ousterhout, p. 91. See also Hahn, 'Seeing and Believing: The Construction of Sanctity in Early-Medieval Saints' Shrines,' *Speculum* 72, 1997, pp. 1079–1106, for ampullae see pp. 1086 and 1105.

93 Hahn in Oosterhout, pp. 91, 93.

94 Jamie Scott and Paul Simpson-Housley, 'Afterword,' in Jamie Scott and Paul Simpson-Housley, *Sacred Places and Profane Spaces: Essays in the Geographies of Judaism, Christianity, and Islam*, New York, Greenwood Press, 1991, pp. 177, 184.

95 Gibson 1989, op. cit., p. 46.

96 Ibid., p. 71.

97 Ibid., p. 77.

98 Ibid., p. 142.

99 Ibid., p. 174.

100 '*Locus* et *imago* sacrals sont indissociables en l'expérience métaphysique du pèlerinage ... si le *locus* met en condition pour celle-ci, l'*imago* en fixe la puissance.' Alphonse Dupront, *Du Sacré: Croisades et Pèlerinages: Images et Langage*, Gallimard, 1987, p. 56.

101 '[*I*]*mago* est reproduction, copie, imitation. Dès lors, dans sa réalité objective, l'image de religion re-présente la présence ... L'image ... donne sa puissance d'accès sacral.' Ibid.,

p. 116.

102 Ibid., p. 484.

103 Hahn 1997, op. cit., pp. 1079–80.

104 Ibid., p. 1097.

105 'The founder of the Priory at Horsham S. Faith, Robert Fitz-Walter, implored the help of S. Faith when he and his wife were captured by robbers on their way back from Rome, and on their safe return dedicated the foundation to S. Faith, to whom they felt they were indebted for their lives.' She appears on the pulpit and wood screen panels. W. W. Williamson, 'Saints on Norfolk Rood-Screens and Pulpits,' *Norfolk Archaeology* 31, 1955–7, pp. 299–346, 299. Duffy disagrees with some of his identifications. Eamon Duffy's work, 'Holy Maydens, Holy Wyfes: The Cult of Women Saints in Fifteenth- and Sixteenth-Century England,' in *Women in the Church*, W. J. Sheils and Diana Wood, eds, Oxford, Basil Blackwell, 1990, pp. 175–96, addresses the issue of women saints on rood screens. In contrast to Norfolk, there are thirty-eight in Suffolk and forty-two in Devon, indicating a strong predilection for such figures in Norfolk. Duffy wonders if 'screens represent popular devotion or that of wealthy donors who paid for them' and concludes that many screens were a corporate effort. '[T]he placing of images in the church was both an expression of and an incentive to a sense of shared value and piety, of kinship and neighborhood between the saints, the parish, and the individual,' pp. 176–7.

106 Gibson 1989, op. cit., p. 41. See also Staley's comments about rood screens, which she likewise argues 'further distanced' the laity 'from the mysteries being enacted at the altar', op. cit., p. 181. She intriguingly suggests that this separation of sacred space from the laity allows it to engage in vernacular devotions.

107 The images at Ranworth of fecundity on the south altar, the Lady Altar, suggests that women would probably have brought their babies and offerings here. 'The three Marys with their holy children were icons of the divine blessing on the earthiness of womanly things, of marriage and child-bearing, of fruitfulness and heaven's blessing on woman's labour. The figure of Margaret beside them also symbolized that blessing, but through a contradictory emphasis on the supernatural power of holy virginity, the untouched and inviolate female body as the meeting-place of earth and heaven, the spousals of human and divine,' Duffy 1990, op. cit., p. 196. On Ranworth, see also Duffy 1992, op. cit., pp. 181–3. Duffy 1992, op. cit., discusses the question of whether rood screens blocked the view of parishioners, thus leading to a non-participatory laity. Duffy ultimately argues that the rood screen was 'both a barrier and no barrier', ibid., pp. 97, 110–14. Squints in some screens would allow for visual access to the sanctuary. And the churches under investigation in this essay are so small and the screens at such a low height that one's view would not be obscured. Duffy also points out how the laity controlled and often owned altars at rood screens. See ibid., p. 159. The laity also influenced which saints would be depicted and would know the saints from legends. Ibid., pp. 165, 173.

108 Carolyn Walker Bynum, *Holy Feast and Holy Fast*, Berkeley, University of California Press, 1987, p. 273; E. Cobham Brewer, *A Dictionary of Miracles*, London, Chatto and Windus, 1884, pp. 49–50. See also Erbe, op. cit., p. 277/8–9: 'Then when þe hed was smytten of, ynstyd of blod ran out whyt mylke.'

109 David Hugh Farmer, *The Oxford Dictionary of Saints*, 3rd Edn, Oxford, Oxford University Press, 1992, p. 473. See also Duffy 1992, op. cit., p. 171.

110 The stories of the virgin martyrs 'provided models of virtue which had disturbingly disruptive implications for the peace of women in late medieval society', Duffy 1990, op. cit., p. 187. Duffy evokes the pornographic aspect of these stories. 'The violent juxtaposition of purity and defilement might seem to suggest a profound, if unacknow-ledged, ambivalence and tension about the relationship between holiness and sexuality in the minds of the married men and women who paid for the screens, and who proposed the saints on them to themselves as exemplars and intercessors.' Ibid., p. 188.

111 Ibid., p. 190.

112 'Surely this transformation produces one of literature's most complex icons, the virgin becomes the bride of the God, and finally the mother of the God, while retaining her virginity,' Oxford, Oxford University Press, 1988, p. 283.

113 Ibid., p. 283.

114 Ibid., p. 283.

115 '[T]he figure of Christina ... does not disparage the role of most medieval women, that of wife and mother. And indeed, her image projects a powerfully complex yet consolidating thesis for medieval women, and one which affirms the value of the opposing traditions of celibacy and the conjugal life,' ibid., pp. 286–7. In the case of Christina, '[t]he miracle of the maternal milk is the emblem that signals the union of [triumphant virgin and spiritual mother]', ibid., p. 288.

116 Duffy 1992, op. cit., p. 175.

117 Farmer, op. cit., pp. 503, 165.

118 Duffy 1992, op. cit., p. 179.

119 'Mary's mother became the exemplary, stable, and loving grandmother for a new age ...' Atkinson, op. cit., p. 106. There were even devotional dolls, 'the figure of St Anne could be opened to find Mary within, and within Mary, the infant Christ ... [Visions and works of art in the early fifteenth century] displayed the central figures of Christianity in groupings based on holy women-mothers and grandmothers', ibid., pp. 160–1. Camille 1985 talks about the increased importance of the iconography of Anne teaching the Virgin how to read coinciding with increased vernacular literacy among women, op. cit., p. 41.

120 Heffernan, op. cit., pp. 285–6.

121 Atkinson, op. cit., pp. 94–5.

122 Duffy 1990, op. cit., p. 193.

123 Victor and Edith Turner, *Image and Pilgrimage in Christian Culture*, Oxford, Basil Blackwell, 1978, p. 23.

124 Alison Binns, *Dedications of Monastic Houses in England and Wales 1066–1216*, Woodbridge, Suffolk, The Boydell Press, 1989, pp. 30, 99, asks, 'Was St Giles a saint to whom women felt a particular devotion?' Gilchrist and Oliva speculate that St Giles and Paul, figures of charity and healing, were chosen as the patron saints of 'some of the [Norwich] diocese's hospitals for women' reflecting the 'association of women as dispensers of charity,' op. cit., p. 82.

125 'Segregation in Church,' in Sheils and Wood, op. cit., pp. 237–94. Sered op. cit., also discusses the male and female division of space at Rachel's Tomb in accordance with Orthodox Judaic proscriptions.

126 'Rood screens in parish churches sometimes depict a range of female saints on the north and male saints on the south, for example, North Elmham, Norfolk, a distinction which was also made in the dedications of chapels in monastic chapels ...' London, Routledge, 1994, p. 134. See also Gilchrist and Oliva, op. cit., pp. 42, 77, 82.

127 Aston, op. cit., p. 239.

128 Aston, op. cit., pp. 274, 280. See also Gilchrist and Oliva, 'Such an association between symbols and holy women was further reflected in the adoption of the north-sided cloister, as well as in the north-sided anchoress's cells in the diocese, a connection which reflected an earlier Christian tradition in which female saints were associated with the north sides of churches,' op. cit., p. 82. See also Duffy 1992, op. cit., p. 171.

129 Gilchrist 1994, op. cit., pp. 150–1.

130 Ibid., pp. 152, 192.

131 Pope Gregory, Jerome, Ambrose, Augustine, Silvester, Pope Clement. See M. R. James, *Suffolk and Norfolk*, London, J. M. Dent & Sons Ltd, 1930, p. 177.

132 Camille talks about the 'collective appreciation' of church art, and even illuminated manuscripts, when a community of viewers receives a visual artistic work. 'Pictorial art becomes a statement or discourse of groups and individuals in history, especially when it

is possible to establish its role within and alongside other systems of communication.'
Camille 1985, op. cit., pp. 33, 44.

133 Harry C. Luke, trans. and ed., *A Spanish Franciscan: Narrative of a Journey to the Holy Land*, London, Palestine Exploration Fund's Office, 1927, pp. 36, 69. The legend goes that the Blessed Virgin, frightened by Herod, lost her milk, and returned in the grotto whereupon she gave suck. Then a drop fell, which later women could use to get their milk back. Brewer, op. cit., p. 260.

134 'The Virgin was credited with some of the capacities, if not the name, of a fertility goddess ...' Atkinson, op. cit., p. 107.

135 Aristotle, *The Generation of Animals*, A. L. Peck, trans., Cambridge, MA, Harvard University Press, 1979, pp. 473, 475. Quoted in Atkinson, op. cit., p. 59.

136 '[After conception] [t]he first thing that develops is a certain vein or nerve which perforates the womb and proceeds from the womb up to the breasts. When the fetus is in the uterus of the mother her breasts are hardened, because the womb closes and the menstrual substance flows to the breast. Then this substance is cooked to a white heat, and it is called the flower of woman; because it is white like milk it is also called the milk of woman. After being cooked in this way, it is sent through the vein to the womb, and there the fetus is nourished with its proper and natural food.' From Helen Rodnite Lemay, *Women's Secrets: A Translation of Pseudo-Albertus Magnus's De Secretis Mulierum with Commentaries*, Albany, SUNY Press, 1992, p. 109. For more on this topic see William F. MacLehose, 'Nurturing Danger: High Medieval Medicine and the Problem(s) of the Child,' in *Medieval Mothering*, John Carmi Parsons and Bonnie Wheeler, eds, New York, Garland Publishing, Inc., 1996, pp. 3–24.

137 Bynum 1987, op. cit., pp. 30, 65, 74, 80, 179, 247, 270–1.

138 Blumenfeld-Kosinski, op. cit., p. 30.

139 Edmund Colledge and James Walsh, trans., *Julian of Norwich Showings*, New York, Paulist Press, 1978, p. 298.

140 Ibid., p. 31, see also p. 32.

141 Atkinson, op. cit. p. 59.

142 Ibid., pp. 121, 142.

143 *Alone of All Her Sex: The Myth and Cult of the Virgin Mary*, New York, Alfred A. Knopf, 1976, pp. 202–5.

144 Erbe, op. cit., p. 247/17–29.

145 Sumption, op. cit., p. 93; Franco Sacchetti, I *Sermoni evangelici. Le Lettere*, LXVIII, O. Gigli, ed., Florence, 1857, pp. 165–6.

146 Duffy 1992, op. cit., p. 180.

147 Atkinson, op. cit., pp. 135–40.

148 Ibid., p. 192.

149 See 'Women, Saints, and Sanctuaries,' *Signs* 3, 1977, pp. 101–12, here p. 105.

150 Ibid., p. 103.

151 Ibid., pp. 106.

152 Ibid., pp. 111.

153 Ibid., p. 112.

154 Sered, op. cit., pp. 20–1.

155 See Duffy 1992, op. cit. pp. 377 ff.

156 'The Laugh of the Medusa,' reprinted in *New French Feminisms*, Elaine Marks and Isabelle de Courtivron, eds, New York, Schocken Books, 1980, p. 251.

2 Legal documentation and restriction

Disruption and control

In *The Condition of Postmodernity*, David Harvey notes how conceptions of time and space reproduce social relations.[1] This social reproduction varies geographically and historically. No single and objective sense of space and time exists, although each culture may privilege one concept of space and time, naturalizing it. Additionally, social meanings are assigned to spatial and temporal practices which can never be neutral.[2] Power relations are always implicated in spatial and temporal practices. The ability to influence the production of space and the representation of space is a way to augment social power.[3] Those who command space control the politics of place. Nevertheless, diversity rules in conceptions about time and space, conceptions which vary according to historical moment and among different societies and sub-groups within a specific society, varying between men and women, country and city, between classes, and so on. Social conflict rises when these diverse conceptions are at odds and coincide temporally.

In his cursory look at the Middle Ages, Harvey reminds us that shifts in conceptions of time and space can overlap, such as with nascent capitalism with its new cultural and economic order. Late medieval spatial organization reflected 'a confused overlapping of economic, political, and legal obligations and rights'.[4] The feudal outlook was disrupted by capitalism in its early form as merchant trading. In England this conflict in the overlapping of conceptions of space is most clearly seen in the fourteenth century when restrictions concerning spatial movement proliferated.[5] During the reign of Edward III, earls, barons, knights and men-at-arms were not allowed to go abroad without permission. These restrictions also held for religious, but not for all, pilgrims until 1344, when they, too, were required to have a licence to leave the country, a requirement reiterated in 1350, 1354, 1355, 1358 and 1381. The fact that it was repeated shows that the law was disregarded, suggesting that the control of space and place Harvey talks about is not monolithic.

It is post-plague England which particularly functions as a period of discontinuity, when traditional power structures are upset and the labouring classes were perceived as unstable, undisciplined and itinerant. As Rodney Hilton and Sarah Beckwith have pointed out, the labourer was now perceived as exercising 'a new subversive volatility and power' and 'was a dangerously mobile figure'.[6] Anxious because of the shift clearly taking place, parliament and the king instituted statutes and laws which tried to retain former hierarchies and controls. This perception of the labourer as unstable becomes evident in laws and proclamations, 'which authorize, naturalize and textualize implied principles of inclusivity and exclusivity. These are the maps, the ceremonies, the proclamations, treatises, manifestos, and principles of censorship ... in which social order is inscribed or rendered readable and therefore thinkable.'[7] The Statute of Labourers (1351) was enacted to compel work and control both wages and the movement of workers.[8] With this statute 'an attempt had been made to restrain desultory wandering, idleness, mendicancy and indiscriminate alsmgiving'.[9] Sumptuary laws, such as the Statute on Diet and Apparrel (1363), attempted to control dress, a visible sign, according to class.[10] As we will see, measures controlling movement were framed for economic reasons[11] and to help prevent changes in the social order from taking place or getting out of control.

Documented women pilgrims

This chapter explores various historical sources for the names of women who planned to travel or did travel on pilgrimage and provides an archive of their names with whatever details exist. Sources include letters of protection, documents granting power of attorney while on pilgrimage, papal letters containing commutation of vows or dispensation, inquisitions post mortem, wills, guild records, household accounts, letters, narratives and various legal records. Some records come from the Close Rolls which consisted mainly of executive orders, conveying in the sovereign's name orders to royal officers about issues ranging in importance from major constitutional decisions to the daily economics of the royal household.[12] The Patent Rolls enroll the letters patent, issued open with the Great Seal, unlike the Close Rolls which were folded and 'closed' by the Great Seal. The Inquisitions Post Mortem were inquests held to determine the death and age of any tenant of the king in order to establish heirs and financial situations. While these texts give us many names of women who travelled on pilgrimage, legal documents are relatively inarticulate when compared to the deep variety of experience in saint's writings or in the reconstruction of art and material culture. The relatively anonymous official voice, preoccupied with economic concerns, records dates, names, and locations. Still, we can draw out some richness from these relatively colourless texts. The overall impression from this extensive material suggests that pilgrimage activity was not undertaken by only a few, exceptional women, like Margery Kempe or Bridget of Sweden; rather, that, while it remained a special experience in one's life, it was a normal social activity for numerous women.

Before we look at specific references to named and individual women pilgrims, we should understand how pilgrimage itself was undertaken. Travelling abroad entailed a certain amount of careful preparation legally and financially, as well as spiritually and emotionally. Much of the documentation we have which includes women pilgrims' names concerns travels taken 'beyond the seas'. A pilgrimage taken abroad would have involved much more money than a local pilgrimage and would have taken much longer; consequently, the possible legal ramifications of departure from home were more complicated than domestic pilgrimage trips. Among the sources to be documented here which specify women pilgrims are the Letters of Protection and those letters acknowledging power of attorney for pilgrims going abroad. You will notice the formulaic wording of such documents when they refer to a pilgrims 'going on pilgrimage beyond seas', that is, abroad with no particular site designated. Other documents cite pilgrims going to specific sites, most often Rome, Santiago or the Holy Land. Vast differences existed in how pilgrims travelled, depending on class and status.

First a pilgrim had to request permission to leave the country. While theoretically everyone was free to leave the realm for business or travel purposes, this freedom was negated if the defence of the realm was in question. The king could forbid anyone to leave without his permission or *licencia*. The prospective pilgrim, if his status or condition warranted it, would first have to obtain the king's permission in a formal document, stating '*Licenciam concedimus et dedimus*', along with the purpose for the permission. Permission was also implicit when people leaving the country received royal protection for their 'men, lands, things, rents' or when they appointed attorneys to act for them in their absence. The letter of attorney typically stated that the holder was about to set out on pilgrimage. These licenses were enrolled on the Close Rolls and Patent Rolls.[13] Pilgrims with any substantial property or wealth generally made provisions for its disposal and management before departure. A pilgrim's lands and property could be under royal protection obtained by formal application to the Exchequer for letters of protection. Some pilgrims made wills before their departure, though it was clear from a decree of Alfonso IX of León in 1229 that some died without having made them. He decreed that sick pilgrims could dispose of their goods as they chose without duress. Pilgrims from Scotland and Wales or who were otherwise alien also needed an English safe-conduct if they entered England or English lands in France.[14]

Constance Storrs notes that many women pilgrims were recorded as travelling while widows, undertaking the journey to pray for their husbands' souls or to fulfil a vow which his death had prevented. Settling their husbands' affairs would take about a year, after which time widows generally made preparations to undertake the pilgrimage.[15] In 1235 Mary Duston of Northhampton obtained her protection to go to Santiago during the reign of Henry III. Alice de Bello Campo received protection to go 'beyond seas' in 1309.[16] Alice Bigod, widow of the Count of Norfolk who died in 1306 and daughter of the count of Hainult, made her preparations to visit Santiago about three years after the earl marshal's death.[17] Until her own death in 1317 she was abroad numerous times, possibly to visit shrines other than Compostella. Eleanor, widow of John de la Mare, received her letters of protection within three years of his death. Launia Atwell, widow of John, went on pilgrimage in 1320 within a year of his death to Santiago. Margaret, the widow of Gilbert de Knovill, received permission to go to St Edmund's in Pontigny, France, in 1322.[18] In 1329 or 1330 Felicia Somerville, the widow of Sir Roger, knight and commissioner of peace for the East Riding, likewise went on pilgrimage.[19] Isolda Belhous, widow of John, has two letters recorded, one in May, 1330, protecting her until Christmas to go to Santiago, and a second for one year later in February 1331, to go to Santiago until the July feast of St Peter ad Vincula. Seventeen years earlier her husband had made the pilgrimage.[20] Alina Burnell, a wealthy widow and holder of numerous manors, obtained letters for her pilgrimage to Santiago in 1330 and 1331.[21]

Matilda, the widow of Robert Banyard, had two letters nominating attorneys in her absence. One dates from 1332 and the other fourteen months later in early 1334. Different attorneys are named in each letter, the first stipulating only that she is going 'beyond the seas' while the second specifies Santiago. It is certainly possible that some event held up her initial pilgrimage endeavour.[22] Another Matilda, Robert Holland's widow, also had letters drawn up to go to Santiago in 1335 and then again less than a year later. She appears less than a year earlier in the records paying to have daily divine services for her and her husband's souls in the chapel of St Katherine. Matilda was an heiress whose father, Alan Zouche, had made a pilgrimage to Santiago in 1308. Robert, her dead spouse, had been in the household of Earl Thomas of Lancaster and had been involved in the conspiracy of 1317. His estates were taken away by Edward II but given back to him by Edward III.[23] Katherine, widow of Thomas III, Lord of Berkeley, went on pilgrimage abroad two years after his death in 1361. She founded both a chantry and a grammar school before her death in 1386, indicating that her evidently pious motivations for pilgrimage may not have been a one-time thing, but were important throughout her life.[24] But not all women pilgrims were widows. Many travelled with their husbands. Robert, son of Walter, and his wife Alice leave for Jerusalem in 1310. They leave matters in the hands of attorneys for three years, which is longer than most letters stipulate.[25] Other couples include Reginald, son of Herbert, with his wife Agnes, and John and Rose de Monte Gomeri heading for Santiago in 1332.[26]

Pilgrimage travel could vary enormously for women depending upon wealth and class. Some couples travelled quite comfortably. William and Cecily Lench left for Rome with two yeomen and four hackneys, while Adam and Katharine Staple travel with two yeomen and three hackneys.[27] Many others apparently travelled alone and with no horse, such as the widow Alice de Waleys[28] and Margery de Ros.[29] Others travelling alone include Constance de Kingston going to Santiago in 1344.[30] But Alice Chandler leaves for Rome with a yeoman and two hackneys in 1367.[31] Elizabeth, the widow of Robert de Assheton, plans to travel to the Holy Land in 1348 with a chaplain and two yeomen[32] and Joan de Nevill in 1350 travels abroad with one horse.[33] Possibly some women chose to travel humbly, even though their means could have provided more sumptuous accommodations, due to their devout wish to be a mean pilgrim. Some seem to be travelling alone, though we may not have the complete records. For example, Joan de Bar, who will be discussed later, had no record of others included on her trip, but it would be extremely unlikely that a countess would travel alone.

Royal women are particularly well-documented in terms of their pilgrimage activity. In 1125, the young empress Matilda, daughter of Henry I of England and the widow of Henry V of Germany, went to Compostela. Her connection with St James is an intimate one. Her possession of James' hand while in Germany ultimately led to the founding of Reading Abbey, which could boast of its relic.[34] Her maternal grandmother, Margaret of Scotland, was also linked with pilgrimage in that she set up a hostel for pilgrims near Edinburgh. Household accounts indicate the pilgrimage activity of Eleanor of Castile, the consort of Edward I, who made a trip to the Holy Land. Presumably she travelled with Edward who in 1271–2 had fought there against the Mamluk sultan Baibars [*sic*].[35] She returned from the east in 1273. In 1286 she offered fermails or brooches of considerable value at the shrine of St Ethelwold at Cerne, 6th of December; St Richard at Chichester, 31st of March; St Denis, 29th of May; St Edmund at Pontigny, 14th of August; and St Martin of Tours, 27th of August; she visited also the shrines of St Wulfran at Abbeville, the chief city of her country of Ponthieu, and of St Eutrope at Xaintes.[36]

She died in 1290. In 1332 Margery de Chaumpaigne plans to go 'beyond the seas' with Eleanor, Edward III's sister.[37] Eleanor goes to Santiago twelve years later, four months after she experiences some trouble: '... disturbers of the peace drove away eight of her horses, worth 40 *l.* at Toucestre, co. Northampton, and also carried away her goods and assaulted her men and servants whereby she lost their service for a great while'. She was the widow of John Beaumont and married the Earl of Arundel a year after her pilgrimage in 1345.[38] Generally, the high-born travelled with extensive parties. Most extravagantly Queen Isabella in 1322 is granted documents which allow for her financial and material security throughout the realm.[39] In the same year she sent one of her clerks, William Boudon, to Santiago.[40] It is also said that after a trip to Canterbury, presumably on pilgrimage, Isabella left her pack of hounds at the monastery for two years, an expense which threatened to impoverish the monks.[41] In 1336 she is granted an indulgence not to fulfil her vow to go to the Holy Land, Rome, and Santiago, though she must carry out her vow of continence and chastity.[42] After her death, King Edward in 1359, asks permission to 'publish the absolution given to his mother, queen Isabella, since deceased, by her confessor, for nonfulfilment of her vow to visit the Holy Sepulchre'.[43] It appears that this was some sort of political issue. Eva de Seint Johan in 1350 travelled with fifteen persons,[44] Maud de Ferrers with seven persons and seven horses,[45] and Ida Lady of Nevill of Essex with twenty damsels and grooms and twenty horses.[46] Andrew Luttrell and Elizabeth his wife in 1361 travel to Santiago with twenty-four men and women and twenty-four horses.

There is also the case of Margaret of Anjou, before the death of her husband, Henry VI, but after his defeat by Edward IV in 1461. They fled into exile to Scotland and also to St Mihiel en Barrois in France. From 1461–71 Margaret raised money and gathered troops in an attempt to put her husband back on the throne, finally succeeding for a few months in late 1470 and early 1471, before her final defeat in May. This papal letter dates from 1467, during this period of crisis. She seeks to be absolved for 'her crimes, excesses and sins and perjuries and transgressions of any vows, and also from all sentences of excommunication'. It is explained that,

> when living in England she, constrained by very many sufferings and tribulations, made divers and almost innumerable vows, impossible of fulfilment by her on account of her weak health, for example many fastings, the observance of which vows very often involves fasting four or five times a week and several pilgrimages to divers places unsafe for her, or rather inaccessible for her without manifest bodily peril, wherefore, as also because she is deprived of her moveable goods, she cannot conveniently fulfil, as is becoming and as she desires, the aforesaid and many other vows taken by her.

She is allowed to commute her vows 'except only the vow of Crusade'.[47] In 1471, after Henry VI's death and her defeat, she was paraded through the streets of London and publicly humiliated. Until she was ransomed four years later and returned to France, she was held in captivity.[48]

In 1468 the third daughter of Richard, Duke of York, and Cecily Neville, who was Princess Margaret, sister of Edward IV, was to marry the widowed Duke of Burgundy. En route to the continent for her marriage she lodged at the Abbey of Stratford (Stratford Priory) and the next day '… she toke hur' pilgremage unto saynte Thomas of Canturbury. And aft' hur dep[ar]tyng toward' Canterbury, it pleasid' the Kyng to send aft[e]r hur and to see hur shippyng.'[49] Sir John Paston, who went on pilgrimage in 1473 to Santiago, writes to John Paston in 1471 that 'the Kyng [Edward IV], and the Qwyen, and moche other pepell, ar ryden and goon to Canterbery, nevyr so moche peple seyn in Pylgrymage hertofor at ones, as men seye.'[50] In the letters relating to the Stonor family, there exists a letter from the second wife of the great-grandson of Alice Duchess of Suffolk, wife of William de la Pole, Duke of Suffolk. Alice is daughter of Thomas Chaucer, who was Speaker of the House of Commons and an eminent person in the reigns of Henries V and VI, and granddaughter of Geoffrey Chaucer. Alice and William had a son, John de la Pole, Duke of Suffolk, who had a natural daughter, Johanna. Johanna married Thomas Stonor who had a son, Sir William Stonor. Sir William's second wife, Elizabeth [d. 1479], sends him a letter in 1478 mentioning pilgrimage. She assures him that she is better and that

> on sonday last past I was at the chirche at my ffadyrs deryge, and soppid with my modyr the same nyght. And Syr, yeff I had ones done my pilgramages I reke nat howe sone I were with you at Stonor: and þerffore, gentil Syr, I praye you þat ye ffayll nat to send me myn horsse on settyrday next …[51]

The religious also went abroad to go on pilgrimage. The Abbess of Elnestowe joins others on a pilgrimage to Santiago in 1329[52] as does the Prioress of Clerkenewell in 1331.[53] The Abbess of Barking nominates attorneys to control her affairs while on pilgrimage to Rome in 1350.[54] Mary, daughter of Edward I, was a nun at Amesbury in Wiltshire and went on pilgrimages to the most famous shrines. She accompanied her stepmother Queen Margaret on a pilgrimage of thanksgiving after having helped the queen during her confinement of her second son, Edmund of Woodstock. Several years later she went on pilgrimage with her niece, Elizabeth de Burgh.[55] Mary has the further distinction of being the one for whom Nicholas Trevet (sometimes Trivet), a Dominican friar, wrote an Anglo-Norman chronicle of world history in 1334. This history is the source for Chaucer's *Man of Law's Tale*, which features Constance, who travels throughout Europe and the Middle East.[56]

Further evidence of women pilgrims comes from another source, papal letters. These generally contained references to the commutation of vows, though not always. In 1328, someone as illustrious as Margaret, wife of Edmund Woodstock, was absolved and given permission to 'commute her vows, except those of pilgrimage to Rome and Santiago'.[57] Some women did not go on pilgrimage themselves but had proxies undertake the journey for them. Queen Margaret had vowed to go Santiago before her death, at which time her son, Edmund of Woodstock, promised to carry out his dead mother's vow. However, for political reasons he found himself unable to fulfil his vow and petitioned the pope to commute his vow for himself and his wife. The pope granted this as long as the earl fulfilled whatever penance his mother's confessor required and that he donate to the cathedral in Santiago a sum equal to the expenses of the unmade pilgrimage.[58] The church is aware of the economic importance of pilgrimage. There is a price to be paid for piety.

Occasionally the woman is permitted to undertake a lesser pilgrimage instead of the one she originally vowed. Sometimes she pays a fine or must undergo some sort of other religious penance, such as fulfil a vow to be chaste. For example, in 1331 it cost Agnes de Rocquefort 133 gold lambs and 5 shillings to evade a pilgrimage she had vowed to Santiago.[59] Various reasons are given for the inability to complete vows. One is age. Sibyl, widow of Roger Boys, is absolved from her vow to visit Rome since she is eighty years old and sent both a religious and a servant on the pilgrimage she had vowed.[60] Another legitimate excuse is family responsibilities such as children, recent widowhood, war or plague. In August of 1336 Queen Philippa of Hainault, wife of Edward III, is granted permission to 'commute vows which she cannot conveniently observe, those of pilgrimage to the Holy Land, Rome, and Santiago, and of continence and chastity excepted'.[61] It is possible that the inconvenience cited concerns child-bearing. If pregnancy were the reason she had to stay home, she must have lost the child in a miscarriage. Her second son, William of Hatfield, died the previous winter in 1336, having survived only a few weeks. Though pilgrimage itself is fairly easily avoided, vows of chastity or continence cannot be ignored, since these, after all, cannot be accomplished by a proxy. Generally another act must be performed instead of pilgrimage.

The letters make clear that dispensation should be given to those, having vowed to go abroad on pilgrimage to Santiago or Rome, who are unable to by reason of 'age, sickness, or wars'.[62] In 1329 it is noted that yet another way to terminate a vow was to grant the ability to 'subsidy against the heretics in Italy'.[63] War is mentioned again in a letter of 1345, specifically allowing English pilgrims unable to fulfil their vows to go on pilgrimage abroad, 'on condition of their giving the cost of their journey to the war against the enemies of the catholic faith and the defence of the faithful in the east'.[64] In 1345 a truce with France was undermined; the following year was the battle of Crécy.

An interesting case arises in 1391. Margaret, while her dead husband Thomas de Naunton, knight, was still alive, was commanded by her husband to vow to visit Santiago. Since that vow, she remarried George Frwngg, knight, who does not consent to her vow to her dead husband. Furthermore, she asks that, 'on account of her age and number of children', she be absolved. It was decreed that she use the same amount of money she would have spent on the journey to Santiago, including offerings she would have made, for the purpose of repairing the churches of Rome.[65] It is unclear how the church views the struggle between rights of the dead husband and the living husband, but clearly the command of the dead husband was not disregarded. Even if a woman makes a vow involuntarily, she is held accountable for it. Furthermore, there is the question as to which is more important, a husband's command or the vow. Clearly the vow is the favoured verbal contract since her present husband's command is not privileged.

A pious couple, William Cressewyc and his wife Alice, both of London and both fifty years old, had made vows to go on pilgrimage in the past, William to Jerusalem and Alice to Rome. William was subsequently absolved from his vow, giving money to repair churches in Canterbury and London. They also sent two men on proxy pilgrimage, one to Jerusalem and the other to Rome. Although absolved, in 1391 they wished to 'tranquillise their consciences'. They were to give money, equal to their travel expenses had they gone and the offerings they would have made, for the church repairs in Rome.[66]

Both males and females are granted the advantageous indulgences of jubilee year 1390, without having gone to Rome. One group of men and women are, in exchange, to visit churches in England on fifteen days, and the other group are also to send the amount they would have paid in offerings to the churches of Rome.[67] While a number of noblemen and women are absolved from 'all sentences of excommunication' and whose vows to go the Holy Land, Rome and Compostela are commuted,[68] not all requests for absolution come from nobility. In 1466, Agnes Cauod, nun of a priory in Dublin

> left the said priory, with license of her ordinary, came to the Roman court as a pilgrim, and visited the shrines of SS. Peter and Paul, Rome; and that she subsequently transferred herself from the said priory to that of Koveney, O.S.B., in the diocese of Lincoln, and there took the habit of the order of St Benedict, and made her profession.[69]

She prefers to stay in the order of St Benedict and the priory of Koveney due to its stricter rule. She requests an appropriate penance so she can stay at Koveney for life. While this case does not concern unfulfilled pilgrimage vows, it does show how religious women went on pilgrimage.

Yet another source useful for finding out the existence of female pilgrims are the *Inquisitions Post Mortem*. These documents generally try to attest to the birth or death date of a person for the purpose of determining property rights. Many testimonies speak to the way of remembering time through events. For example, three men claim to know the date of a girl's baptism because 'on the same day they set out on a pilgrimage to Canterbury'.[70] The use of remembering pilgrimages suggests several things about taking a pilgrimage in late medieval English society. Pilgrimage was a memorable event, that is, an event worth remembering, an event out of the ordinary so that one would remember, just as breaking an arm or getting married is extraordinary. It was at the same time a common enough event to appear regularly in such documents. Finally, pilgrimage was recognized legally as both an unusual, that is to say, memorable, event, and as a socially recognized activity. The problem with such documents is that the testimony comes, virtually exclusively, from men. So John Smith may go on a pilgrimage, and occasionally testifies that he started his pilgrimage to Santiago the month of the baptism of X with Y, but never is the name of a female companion mentioned (in my searches). Occasionally a testifier may say that he began his pilgrimage to Santiago 'with neighbours' or 'with others', who may or may not of course be women.

Despite the limitations of such documents, occasionally one does glean useful titbits. One case, in the mid-1350s, concerns the complicated property rights of a tenement given to Annabel le Botiller by Alexander de Synton, the rector of a church, but which the Carmelite Friars of London also had claim to.

> Annabel was espoused to John Laughton, saddler, and they held the tenement in her right … Afterwards Annabel went on pilgrimage and passed beyond sea, and has not returned; and the prior and friars aforesaid, supposing her to be dead, claimed the tenement and under the bequest John Laughton gave them 20 marks not to proceed with their claim, and afterwards by his charter enfeoffed William de Bathe of the tenement in fee, and he now holds it. It is held of the King in free burgage, as is the whole city of London. Alexander has no heirs surviving, as the jurors understand.[71]

Evidently, the legal arrangements Annabel made were not specific enough to resolve this property claim without some legal action. Another document concerns 'Wenteliana sister and heir of John son of John de Keynes, knight'. We are told that 'She died on Sunday after St Mary Magdalen, 49 Edward III. Elizabeth de Keynes, her aunt, would have been her heir had she lived; but in Christmas week, 47 Edward III, the said Elizabeth with some neighbors of hers set out for the Holy Land, and the neighbors returned a year ago and said very truly that she was dead, as the jurors also say …'[72] So we do have evidence of two women pilgrims from such documents, both of whom were (presumed) dead.

Wills are a fruitful source for evidence of pilgrimage activity, including this type of proxy pilgrimage. Women stated in wills their desire for pilgrimages to be made for the sake of their souls upon their death. In 1418 Lady Cecily Gerbridge of St Michael's Coslany left ten marks for a proxy pilgrim to go to Rome and to pray for her soul there.[73] Lucia Visconti, Countess of Kent and Lady of Wake, widow of Edmund de Holand, Earl of Kent, leaves stipulated in her will dated April 11, 1424: 'Item lego Nicholao de Aliardis de Verona armigero, senescallo meo … et hoc sibi do quia michi promisit et iuravit quod ibit in perigrinagio ad Sanctum Antonium, ad Ierusalem et ad Sanctum Iacobum pro anima dicti domini comitis Kancie et pro anima mea.'[74] Her seneschal is designated as her proxy in performing pilgrimages to places such as Jerusalem and Compostela and praying for the souls of her husband and herself. In 1484 Margaret Est bequeathed money to Thomas Thurkeld to undertake pilgrimages to

> the holy seynt Wandrede; and aft my dissease he xall go unto seynt Thomas of Canterbury, and ther to prey for me to relesse me of my vowe whiche I made thirdyr myself. And from thens the same Thomas xall go for me on pylgrymage unto the Abby of Chelkey [Chertsey] ther as Kyng herry lyth, yf my goodys wyll stretch so ferr for his costs. And so be hys pylgrymages that I may be relessyd of myn avowes.[75]

Here she specifically cites the vow she had made to go on pilgrimage herself, which her proxy can release her from.

In Trimingham, Norfolk, the priests claimed to have had the head of John the Baptist and, consequently, pilgrims flocked there. In her will dated 1478, a woman from Horstead, Alice Cooke, sent a man to do pilgrimage there, among other places. Cooke wants her deputy pilgrim to go to

> Our Lady of Rafham, to Seynte Spyrite [of Elsing] to St Parnell [Petronella] of Stratton, to St Leonard without Norwich; to St Wandred of Byskeley, to St Margaret of Harstead, to our Lady of Pity of Harstead, to St John's Head at Trimingham, and to the Holy Rood of Crostewyte.[76]

Agnes Parker, a widow of Keswick, in a will dated 1507 stipulated 'Item, I owe a pilgrimage to Canterbury; another to St Tebbald of Hobbies, and another to St Albert of Cringleford.'[77] Wills indicate that women bequeathed goods and moneys to pilgrimage shrines, sometimes while they were still alive. The account rolls of the Abbey of Durham record gifts made by two women pilgrims. 'Item ij monilia ex dono duarum mulierum peregrinancium, valoris, x *s* (ten shillings) …'[78]

Women married and unmarried, rich and poor, are recorded as having been in Rome. While the popular assumption that John Shephard founded the Hospital of the English in Rome is questionable, it is clear that John and his wife Alice ran the hospice and vowed to leave their property to the hospice upon their deaths. For the first one hundred years of its existence, we have no names of pilgrims who stayed there and the fullest account of the hospice is given by Margery Kempe from her trip around 1415. But numerous English women lived in Rome and a list of their names – buyers, sellers, witnesses, etc. – from 1333 to 1469 is accessible from property deeds and other legal documents.[79] A receipt book dating from 1446 lists contributors and enrolled members of the confraternity of St Thomas. This is not necessarily a list of pilgrims to Rome, but lists according to English dioceses the confraternity members including hundreds of women.[80] The dioceses include the parishes of Sutton Valens, Kent, York, Norwich, St Edmund in Lumbardstrete, Willesden, Worcester. One sample entry for the Norwich diocese lists for 16th March 1492:

> Richard Brome and Elizabeth his wife
> The Prioress of Tampsey
> Mistress Anne Hasset
> Parnell Fulmerston
> Alice Cook
> Elizabeth Everard
> Elizabeth Jenay
> Elizabeth Norwich
> Margaret Harman
> Anne Bumstead[81]

The English Hospice could hold approximately one hundred pilgrims, though the biggest number of guests was recorded on Passion Sunday 1525 when 169 pilgrims were present. Being in Rome for Easter meant leaving England in January or February. In the first records of the pilgrims, starting in 1479, there was no distinction made between noble and poor, which was established in records there only in 1504. The Lists of Pilgrims May 1479 to May 1484 and November 4, 1504 to May 4, 1507, include the names of numerous women (dozens) from Wales and England. Some are widows, some travel with husbands, sons, other women (apparently, as when groups of women are listed coming from the same place) or (apparently) alone.[82] Numerous sick are recorded but not named, so some could be women, some of whom could have died in childbirth. One pilgrim, Alice Melton, washerwoman, died June 12, 1483, and she is recorded as travelling with two companions (anonymous).

Post-plague restrictions

Attempted control of pilgrimage can be seen not just in papal letters or letters of protection. While measures were framed from an economic standpoint,[83] pilgrimage was inevitably affected in the effort to control physical movement and the movement of monies. Just as with attempts to control dress and movement, statutes and laws directly manage the activity of pilgrimage in the post-plague period. Royal proclamations from around 1350 limit departure from England for any reason, including pilgrimage, citing economic loss as operative. Of the two following proclamations, one is addressed to the mayors and bailiffs of various port towns and the other to the sheriffs of London and port towns. [See Appendix A for complete texts of documents excerpted or referenced below.]

One proclamation dated January 28, 1350 [Appendix A. 1] is addressed to the 'Mayors and bailiffs of Sandwich', who are commanded 'upon pain of forfeiture not to permit men at arms, pilgrims or any others of the realm to cross from that port without the king's special order'. If detected, these unlicensed travellers shall be arrested along with all of their goods, including money and jewels. There is a great deal of anxiety to be noted in this proclamation.

> [N]o small portion of the people has perished in the present plague and the treasure of the realm is much exhausted, as the king has learned, and several people betake themselves to parts beyond with their money, and if this were permitted the realm would be so stripped both of men and treasure that grave danger might easily arise.[84]

The economic threat to England's well-being, particularly shaky after the worst of the plague, justifies the king's command. Six months later another proclamation is rendered [Appendix A. 2] to the sheriffs of London, in which 'no earl, baron, knight, man at arms, pilgrim or any other, shall cross from the realm to parts beyond before the quinzaine of Michaelmas next, upon pain of forfeiture, without the king's special order'.[85] Pilgrims are not the only group singled out for special mention. But it is notable that those mentioned are ones who would have money, either those of the nobility or those heading off on a pilgrimage. After all, pilgrims had to travel with enough money to last their entire sojourn. If travelling to the Holy Land, such a trip would last months and finances would have to cover that entire period.

We clearly see the attempt to control pilgrimage in the official decrees of the fourteenth century. Before any pilgrim could leave for pilgrimage abroad, there had to have been a vessel available for her departure. One source which provides information about pilgrimage travel are the licences granted to shipowners to take pilgrims over the sea. While the pilgrims are not mentioned by name, they undoubtedly included women. In 1368 lay people are often stipulated to be the sole passengers allowed for the trip undertaken, most often to Santiago. A series of such licences appears in 1368, which specifically allows 'pilgrims of middling condition with no great estate' to go on pilgrimage, excepting 'all clerks, knights, esquires and other nobles'. A year later a merchant of Bristol is licensed to take 'as many pilgrims (*pelegrinos*) as the ship will hold'. No references to the class of pilgrims are made, but he is commanded not to take 'horses, gold or silver or other thing prejudicial to the king'.[86] Six weeks later another merchant from Bristol is similarly allowed to take pilgrims, but he may not take 'horses, gold or silver, bows, arrows or other armour, or anything prejudicial to the king and crown'.[87] This attempt to control who leaves the realm and with what monies or weapons came about due to the Hundred Years' War with France and the desire to control the finances and the fighting classes who would be helpful in that ongoing dispute.[88] The Black Prince's invasion of Castile in 1367 had exhausted English resources. The Treaty of Brétigny (1360) failed with the resumption of the war again in 1369,[89] when some of these licences are issued. Mention is also made of allowing this pilgrim traffic to continue 'provided that the ship be not arrested for the king's service', clearly to aid the war effort.[90] In the early 1390's several licenses specify that 'lieges of the king' may travel, but 'the pilgrims must not carry gold or silver, in bullion or money, or other things contrary to statute'.[91] In the wake of anti-papal legislation in England in 1390 and 1393,[92] numerous licences in 1393 and 1394 allow pilgrims to leave, providing they are lay folk, and not 'clerk or religious'.[93] The usual money restrictions apply. Women are included among those documented as having travelled by ship such as Margery Kempe who describes her plight on board various ships.[94]

Domestic statutes were written controlling the movements of pilgrims at home. Municipal authorities in London in 1369 issued a precept 'for mendicants, vagrants and pilgrims to leave the city'. That society perceived itself as disordered can also be seen in the Commons' Petition against Vagrants (1376) which forbad aiding false beggars, many merely wandering vagrants in disguise. The Statute of Westminster (1383) ordered inquiry concerning vagabonds 'wandering from place to place, running in the country more abundantly than they were wont in times past'. In 1388 a statute of Richard II stipulated the arrest of any persons claiming pilgrim status but who could not produce specially stamped letters of passage.[95] This act declared that those who 'go in pilgrimage as beggars' when fit for employment, should be dealt with by being jailed or placed in the stocks. The government attempted to check this in 1391 by requiring that these people carry letters patent stating the purpose of their journey and the date of their return.[96] One fear was that pilgrimage could be a mere pretext for servants and labourers to leave their manorial service, breaking their terms of hiring, in order to seek out better wages, particularly after the Statute of Labourers.

In March 8, 1391 [Appendix A. 9], it is ordered that 'no servant or labourer, man or woman, shall go forth from the hundred etc. where he dwells before the end of his term to serve or dwell elsewhere or under pretense of pilgrimage unless he carry a letter patent under the king's seal appointed for the purpose, containing the cause of such passage and the date of his return, if he ought to return…'[97] The restrictions here clearly attempt to control the activities, not of the upper classes, but of the labouring classes, whose movements away from places of work, only ten years after the Peasants' Revolt, were perceived as disruptive. This order also reflects the suspicion that pilgrimage activity may be a mere ruse and shows the attempt to control the activities of pilgrims. In November 6, 1399, another order [Appendix A. 10] restipulates a parliamentary ordinance that 'no pilgrim pass out of the realm except at Dover'.[98] This port restriction would help control the departure of pilgrims from England. A year later, on September 10, 1400 [Appendix A. 11], an order exists that pilgrims may not pass out of the realm without special license no matter what 'estate or condition'. Of course, this last document comes just a year after Bolingbroke took the throne as Henry IV. His specific anxiety is that those leaving the realm 'take with them no letters or aught else to the prejudice of the king or realm'.[99]

Exporting money was controlled, so that some personal licenses included permission to take out money. If she took out money without this permission, a pilgrim or traveller risked arrest and confiscation of the money. Those who went to Castile, an ally of France, en route to Compostella during the Hundred Years' War, had to promise that they would not betray secrets of the realm or procure anything detrimental to the Crown. They also had to promise not to take out gold or silver in bullion or specie in excess of their reasonable need.[100] Commissions state in strong terms the necessity for controlling those who leave the realm and their monies and the punishments they would receive in disobeying the royal command. Santiago in particular comes under great suspicion. In early 1376, one proclamation [Appendix A. 6] declares that no one will travel out of the realm carrying 'gold or silver, jewels or letters of exchange' without the king's special licence.[101] Yet another proclamation dated June 15, 1389 [Appendix A. 8], most strongly expresses anxiety concerning those departing from England.

> To the keepers of the passage in the port of London and the river Thames. Order under pain of forfeiture to suffer no lieges in that port and river to pass to any foreign parts save known merchants, any previous command of the king notwithstanding; as the pope has excommunicated all them of Spain who are the king's enemies and notorious schismatics, and all others who repair to them or have communication with them, and great number of king's lieges are minded to go on pilgrimage and for other causes to Santiago in Spain and other foreign parts, taking with them divers sums of money in the lump, in plate and in coin contrary to the king's order and prohibition.[102]

The intensity of the wording here, making reference to the 'king's enemies' and 'notorious schismatics', for example, becomes understandable when one considers that only a year earlier, some of Richard II's closest advisors were removed during the 'Merciless Parliament' and Thomas Usk, a supporter of the king, was executed. Richard II's regality was only returned to him on May 3, 1389, six weeks before this proclamation is made.

Pilgrimage continued even during times of war and unrest. During a two-year peace between Henry VI and Charles of France, the truce stipulated the control of activities among the peoples of each country, with a specific address to the movement of pilgrims. This truce [Appendix A. 12] would last from the date of its publishing, May 28, 1444, until April 1, 1446.

> [T]rue pilgrims may visit the ancient shrines of saints as pilgrims were used to do in companies great or small, and it shall be sufficient for them and for merchants and poor and humble men to ask leave of the porters to enter towns, castles, etc ...[103]

It was in France's interest to allow English pilgrims onto French soil. Not only would it foster goodwill, but pilgrims provided economic advantages to the shrines and cities and towns along pilgrimage routes.

Personal piety in public space: crime and punishment

According to Georges Duby, from the eleventh to thirteenth centuries, anyone who attempted to 'construct his own private enclosure' was looked at as unusual, either positively or negatively. Nevertheless, those who were alone or isolated, who were not part of a community, were considered 'deviant or possessed or mad; it was commonly believed that solitary wandering was a symptom of insanity'. Where does pilgrimage fit in here? After all, many pilgrims travelled alone. More, though, travelled in groups or at least with one other person, for protection but also to create a community which reflected the social order. Pilgrimage routes frequently went through rural areas, woods and forests. Were these uncultivated areas 'outside the law'? If so, Duby shows, '[c]riminals and heretics supposedly sought refuge in these realms of disorder, fearfulness, and desire, as did those deranged by passion, driven out of their minds'.[104] But could it be that, since the routes linked established areas of order, a city and a cathedral for example, they did represent God's order? Pilgrimage challenges easy divisions.

In the fourteenth and fifteenth centuries, with the rise of increased subjectivity, the issue of perceived dangerous spaces carries over. Duby writes,

> Self-consciousness is born when the individual can see himself in perspective, set himself apart from his fellow man; it can lead to a radical questioning of the social order. Those who risked abandoning their position in society, who took to the roads and the forests, lost their social status. The restless wanderers, shady characters, and madmen who fill the pages of the romantic adventures so widely read in the waning Middle Ages were not alone in the forests of disorder, where charcoal burners, outcasts, and hermits avidly seeking another world also roamed.[105]

Those also leaving home were pilgrims, but they did not lose their social status. In fact, who they were in society before leaving on pilgrimage informs how they travelled while on pilgrimage. But the taint of disorder becomes associated with those setting themselves apart through an act of personal piety, those performing pilgrimage. Their subjectivity is deeply informed by the church and its strictures concerning relics, pilgrimage and sainthood, but the very act of personal devotion, shown in pilgrimage, becomes suspect in a society where the stability of the community is perceived as being threatened as in the post-plague period in England.

Duby suggests that '[m]en and women who travelled the roads without escort were believed to offer themselves up as prey, so it was legitimate to take everything they had'.[106] Certainly pilgrims were not immune from criminal activity, both as victim and perpetrator. Pilgrims, while ostensibly on a religious journey, were not necessarily the holiest of creatures. A statute of Richard I from the late twelfth century covers certain crimes which might be committed on a ship journey to the Holy Land. This statute proclaims that

> if a pilgrim kill another, he shall be bound to the body of his victim and flung into the sea; that if a pilgrim attack another with a knife or so as to draw blood, his hand shall be cut off; that if a pilgrim strike another with the palm of his hand or so that no blood be drawn, then 'he shall be plunged in the sea three times.'[107]

A crime involving a husband and wife lies at the heart of a church dedication. Robert Fitz-Walter and his wife had gone on pilgrimage to Rome. On their return trip, they were captured by robbers. After safely returning to England, they founded a Priory at Horsham, dedicating it to St Faith, whom they credited for their lives. St Faith appears on the pulpit and wood screen panels.[108] Agnes Paston informs John Paston in a letter from March 11, 1450 that

> Rychard Lynsted cam thys day from Paston, and letyt me wete that on Saturday last past Dravale, halfe brother to Waryn Harman, was takyn with enemyis, walkyn be the se syde, and have hym forthe with hem; and they tokyn ij. pylgremys, a man and a woman, and they robbed the woman, and lete hyr gon, and ledde the man to the see, and whan they knew he was a pylgreme, they geffe hym monei, and sett hym ageyn on the lond ...[109]

But while these crimes could be committed by or against either men or women, there were certain crimes women were typically the victims of. Pilgrimage was not always liberating nor did it free one from hierarchies, particularly gender differences.

Gender was always an issue for female pilgrims, something we can see in criminal records. Women had special risks as pilgrims, especially the danger of rape by fellow companions or those she might meet along the way. Under Richard II [1398/9] Thomas Walsham, a former canon of Walsingham, '[is accused of having] raped against her will Emma, wife of William Bole of Walsingham, coming on pilgrimage to Canterbury, and took goods and chattels from her purse to the value of £20, and is a common thief'.[110] Margery Kempe explicitly cites her fear of rape and theft numerous times while on pilgrimage.[111] St Birgitta's daughter, Catherine, also feared being raped while en route to Rome to meet her mother.[112] A prioress on pilgrimage to Jerusalem, it is related in the life of Saint Altmann, was raped and killed by the infidels.[113] Sometimes the woman pilgrim might be killed by someone she trusted. In 1433 John Carpenter disembowelled his bride while on a pilgrimage.[114]

The very popularity of a pilgrimage shrine could prove dangerous for women pilgrims. In a poem written about Fécamp, the Benedictine shrine on the coast of Normandy, tells how it was overcrowded at Christmas and how a woman pilgrim was seriously wounded when trampled by other pilgrims.[115] In 1221 a case was presented to the king's justices concerning toll-exaction from carts carrying pilgrims in Worcester. In one scandalous case a woman who was carrying out a pilgrimage with difficulty in a cart was charged two shillings.[116] We learn of another woman pilgrim from 1261, who, with her son, John le Chaumpeneys, was on her way to Walsingham. In Bintree John was attacked by their landlord and accidentally killed him in defence.[117]

Unusual juridical proceedings also could prove hazardous for women. Around 1300 a husband and wife from Exeter came to Canterbury on pilgrimage. They had drinks at the house of Ralph of Canterbury. While there someone named Romeus asked for something to drink and the wife from Exeter gave him the dregs of her goblet, whereupon he exclaimed, 'It would be better for you to be somewhere else with Colman, your husband, than here with another man.' Furious at this insult, her husband threw Romeus out, who in turn told people that 'unlawfully wedded and incestuous people had entered the town under cover of pilgrimage'. Accused of adultery, the couple was taken into custody. The dean of the church courts then questioned them separately. 'To the woman he said: "How many children have you had from this man?" To which she replied: "Four". After she had been taken away he interrogated the man about the number of his children, who answered: "Two," remembering the two who had survived and not the two who had died. So the dean judged that they were convicted.' They were then locked up.[118] The crux of the interrogation – how many children they had – reveals not only how tricky investigations can be, but how the husband and wife viewed their progeny. The husband counted as his children only his living ones, his heirs, while the wife included the dead or miscarried ones as well.

Other types of crimes, such as robbery and kidnapping, also plagued women. One case is recorded of a widowed noblewoman from the Ile-de-France, who was separated from the group of people she was on pilgrimage with, kidnapped and subsequently spent several days in the municipal brothel, the Grande Maison, in Dijon.[119] A plea before the King's Bench in 1414 tells of the bizarre kidnapping and robbery in 1410 of 'Alice Pykemere of the county of Chester … as she came from a pilgrimage to the Blessed Mary of Walsingham, together with other pilgrims, towards the aforesaid county of Chester'. John Yardley and 'others' were counselled and abetted by 'Thomas of Yardley and Richard Skyptum, fellow-monks of the abbot of St Werburgh, Chester, apostates to the truth who have been in apostasy for the last ten years past and squanderers in common of the ecclesiastical property of the aforesaid abbey'. They took Alice to numerous villages. Finally they came to

Bescot manor, wherein the Lady Hilary was staying; and they kept her there for a fortnight until the said Alice had made them a certain deed of quitclaim with regard to all actions, personal and real, on account of the aforesaid trespass and robbery, and they forced the said Alice to swear on the Book that she would definitely not prosecute by common law against them or any one of them for the aforesaid trespass and robbery inflicted upon her in the aforesaid manner, in derogation of the aforesaid king and in manifest contravention of the common law.

John Yardley was pardoned due to a pardon issued in 1413 'for wrongdoings committed before 9 April 1413, murders and rapes excepted'.[120]

One of the most incredible cases concerning a woman in the Holy Land is revealed in a Papal Petition to Urban V (1366).

Isolda Parewastel, of Bridgwater. For three years she has daily visited the Lord's Sepulchre and other holy places of the Holy Land, and has there been stripped and placed head downwards on a rack, and beaten; then, half dead, she miraculously escaped from the Saracens, and now proposes to build a chapel at Bridgwater in honour of the Blessed Virgin, and for her soul's health, and for those of her ancestors, and to endow it for one priest with a yearly rent of 36 florins. She therefore prays for license to found and endow the same, and to
. reserve the right of patronage to herself and her heirs.

Put up an altar in the church of the parish in which you wished to build and found the chapel.

Avignon, 13 Kal. Feb.[121]

Anthony Luttrell has discussed Isolda Parewastell and suggests that there is no evidence that she ever founded a chapel or chantry at Bridgwater subsequent to her ordeal,[122] though the papal decision could have meant that she simply found an altar within a parish church rather than found a separate chapel. The many examples of crimes mentioned above show us that women suffered crimes both equally with men and also some peculiar to their gender, such as rape, while on pilgrimage. This evidence indicates that gender remains a factor even if pilgrimage theologically renders all neither man nor woman.

Sea journeying could also be hazardous. Cardinal Jacques de Vitry was told in the thirteenth century

how certain abominable traitors, having received payment to furnish the pilgrims with victuals even to the port [of their destination] have stocked their ships with but little meat, and then, after a few days' journey, have starved their pilgrims to death and cast them ashore on an island, or [most cruel of all] have sold them as manservants or maidservants to the Saracens.

It was also known that

certain sailors bound for the city of Acre … had hired a ship from a man on condition that, if it perished on the sea, they should be bound to pay naught. When therefore they were within a short distance of the haven, they pierced the hold and entered into a boat while the ship was sinking. All the passengers were drowned: and the sailors, having laden their boats with the money and goods of the pilgrims, put on feigned faces of sadness when they drew near unto the haven. Therefore, having drowned the pilgrims and carried away their wealth, they paid not the hire of the ship, saying they were not bound thereunto unless the vessel should come safe and sound to haven.[123]

These cases cited are doubtless exceptional, since the majority of ship owners simply wanted to make money by handling as many pilgrims as quickly as possible. Clearly a captain who made a habit of enslaving his pilgrims or drowning them would not be in business terribly long. Papal letters record another unfortunate case. In 1330, Matilda de Bionie of London, who, on her way

to visit the Holy Sepulchre, Santiago, and Assisi, [whereupon she] was, after leaving Valence, upset out of a boat on the Rhone, when some of her fellow-pilgrims were drowned, and her money lost so that she could not prosecute her pilgrimage. Dispensation to enter some convent instead of fulfilling her purpose.[124]

She was lucky not to have drowned and was able to transmute her vow into entry to a convent.

Political events often played havoc with pilgrims. During the Peasants' Revolt, a large number of the rebels left Canterbury on the morning of June 11, 1381 and marched to London. Naturally they were walking on the same route as that of the pilgrims who made their way to or from the shrine to Thomas Becket. Thomas Walsingham's history of the revolt tells how

[the Kentishmen] blocked all the pilgrimage routes to Canterbury, stopped all pilgrims of whatever condition and forced them to swear: first, that they would be faithful to King Richard and the commons and that they would accept no king who was called John: – on account of their hatred of John, duke of Lancaster who called himself 'King of Castile' because of his marriage to the daughter and heiress of Peter, King of Castile. The pilgrims also had to swear that they would come and join the rebels whenever they were sent for, and that they would induce their fellow citizens or villagers to join them; and that they would neither acquiesce nor consent to any tax levied in the kingdom henceforth except only for the fifteenths which their fathers and ancestors had known and accepted.[125]

Henry Knighton's chronicle tells how the rebels broke open the Marshalsea prison. 'They compelled all the prisoners to join and help them; and also forced all those they met, whether pilgrims or men of whatever condition, to go with them.'[126] Canterbury pilgrims were also apparently guilty of spreading rumours that John of Gaunt had enfranchised all his villeins. According to one conspirator's confession, this false report caused rebels allegedly to replace Richard after a deposition with John.[127]

While the pilgrims in these reports are ungendered, there is one woman pilgrim specifically mentioned in the various accounts of the revolt. Jean Froissart's account is not to be accepted as strictly factual, but he does tell of Joan of Kent, the widow of the Black Prince and mother of Richard II.

> The same day that these unhappy people of Kent were coming to London, there returned from Canterbury the king's mother, princess of Wales, coming from her pilgrimage. She was in great jeopardy to have been lost, for these people came to her chare and dealt rudely with her, whereof the good lady was in great doubt lest they would have done some villany to her or to her damosels. Howbeit, God kept her, and she came in one day from Canterbury to London, for she never durst tarry by the way. The same time Richard her son was at the Tower of London: there his mother found him ...[128]

While Joan of Kent survives this treatment, other women pilgrims were not always so lucky.

The many examples above illustrate how pilgrims were vulnerable away from home. And it is clear that in the eyes of the law the status of pilgrim was an important one, since legal documents detailing crimes committed against pilgrims identify those who are on pilgrimage. Pilgrimage confers a distinctive status, signifying something other than mere movement. It is not the simple act of leaving home, as documents criticizing false pilgrims demonstrate. However, pilgrims do not seem to be specially defended when they are victims of crime. Rather than singling out those who attack pilgrims for special punishment, pilgrims are singled out in documents for social control. Their presence needs intervention by the state since it gives rise to crime. The fact that pilgrims are victims as well as perpetrators does not seem to be an issue. Ultimately, pilgrimage itself is perceived as disruptive and in need of state control.

England was not the only country to attempt controls over pilgrimage activity. In the 1450s and 1460s in Germany, Charles Zika has shown how discussions of sacred space by such men as John Hus and Heinrich Tocke, a Magdeburg canon and theologian, reflect fears of social disorder, describing pilgrims in terms of irrationality. In his description of the Wilsnack pilgrimage of 1475, the Saxon Augustinian, Johannes Dorsten, interprets it as societal chaos.[129] Pilgrimage was perceived as a subversion of the 'natural' authority of priest, lord and spouse.[130] As Zika comments on the differences between church organized processions and pilgrimages,

> Procession emphasized the community's celebration of its sacred objects throughout prescribed political space; pilgrimage signified a potentially uncontrollable journey beyond the borders of one's territory (or through one's territory) to a foreign location sanctified by the relics and wonders of others ... The pilgrimage into foreign parts, much of it beyond ecclesiastical control and prescription, its end a locally embedded object dependent upon miraculous powers for its truth, is more and more frequently regarded as a danger and a threat.[131]

Attacks on sacred mobility increase in Germany throughout the fifteenth century, and the authorization of pilgrims, as opposed to mere travellers, is stressed.[132] Similarly, in England, reflecting the fear of social disorder heightened by the plague and the undermining of traditional authorities, the perception that pilgrims could be false continued into and through the fifteenth century.[133] Pilgrims had to be licensed. One document from 1473 [Appendix A. 13], explains why false pilgrims are so dangerous.

> Forasmuch as this day many persons being strong of body to service in husbandry and other labours feign them to be sick and feeble and some ... [*sic*] in going of pilgrimages and not of power to perform it without alms of the people, and some also feign to be clerks in universities using study and not of power to continue it without help of the people; by means of which feigning, divers fall into the said beggings in cities, boroughs and other places, and so living idly will not do service, but wander about from town to town in vagabondage, sowing seditious languages whereby the country people be put in great fear and jeopardy of their lives and losses of their goods, and many other inconveniences follow by occasion of the same, as murders, robberies and riots, mischievous to the disturbance of the people and contrary to the king's laws and peace. Our sovereign lord ... straightly chargeth and commandeth ... that no person go in pilgrimage, not able to perform it without begging, unless he have letters testimonial under the great seal ordained for the same, testifying the causes of his going and the places whence he came and whither he shall go: and that no clerk of any university go begging for his sustenance, unless he have letters testimonial of the chancellor, witnessing that he is a clerk of poverty intending his learning not able to continue without relief of begging ...[134]

The linkage of pilgrims begging and clerics begging may seem to be an odd twinning, but as early as the fourteenth century theologians had commented on the problems inherent to clerical begging. André Vauchez shows how poverty became less of a virtue in canonization proceedings in the late medieval period. The general master of the Dominicans, Harvey Nédellec, wrote to Pope John XXII concerning clerical begging which could turn a cleric from God in his increased preoccupation with simply surviving. Nédellec wrote, 'to trust to chance for the necessities of life when one can do otherwise, seems dangerous'.[135] The reliance on others for sustenance by clerics or pilgrims was potentially fraught with exploitation and deviation from piety.

While the church is concerned with spiritual deprivation brought about by begging, English documents expresses anxiety about both political insurrection and social disorder. This one from 1493 [Appendix A. 14] reflects the anxiety and perception that pilgrimage was being used as a disguise for beggars, murderers and thieves:

> The kyng our soverayne lord is informed that full heynes murdres, and robries, thefte, decaye of husbaondrye and other enormyties and inconveniences daily increase within this his realme to the greate offense unto God, displeasour to his highnesse, hurt and impoverisshing vexacion and troble of his subgjettis by the mean of idelnesse and specially of vagabundes, beggers able to werk and by faitours; summe excusyng them self by colour of pylgrymages.[136]

Here a statute from the time of Richard II is invoked as support for Henry VII's insistence that legal officers examine questionnable folk. In fact, if they do not interrogate these creatures, they stand to lose 20 *d* themselves.

The statutes and proclamations which attempted to control the social order and movement were enforced at least some of the time. We have evidence of those who disobeyed decrees which attempted to control pilgrimage. One woman, the lady of Segrave, crossed the channel in defiance of Edward III's prohibition shortly after the plague when these restrictive measures were starting to proliferate [Appendix A. 3]. In another proclamation [Appendix A. 4], Edward III angrily recognizes that the warden of the Cinque Ports and constable of Dover castle has not fulfilled his duties in stopping people from leaving the realm without a licence. The king demands the names of those who have gone. A most suggestive document [Appendix A. 5] from 1369 tells the story of a woman Joan, wife of Thomas de Burton of London. She was apparently ignorant of the ordinances about not taking money out the realm without a license. Her husband had departed on a pilgrimage for the Holy Land only to be imprisoned and ransomed. To set him free, Joan sold property and goods and attempted to take the money abroad, whereupon she was searched and arrested. Ultimately, Edward III orders her money returned to her on May 22 of that year.

The lollard view of pilgrims

The impression that pilgrims were disruptive and not necessarily devout was a view espoused not only in official documents but also in anti-official proceedings. The famous heresy examination of the itinerant Lollard preacher William Thorpe before Thomas Arundel, Archbishop of Canterbury, in 1407, carries numerous references to pilgrims. True pilgrimage for Thorpe lies in one of two manners: travelling toward the bliss of heaven and doing works of mercy. 'Pilgrimage of God' lies in the delight of hearing of saints and virtuous men and women, forsaking prosperity of life, withstanding the fiend, restraining fleshly lusts, and being discreet in acts of penance, patient in adversity and prudent in counselling men and women. Most male and female pilgrims do not act this way, asserts Thorpe. Out of twenty pilgrims, only three can say the *Pater Noster*, *Ave Maria* or Creed. Both male and female pilgrims go

> more for the health of their bodies, then of their soules; more for to have riches and prosperitie of this worlde, than for to be enriched with vertues in their soules; more to have here worldly and fleshlie friendship, then for to have friendship of God & of his saints in heaven: for whatsoever thing man or woman doth, the friendship of God, nor of any other saint, cannot be had, without keeping of Gods commandements. Further, with my protestation, I saie now as I said in Shrewsbury, though they that have fleshly wils, travell for their bodies and spend mikle mony, to seeke and to visite the bones and images (as they saie they do) of that saint or of that, such pilgrimage-going is neither praiseable nor thankfull to God, nor to any saint of God, since, in effect, all such pilgrimages despise God and all his commandements and saints … [S]uch fond people waste blamefullie Gods goods in their vaine pilgrimages, spending their goods upon vitious hostelars, which are oft uncleane women of their bodies; and at the least,

those goods, with the which they should doe workes of mercie, after gods bidding, to poore needie men and women.[137]

His most famous comment from this examination reminds us of the musical Miller in the *Canterbury Tales*.

> I know well that when divers men and women will go thus after their own wills, and finding out one pilgrimage they will ordain beforehand to have with them both men and women that can well sing wanton songs. And some other pilgrims will have them bagpipes so that every town that they come through shall know of their coming, what with the noise of their singing and the sound of their piping, what with the jangling of their Canterbury bells, and the barking out of dogs after them. They make more noise than if the King came thereaway with all his clarions and many other minstrels.[138]

Whether or not Thorpe is accurate about pilgrim misbehaviour, it is clear that he condemns both men and women and that neither sex is more harshly condemned than the other. Pilgrims are noisy, liars, and not turned to God.

The fundamental belief in the efficacy of images, inspiring pilgrimage not only to shrines with relics but places with painted or crafted images of saints, stands in strong contrast to heretical arguments such as Thorpe's. While official doctrine promoted the positive effects of images, sometimes tempered with warnings against idolatry, Lollard treatises unequivocally objected to pilgrimages and images and their misuse. Anne Hudson emphasises the spectrum of beliefs Lollards held concerning images and pilgrimages, ranging from iconoclasm to more cautionary fear of abuse.[139] Essentially, a Lollard's attitude towards pilgrimage depended on his or her attitude toward images.[140] Genuine meritorious physical pilgrimage should be performed by visiting the poor, sick and infirm, not relics or images. Not only do Christians risk being idolators by going on pilgrimage to venerate a particular image, but they risk being exploited as well. One Lollard homilist asserts that if 'a wife lose a keye of valew of thre pens, anon she wil hete to seke seynt Sithe, and spende a noble or ten schilyngis in the iurney'.[141]

Underlying all of this suspicion is a fundamental sense of the futility of 'blessed places'. God created the entire world and did not favour one spot over another. If he had and if a special place could be saved, then the Garden of Eden would have been preserved and Eve never would have bitten the apple. Walsingham in particular was singled out for attack by Lollards: 'Wherefore it is a vein waast and idil for to trotte to Wa(l)singham rather than to ech other place in which an ymage of Marie is …'[142] This suspicion of place also extends into Lollard views on baptism. Some Lollards felt that a boy born to a married couple needed no baptism.[143] The East Anglian heresy investigation of 1428–31 revealed that a number of suspects likewise believed that baptism was not obligatory. A clerk, Thomas Bikenore, investigated in 1443, suggested that baptism is not required when the mother is a Christian 'because the Holy Ghost is transmitted to the child in the womb'.[144]

Sources showing women who were against pilgrimage include the trials of sixty men and women prosecuted for heresy in Norwich 1428–31. This period coincided with other anti-Lollardy activities elsewhere in England, including the province of Canterbury. One of the most extreme incidents took place in spring 1428 when the Bishop of Lincoln had Wyclif's supposed bones dug up and burnt. The major belief of the defendants in Norwich in attacking images and pilgrimages was the implication that earthly objects (images) or bones of dead men (relics) were somehow holier than other objects or bones. The accused Lollards usually qualified their attacks by allowing that poor people were justified in going on pilgrimage, or that the expenses of a pilgrimage should be given to the poor. The most frequently criticized shrines were Our Lady of Walsingham, Our Lady of Woolpit and St Thomas of Canterbury – 'sometimes punned as "the Lefdy of Falsyngham, the Lefdy of Foulpette and Thomme of Cankerbury"'.[145] Defendants included fifty-one men and nine women, four from Martham alone. Most of the defendants came from a group of small towns and villages in south and east of Norfolk and northeast Suffolk. Fewer came from larger towns.[146] Hawisia Moone, wife of Thomas Moone of Loddon, states in her testimony that

> no pilgrimage oweth to be do ne be made, for all pilgrimage goyng servyth of nothyng but oonly to yeve prestes good that be to riche and to make gay tap[s]ters and proude ostelers.
>
> Also that no worship ne reverence oweth be do to ony ymages of the crucifix, of Our Lady ne of noon other seyntes, for all suche ymages be but ydols and maade be werkyng of mannys hand, but worship and reverence shuld be do to the ymage of God, whiche oonly is man.[147]

John Foxe records an incident dating from about 1518 to 1521 wherein a man named Cotismore of Britwell in Oxfordshire made a vow during his last illness to go on pilgrimage to Walsingham; should he not survive, a servant should go for him. After the man's death the chaplain, Sir John Hakker, tried to make arrangements with his widow.

> Sir John, a priest, and also Robert Robinson, detected Master Cotismore, of Brightwell. Also Mistress Cotismore, otherwise called Mistress Dolly, for speaking these words to one John Bainton, her servant: That is she went to her chamber, and prayed there, she would have as much merit as though she went to Walsingham on pilgrimage. Item, when the said Sir John came to her after the death of Master Cotismore, his master, requiring her to send one John Stainer, her servant, to our Lady of Walsingham, for Master Cotismore, who in his lifetime, being sick, promised in his own person to visit that place, she would not consent thereto, nor let her servant go. Item, for saying, that when women go to offer to images or saints, they did it but to show their gay gear: that images were but carpenters' chips; and that folks go on pilgrimage more for the green way, than for any devotion.[148]

Royal proclamations which ordered the control of physical movement had economic motives and also reflected a clear anxiety about the disruption of the social order. Oddly, control over pilgrims was demanded both by the state and by the state's enemy, heretics such as Lollards. Interior motivation for pilgrimage was not controllable, recognized by Lollards in accusations that some pilgrims go more for pleasure than faith (but how can that be proven?), and recognized by the state in references to false pilgrims (how can that be verifiable?). The government attempted control over pilgrimage by recording its practitioners through licenses, while the Lollard attempt at control was through the dismantling of the system rhetorically. One such device was sarcasm or ridicule. Shannon McSheffrey, in her book *Gender and Heresy: Women and Men in Lollard Communities 1420–1530*, discusses the problems faced in mixed marriages, wherein one spouse was orthodox and the other Lollard. Lollard husbands may have feared that their wives might testify against them, but this did not prevent them from discouraging their wives from going on pilgrimage. When the wife of William Dorset is about to set out to Our Lady of Willesdon, he comments, 'Our lady is in heaven.' Another husband assures his wife that priests only have economic motives in encouraging pilgrimage.[149] When Alice Gardner asked her godson, John Tyball, to go with her to Ipswich on pilgrimage, he pointed out she should give money to poor people and not dead images.[150] Isabel Morwyn tried to convert her sister, Elizabeth, who, questioning the Lollard aversion to pilgrimage, asked why 'pilgrimage was ordained by doctors and priests? [Isabel] said, for gain and profit.'[151] The rhetoric thrust of much of these criticisms of pilgrimages is economic in base. Just as the royal proclamations linked money with movement, so too did Lollard critiques of pilgrimage.

In orthodox and heterodox opinions agreeing that pilgrimage needed controls, whether economic or in being outright eliminated, these rhetorical acts affected women pilgrims. Lollard speech undermines the pilgrimage act itself, ridiculing 'the gullible layperson – often enough specifically a woman – who believed that the saints could save him or her'.[152] The post-plague restrictions advocate controls, suggesting that men and women pilgrims are out of control. In the next chapter we will see how this uncontrolled pilgrim becomes centred on the sexual active woman pilgrim in secular texts.

Pilgrimage: group or individual activity?

The documentation in this chapter amply illustrates the actual participation on pilgrimage by women. Going on a pilgrimage, a woman was not an oddity and even, in some cases, would be part of the majority of pilgrims to a particular shrine. But can we theorize pilgrimage as a social activity or an individual activity? Eamon Duffy's *The Stripping of the Alters: Traditional Religion in England c.1400–c.1580* argues for the fertile state of medieval Catholicism before and even during the early Reformation period. One of Duffy's most crucial arguments concerns the question of individual as opposed to corporate religious devotion. While many scholars have emphasized the growth in private piety as the basis for the decay of late medieval Catholicism, giving way eventually to the Reformation, Duffy emphasizes the corporate aspects of late medieval devotion, concluding that 'late medieval Christians identified individual spiritual welfare with that of the community as a whole'.[153] Duffy offers much evidence for this communal nature of late medieval piety. As Philip M. Soergel puts it in a review of Duffy's book,

> English historians in particular have recently toyed with the notion that a new birth of individualized religious sentiment appeared during the fifteenth century, a factor that prepared many, especially urban elites, for the later introduction of Reformation principles. Duffy's work shows how scant the evidence is for this 'Revolution of the Individual.' Late-medieval English men and women retained passionate attachments to forms of group-centered piety. Gilds, parishes, and other kinds of religious associations were the essential vehicles though which both high and low witnessed, participated, and acted upon the central rituals that formed their faith.[154]

This type of group activity we saw in English Hospice which recorded confraternity members. We can also see it in guild records, wherein members' pilgrimage activities are economically supported.

Financing a pilgrimage abroad could be very expensive. Pilgrims would have to pay for a sea passage to the continent, depending upon their ultimate destination. If they had a long land route, which most did, they had to find and pay for lodging and food along the way. Some English received royal gifts, such as Margaret Norton, who received ten shillings by Edward II in 1321. Someone might inherit money on condition that he or she carry out a pilgrimage by proxy for the dead soul. As we have seen, money taken out of the country was strictly controlled, with particular restrictions on good silver money.[155] Others received alms.

Still oth[er ... relied on their guilds or confrater]nities to subsidise the trip. Guilds and guild re[...] men acted as pilgrims or otherwise participated [...] ggest that virtually all of the nearly five hundre[d ...] male and female members. Women were admit[ted ...] ng those run by priests. They had many of the [...] Guild members went on pilgrimage and aided t[hem ...] financially, such as releasing them from their [...] Holy Land as in the Guild of the Blessed Vir[gin ...] was founded in 1357 by ten men and twelve [...] Resurrection of the Lord, Lincoln, would recei[ve ...] rs if she went to Rome, St James of Galicia, or [...] l of the Fullers of Lincoln also gave a halfpenny [...] ge to Ss. Peter and Paul. The Guild of the Tailo[rs ...] give a penny to those in the guild going to the [...] ne, a halfpenny. Others helped out with drink, [...] l of the Holy Cross, Bishop's Lynn. Other guild[s ...] try, aided pilgrims coming to their town or wh[ere ...] . The Coventry guild kept a house where poor [...] the Guild of St Benedict and the

BARCODE: DCPL9000088274
TITLE: Women pilgrims in late Medieval E
DUE DATE: 18 Sep 2021

Current Check-Outs summary for Keely, Dr
Sat Aug 28 10:31:20 BST 2021

Guild of the Tailors, both of Lincoln, if a pilgrim were to die on pilgrimage abroad or away from home, the pilgrim should be prayed for as if she were at home.[157] These guild records support Duffy's emphasis on group piety. In the organization of guilds, economic and spiritual aims and endeavours fused. Economic entities, such as guilds, were a means for pursuing spiritual activities.

Functioning as a kind of diptych with Duffy's work, Anne Hudson's seminal book, *The Premature Reformation: Wycliffite Texts and Lollard History*, investigates the state of heterodox opinion in pre-Reformation England. These two books present opposing yet ultimately complementary visions of late medieval England. While Duffy emphasizes the dissenting voices to the Henrican Reformation, that is, Catholic orthodox opinion resisting the changes of the 1530s and 1540s, Hudson focuses on dissension prior to the dismantling of the Catholic Church in England, concluding that the Lollard 'Reformation', had it succeeded, would have been far more extreme in its measures than the Henrican/Edwardian one.[158] Furthermore, Hudson, admittedly hampered by inadequate records, investigates the tension and interplay in Lollard society between individual and group activity. She brings out the importance of family in Lollard society and the domestic element. In a Lollard group, at least one member would most likely be able to read, for example.[159] But fundamental to Lollard thought was a theology based on Scripture, each believer deducing his or her own theology from Scripture. Thus, individual conscience is the basis of Lollard thought, leading, Hudson suggests, to an inevitable fragmentation inherent to any Lollard movement.[160]

Taking Duffy's and Hudson's views into consideration, can we understand pilgrimage as an individual or group phenomenon? All the sources cited above have one thing in common aside from pilgrimage: money. In investigating sources for women pilgrims, the economics of the pilgrimage act are unavoidable. Pilgrimage is never a wholly personal act; it collides with financial reality on some level, whether in a letter of protection, granting power of attorney, wills, or *inquisitions post mortem*.

These documents show how certain things were documentable and others were not and perhaps could not be, thus indicating to us the limitations in trying to find historical women pilgrims. Things which are able to be documented are financial and political. While the personal dimension may be hidden from us, the social aspects of this documentation do reveal a lot. For example, these documents show how the bodies of people and their goods moving in and out of the realm needed to be controlled. Pilgrimage was interpentrated with economic and dynastic concerns. We can perceive an attempt on the part of the state to control pilgrimage activities.

Women pilgrims in particular are recorded in a gender-specific way. That is, if they are married or widowed, they are identified in connection with their husband, dead spouse or religious profession. Male pilgrims in such documents, on the other hand, are recorded as individuals or in terms of their profession or title. One aspect in which men are read separately depends on class. Knights, esquires, etc., are separated from other travellers since their ability to fight for (or against) and defend the kingdom in times of war was deemed vital to the realm. These ways of typing pilgrims are 'social', in that legal documents wed the party described to a particular class or marital status, both aspects of societal structure. But women are peculiarly identified by their bodies, bodies which are the property of their husbands or wedded to Christ. Even in legal documents which otherwise do not distinguish between the sexes in recording letters of protection, for example, gender matters. At the same time, though, the church and state see pilgrims, male or female, as economic agents who will spend money or not. A woman's ability to spend money puts her on equal footing with men. Men and women are seen equally in terms of vow-making. This would argue against reading women pilgrims as an individual class. Thus, a tension exists between reading women pilgrims separately from men, in that, say, they identify with certain saints, and reading them as genderless spenders.

This private act of piety becomes publicly documented and of social importance. That which is recordable is controllable, in that it is traceable and comprehensible, yet religious devotion, while documentable to a certain extent, could not, ultimately, be controlled by church or state. The very control the church or state attempts to exert over pilgrims shows how it is a social phenomenon, in that there are economic and legal controls placed on it, but also individual since the personal motivation can range from the devout to the subversive, motivations which can be moulded or informed by culture but not mandated by official bodies such as the government or church.

The fact that the state is exerting control demonstrates how little control the state had, in reality, over other, undocumentable, aspects of people's lives. Matters of faith are not really documentable unless someone's visions are written down, as in the case of Julian of Norwich or Margery Kempe, or taken down in heresy trials. Why did the women, for whom we only have letters of protection, go on pilgrimage? Were they devout souls or interested only in getting away from home? Were they experiencing mystical unions with Christ or simply carrying out a vow to a dying husband? There is no way of knowing these matters from the material we have. The state can control the body or monies of someone, but not that person's spirit, mind or faith. The documents which list women's names intending pilgrimage illustrate both the control of the government and church over their activities, and the lack of control those entities ultimately wield, hence the suspicion towards pilgrims shown in legal and literary texts, as we will see. Pilgrimage exposes the way the binary of control/lack of control breaks down. Pilgrims were both controlled, by being recorded, but also were free, in that much of their activity on pilgrimage was not able to be controlled, such as personal reaction to a shrine visit.

Pilgrimage as creative endeavour

The Lollard denigration of the cult of the saints and the practices associated with it was not, ultimately, favourable to women. McSheffrey argues that men were more attracted to Lollardy than women. Lollards

> attacked various aspects of medieval piety that have been associated particularly with female religiosity: eucharistic devotions, ascetic practices, and veneration of saints. Whether such aspects of medieval Catholic religion can indeed be identified as specifically female is still an open question. Nonetheless, Lollard opposition to nonscriptural Catholic practices, particularly the cult of saints, took away

from women one of the only spheres of religious activity over which they had a significant measure of control.[161]

Even the many religious rituals associated with childbirth and being churched were put down by Lollard rhetoricians. Practices connected with the cult of saints, such as pilgrimage, offered women some autonomy and creativity in their religion. By criticizing these, women were being denied an outlet for control and power. This chapter concludes with a more detailed look at three women pilgrims. We can, perhaps, understand more about the motivations of Margery Kempe (who will be discussed at greater length in a later chapter), Elizabeth de Burgh and Elizabeth of York for endorsing pilgrimage since we, quite simply, have more material to draw from due to their social prominence. These three women illustrate how pilgrimage activities provide a path to self-creation and expression.

Margery Kempe

One of the most famous sources concerning women pilgrims is *The Book of Margery Kempe* which dates from the first half of the fifteenth century. While it has generally been assumed that Margery, an apparently illiterate merchant-class woman from Lynn in Norfolk, dictated her life to various amanuenses, Lynn Staley's recent book, *Margery Kempe's Dissenting Fictions,* suggests the view that Kempe the 'author' and Margery the protagonist are radically different figures, thus making the *Book* a more consciously crafted work than previously considered. Whether or not we read Kempe's *Book* as it presents itself on the surface – the simple retelling of the spiritual and literal pilgrimages of an early fifteenth-century woman – or as a subversive criticism of an increasingly mercantile society as Staley does, with the speculation that Kempe may not have even gone on the pilgrimages she claims[162] – we do gain insight into the nuts and bolts of some aspects of pilgrimage in late medieval England. For example, Kempe needs permission from her husband before she can go on pilgrimage.

> Sone aftyr þis creatur was meuyd in hir sowle to go vysyten certeyn places for gostly helth in-as-mech as sche was cured, & mygth not wyth-owtyn consentyng of hir husbond. Sche reqwired hir husbond to graw[n]tyn hir leue, &, he, fully trostyng it was þe wyl of God, sone consentyng, þei went to-gedyr to swech place as sche was mevyd.[163]

She must also have her debts paid before she leaves on pilgrimage to the Holy Land, since her financial status must be clear before she departs.

> Whan tyme cam þat þis creatur xuld vysiten þo holy placys wher owyr Lord was whyk & ded, as sche had be reuelacyon ȝerys a-forn, sche preyd þe parysch preste of þe town þer sche was dwellyng to sey for hir in þe pulpyt þat, yf any man er woman þat cleymyd any dette of hir husbond or of hir þei xuld come & speke wyth hir er sche went, & sche, wyth þe help of God, xulde makyn a-seth to ech of hem þat þei schuldyn heldyn hem content. & so sche dede.[164]

She goes to 'diuers placys of relygyon',[165] which for Kempe signify both pilgrimage sites and places where religious live, such as monasteries, or anchorite cells, like that of Julian of Norwich. The Lord commands her to go to the three major pilgrimage sites of the Middle Ages: Rome, Jerusalem and Santiago de Compostela.[166] The Bishop of Lincoln cites her impending pilgrimage to Jerusalem as a means of proving herself and being recognized.[167]

On her way to Yarmouth, where she boards a ship to the continent for her trip to Jerusalem, she goes to Norwich, making an offering at the Cathedral of the Holy Trinity, and then at an image of Our Lady in Yarmouth. It is impossible to know if other pilgrims were mean to Kempe or not, as she suggests. But certain aspects of the trip coincide with historical records and other pilgrims' diaries. The group she travels with makes it to Venice where they must wait thirteen weeks. Windeatt comments that, calculating from other pilgrim records, it may have taken Kempe six to eight weeks to go from Lynn to Venice. The pilgrims' ships normally left Venice in spring or early summer.[168] The various sights she witnesses in the Holy Land – from seeing the Mount of Calvary to where Christ was born, from viewing where Christ reputedly celebrated the Last Supper to riding an ass into Bethlehem – are all familiar events in the experiences of other pilgrimage accounts. Later on she sees the Virgin's veil in Assisi and goes to the Hospital of St Thomas of Canterbury in Rome, a pilgrim hospice, where she is first beloved and then kicked out.

The threat of thieves is paramount in her text. While in Rome she is asked by women 'ȝyf malendrynes had robbyd hir, & sche seyd, "Nay, madame"'.[169] Later on she returns home and wants to go to Santiago. She received donations for her journey, but 'þan was it seyd in Lynne þat þer wer many theuys be þe wey. Þan had sche gret drede þat þei xulde robbyn hir & takyn hir golde a-wey fro hir'.[170] The Lord reassures her. She has to wait in Bristol for a ship. This was a usual port for Santiago. She also makes pilgrimages to see the Blood of Hailes, where Christ's blood – supposedly – existed in Gloucester, to Canterbury, to York for St William's shrine, to Ely, to Walsingham, to Aachen and to Wilsnack. We get little description, however, of these pilgrimage sites, though she frequently augments her elaboration of the place with complaints of how she was treated there or emotes on the spiritual revelation she experienced. We do get a hint at the fatigue brought on by pilgrimage. En route to Wilsnack she tells us how it was a great marvel that a sixty-year-old woman could keep up walking with a young man, though she falls ill. Finally some pilgrims travel in a wagon and let her join them.[171] These details of the quotidian aspects of pilgrimage are, in themselves, important for confirming other pilgrimage accounts and historical documents as to the actual means of pilgrimaging. Margery Kempe's text is more suggestive about the state of medieval pilgrimage and woman's place in it beyond the level of how one goes on a pilgrimage. As we will see in Chapter 5, theoretical issues touching on space and performance can be teased out of her text, illuminating not only her life and work, but the position of medieval women pilgrims in general. We also see that, while women pilgrims were under the control of men (Kempe had to ask her husband's permission to go on pilgrimage), women pilgrims thought of themselves not just as pilgrims, but also as women.

Elizabeth de Burgh

One prominent woman linked to pilgrimage is Elizabeth de Burgh, born in 1295 to Gilbert de Clare, ninth earl of that title, and Princess Joan, daughter of Edward I. Elizabeth was niece to Edward III. Married three times and heiress to one-third of the Clare lands, she was a very wealthy and important dowager until her death in 1360.[172] Her household accounts are extensive and well documented. Other documentation concerning her pilgrimage activities exists as well. One papal letter asks that she 'may choose a confessor, who shall transmute the vow she made in her husband's lifetime to visit the Holy Land and Santiago di Compostella, which, being forty, she cannot hope to fulfil, to some other works of piety, and to absolve her'. She is absolved and the bishop of London is to 'forward to Santiago the oblation which she would have given.'[173] She was really forty-eight years old, which is relatively young when one considers Margery Kempe travelling in her sixties. Elizabeth has left ample evidence of her connections to pilgrimage sites. Jennifer Ward, who has written extensively on the household account illustrating numerous aspects of her – and other noblewomen's – lives, reports that Elizabeth went on pilgrimages to Canterbury, Walsingham, and Bromholm, with its shrine of the Holy Rood.

Elizabeth's connection to Walsingham was deeply rooted. She established a Franciscan priory there in 1347, much against the will of the Augustinian canons who enjoyed a lucrative relationship with pilgrims. Her patronage supported goldsmiths creating jewellery, plate, images, and religious vessels.[174] In fact, one document recording her payment to such artisans records a pilgrimage.

> John de Lenne [clerk of the wardrobe] accounts for payment to Robert the illuminator and Thomas the goldsmith staying behind at Bardfield, the lady being at Clare and going on pilgrimage to Walsingham, from 21 August to 3 October inclusive, namely for 42 days, each taking 2*d* a day, 14*s* 8*d*.[175]

Other records list her extensive religious expenditures.[176] For example, Elizabeth's private expenditures for 1351 include 'Item, for the offering by my lady and Lady Bardolf and Lady Athol on the feast of St Thomas [29 December], 3*d*.'[177]

But Elizabeth de Burgh's connection to pilgrimage may not only be limited to her own activities. In October 1344, Margaret, Countess of Hereford and Essex, and widow of John de Bohun, nominates attorneys for her planned pilgrimage to Santiago and other holy places. It is said that her husband had often seen much of his cousin, Elizabeth de Burgh, first cousin to Edward III and who was involved in pilgrimage activities herself. Perhaps Elizabeth's intense interest in pilgrimage sparked her cousin-in-law's desire to go abroad.[178]

Joan de Bar, countess of Surrey and Sussex, receives a safe-conduct letter in 1350 to go to various shrines.[179] The granddaughter of Edward I and married at the age of ten, she had been threatened with divorce by her husband, John de Warenne, who had children by a mistress. He died three years before she planned this pilgrimage. Like Margaret de Bohun, Joan was friendly with Elizabeth de Burgh who even bequeathed her a golden image of St John the Baptist in the desert.[180] In fact, she is recorded as having visited Elizabeth de Burgh from May 8 to May 11, 1350. The safe-conduct letter is dated May 30, 1350, shortly after this visit, again suggesting that Elizabeth may have influenced Joan's activities.[181] In 1355 Joan is granted dispensation for a year and a half from a pilgrimage vow. She explains the request for delay: 'Whereas she, while at sea between England and France, vowed not to return to England until she visited Santiago, and afterwards on hearing of her husband's death returned to look after his property in England without fulfilling her vow.'[182] Here financial matters intervened preventing her religious endeavours.

Yet another pilgrim connected to Elizabeth de Burgh is her granddaughter, Agnes Bardolf, Lady of Wormgay, the widow of Thomas Mortimer. Elizabeth bequeathed her numerous goods 'to help her to marry', including several religious items, such as 'one silver cross ... one great almsdish ... one incense-boat, one censer, one clasp with the Annunciation depicted on it ...'[183] In 1403 Agnes received a licence to go on pilgrimage to Rome, Cologne, and other 'foreign parts' with twelve men and twelve horses, as well as ample money.[184] Considering their close relationship, including religious activity, it would be surprising if Elizabeth's support of pilgrimage had not affected Agnes in her decision to go on pilgrimage.

With Elizabeth de Burgh, the social aspects of pilgrimage mean not just whom she travelled with or how her activities were recorded. Her possible influence on other women's pilgrimage activities suggests how pilgrimage for women was a bonding experience even if carried out individually. Pilgrimage did not create just an inner spiritual feeling, but also spun a web among women of a certain class, connected by blood, marriage and pilgrimage.

Elizabeth of York

While her position as princess and then queen designates her as atypical of most women in late medieval England, Elizabeth of York (1465–1503), daughter of Edward the IV and wife of Henry VII, nonetheless represents many facets typical of women pilgrims in the period before the Reformation as talked about in this chapter. In the mid-1490s she went on pilgrimage to Walsingham after the deaths of her four-year-old daughter, Princess Elizabeth, and an infant son.[185] As we have seen, Walsingham was a shrine which had a particularly attractive resonance for women, in particular, women in conjunction with childbirth, children, and fertility. She and her mother-in-law, Margaret Beaufort, commissioned the printing of prayers by Saint Birgitta of Sweden, the well-known and influential pilgrim-mystic of the fourteenth century. Like many other women pilgrims, most famously Margery Kempe, Elizabeth was affected by this pilgrim's spiritual guidance and experiences, so much so that she and her husband's mother commanded William Caxton in 1490 to produce this volume.[186]

But it is in the Privy Purse Expenses of the Queen, which exist from 1502–3 until her death, where we find even more evidence for the role of pilgrims and pilgrimage in this woman's life. Without the privy purse expenses of other queens it is impossible to compare her to them and decide if she were more or less devout than other consorts. She is clearly no ascetic. We can see this in that she gives money for her fool,[187] for the 'boy bishop',[188] for payment of her debts from gambling at dice and cards,[189] to rewards offered the Lord of Misrule for Christman celebrations,[190] to her minstrel,[191] and a Spanish dancing girl.[192] She also payed for a 'disare' or tale teller, who 'played the Sheppert before the Quene', apparently the shepherd in the adoration.[193]

We can also see in her expenses a reflection of her life, one in which the church calendar provides both chronological structure and the reminder of offerings to be made at various churches. For example, the first entry in the Privy Purse Expenses concerns money to be donated to poor women upon Shire Thursday. Thereafter follow offerings to be made upon Good Friday, upon Easter to the cross and during Easter week on Monday, Tuesday and Wednesday, as well as money to be given to an anchoress.[194] She pays Robert Fayrfax 'for setting an Anthem of oure lady and Saint Elizabeth'.[195] Clearly, her spiritual activities are not merely duties, since she has had religious music created in honour of the Virgin and, most probably, Elizabeth of Hungary, whose relics drew pilgrims in Marburg.[196]

We also get specific mention of pilgrimage. Sir William Barton, priest, is given money to present offerings of the Queen to shrines at Windsor (Our Lady and Saint George and the Holy Cross), Eton (Henry VI and Our Lady), Reading (Child of Grace), Caversham (Our Lady), Cockthorpe (Our Lady), the Holy Blood of Hailes, Prince Edward (the son of King Henry VI who was killed in the battle in Tewksbury in 1471), Worcester (Our Lady), Northampton (Holy Rood and Our Lady of Grace), Walsingham (Our Lady), Sudbury (Our Lady), Woolpit (Our Lady), Ipswich (Our Lady), and Stokeclare (Our Lady). This vicarious pilgrimage or pilgrimage by proxy, quite common in the Middle Ages and often set out in wills, took the priest twenty-six days to accomplish, the expenses for which he received tenpence a day.[197]

She also pays Richard Mylner of Bynfeld, apparently not a priest, to offer money to various shrines in Kent:

> to our lady of Crowham ... To the roode of Grace in Kent ... to Saint Thomas of Canterbury ... to oure lady of undrecroft there ... to Sainct Adrean ... to Saint Augustyn ... to our lady of Dover ... to the roode of the north dore in Poules ... to our lady of Grace there ... to Saint Ignasi ... To Saint Dominik ... To Saint Petre of Melayn ... to Saint Fraunces ... to Saint Savioure ... to oure lady of Piewe [of pity or grace at Westminster] ... to our lady of Berking ... and to our lady of Willesdone ... [198]

These pilgrimages took him eight days. In February, 1503, the month of the queen's death in the aftermath of childbirth, a man is paid for having gone on pilgrimage at the commandment of the queen to 'Our Lady of Willesden'.[199] Her evident devotion to the Virgin, as we can see in the overwhelming choice of pilgrimage sites chosen, particularly in the month of the birth of her child, is not accidental. The Virgin was a particularly potent symbol for childbearing women in their pilgrimage activities, whether undertaken by themselves or by proxy.

R. N. Swanson suggests that some of her accounts, particularly those for offerings made at feasts, have a 'ritualized quality', suggested a lack of spontaneity on her part. However, other payments arise erratically suggesting her immediate personal choice, as in money given to the anchoress of St Peter's at St Albans.[200] Like many other medieval men and women, she has offerings made during an illness to induce saints to intercede on her behalf.[201] She particularly targets the Virgin as her patron saint in her time of illness. The offerings are made to Our Lady at Northampton, money given to five priests to perform five masses before Our Lady there. Additional money is given as an offering to the Rood at Northampton and Our Lady at Linchelade. Elizabeth may have sought out the Virgin's help in an illness related to her pregnancy (the payments are made in August 1502 and she gives birth and dies in childbirth in February 1503). As we have seen, women were particularly attracted to the Virgin and sought her help in times of childbirth and its related complications. We have further evidence of this with Elizabeth in her payment to a monk in December 1502, two months before her delivery, for a 'Lady gyrdelle'.[202] Nicolas comments that it was

> [p]robably one of the numerous Relicks with which the monasteries and abbies then abounded, and which might have been brought to the Queen for her to put on when in labour, as it was a common practice for women in that situation to wear blessed girdles[203]

which may have helped to ensure a safe delivery.[204] This purchase and these offerings suggest a personal relationship and identification between women and saints' images and talismans. Late medieval women pilgrims practised many of the activities which Elizabeth of York has been shown to have undertaken. Women paid for proxy pilgrimages, they made pilgrimages – Walsingham being a particularly significant one – they offered money to saints with whom they felt a special personal relationship, and identified with saints and their images.

The study of women pilgrims raises the question of whether or not we should take gender into consideration when examining an apparently gender-neutral church-supported activity of veneration. Equality seems to exist in economic terms. That is, both church and state are interested in pilgrims as economic creatures, regardless of sex. We can also see that women, despite the attempt at controlling pilgrims as a class, were able to exercise some autonomy in their worship practice, especially if they were widows with money. While women pilgrims went to the usual pilgrimage sites along with men, there is evidence that pilgrimage must be looked at in a gender-specific way. Women tended to gravitate toward woman-centred shrines, as in the case of Elizabeth of York's devotion to Mary. Her case illustrates how pilgrimage is more than merely economic or a generic expression of piety. It suggests a kind of individual understanding of worship practice informed by gender consciousness.

Notes

1 Cambridge, MA, Blackwell, 1989, p. 247.
2 David Harvey, op. cit., p. 239. Henri Lefebvre, *The Production of Space*, Donald Nicholson-Smith, trans., Oxford, Blackwell, 1991, also argues that perceptions of space – and how they affect experience and activity and their representations – vary according to society and culture. Space reproduces social order which differs geographically and historically. His views will be discussed at more length in Chapter 3.
3 David Harvey, op. cit., p. 233.

4 Ibid., p. 241.

5 It should be noted that starting in the thirteenth century the number of documents in general increases dramatically. Georges Duby, ed., *A History of Private Life*, Vol. II, *Revelations of the Medieval World*, Arthur Goldhammer, trans., Cambridge, MA, Belknap Press, 1988, pp. 535, 549–550. Barbara H. Rosenwein argues that starting with the reign of Edward IV (1461–83) through the seventeenth century, 'kings increasingly claimed to control the nature of English space'. Reforms under Henry VIII 'suggest the new ways that the state was conceptualizing, organizing, and controlling space'. She is concerned here with the rights an individual has within his house. See *Negotiating Space: Power, Restraint, and Privileges of Immunity in Early Medieval Europe*, Ithaca, Cornell University Press, 1999, pp. 204–7.

6 Sarah Beckwith, *Christ's Body: Identity, Culture and Society in Late Medieval Writings*, London, Routledge, 1993, p. 26. Rodney Hilton, *Class Conflict and the Crisis of Feudalism: Essays in Medieval Social History*, London, The Hambledon Press, 1985, pp. 247–8. '[A]lthough contemporaries may have felt it necessary to define social boundaries, the problem was not one of insecurity caused by increased social mobility. The problem, especially between 1380 and 1450, was seen by contemporaries as a general upward move of the whole of the lower class, as much as social climbing by individual parvenus … If there was a threat, it came not from individuals but from a whole class or classes.'

7 Patricia Badir, 'Playing Space: History, the Body, and Records of Early English Drama,' *Exemplaria* IX, 1997, pp. 255–80, here p. 263.

8 The act of labourers selling their commodity for the highest price reflects Lefebvre's concept of the 'space of accumulation', where capitalistic activities are enacted.

9 Rotha Mary Clay, *The Medieval Hospitals of England*, London, Frank Cass & Co. Ltd, 1966, p. 6.

10 See Paul Strohm, *Social Chaucer*, Cambridge, Harvard University Press, 1989, pp. 5–8.

11 Clay, op. cit., p. 7.

12 All descriptions from M. S. Giuseppi, ed., *Guide to the Contents of the PRO*, Vol. I, London, Her Majesty's Stationery Office, 1963.

13 Constance Mary Storrs, *Jacobean Pilgrims From England to St James of Compostella from the Early Twelfth to the Late Fifteenth Century*, Santiago de Compostela, Xunta de Galicia, 1994, pp. 62–3.

14 Ibid., pp. 67–8.

15 Ibid., pp. 150–1. Some of the widows mentioned below Storrs treats here.

16 *Calendar of the Patent Rolls, Edward II, 1307–1313*, prepared under the supervision of the Deputy Keeper of the Records, London, Her Majesty's Stationery Office, 1894, p. 122.

17 Ibid., p. 195.

18 *Calendar of the Patent Rolls, Edward II, 1321–1324*, prepared under the supervision of the Deputy Keeper of the Records, London, Her Majesty's Stationery Office, 1904, p. 181.

19 *Calendar of the Patent Rolls, Edward III, 1327–1330*, prepared under the supervision of the Deputy Keeper of the Records, London, Her Majesty's Stationery Office, 1891, pp. 454–5.

20 Ibid., pp. 70, 523.

21 Ibid., pp. 454–5, 514 and *Calendar of the Patent Rolls, Edward III, 1330–1334*, prepared under the supervision of the Deputy Keeper of the Records, London, Her Majesty's Stationery Office, 1893, p. 69.

22 *Calendar of the Patent Rolls, Edward III, 1330–1334*, op. cit., pp. 379, 513.

23 *Calendar of the Patent Rolls, Edward 1334–1338*, prepared under the supervision of the Deputy Keeper of the Records, London, Her Majesty's Stationery Office, 1895, pp. 163, 235, 33. Also Storrs, op. cit., p. 151.

24 David C. Fowler, *The Life and Times of John Trevisa, Medieval Scholar*, Seattle, University of Washington Press, 1995, p. 88.

25 *Calendar of the Patent Rolls, Edward II, 1307–1313*, op. cit., p. 233.

26 *Calendar of the Patent Rolls, Edward III, 1330–1334*, op. cit., pp. 247, 252.

27 *Calendar of the Patent Rolls, Edward III, 1367–1370,* prepared under the supervision of the Deputy Keeper of the Records, London, His Majesty's Stationery Office, 1913, p. 71.

28 *Calendar of Patent Rolls, Edward III, 1348–1350,* prepared under the superintendence of the Deputy Keeper of the Records, London, His Majesty's Stationery Office, 1905, p. 571.

29 Ibid., p. 581.

30 *Calendar of Patent Rolls, Edward III, 1343–1345,* prepared under the superintendence of the Deputy Keeper of the Records, London, His Majesty's Stationery Office, 1902, p. 209.

31 *Calendar of the Patent Rolls, Edward III, 1367–1370*, op. cit., p. 71.

32 *Calendar of Close Rolls, Edward III, 1346–49,* prepared under the superintendence of the Deputy Keeper of the Records, London, Mackie and Co., (His Majesty's Stationery Office), 1905, p. 501.

33 *Calendar of Close Rolls, Edward III, 1349–1354,* prepared under the superintendence of the Deputy Keeper of the Records, London, Mackie and Co., (His Majesty's Stationery Office), 1906, pp. 271–2.

34 Vera and Hellmut Hell, *The Great Pilgrimage of the Middle Ages: The Road to St James of Compostela*, London, Barie and Rockliff, 1964/1979, p. 18.

35 Ronald C. Finucane, *Soldiers of the Faith: Crusaders and Moslems at War*, New York, St Martin's Press, 1983, p. 28.

36 Beriah Botfield, *Manners and Household Expenses in the 13th and 15th Centuries*, London, William Nicol, 1841, p. lxvi.

37 *Calendar of the Patent Rolls, Edward III, 1330–1334*, op. cit., p. 275.

38 *Calendar of the Patent Rolls, Edward III, 1343–1345*, op. cit., pp. 224, 183. Also Storrs, op. cit., p. 151.

39 *Calendar of the Patent Rolls, Edward II, 1321–1324*, op. cit., p. 227.

40 Storrs, op. cit., p. 59.

41 A. R. Myers, *England in the Late Middle Ages*, Harmondsworth, Penguin, 1963, p. 64.

42 *Calendar of Entries in the Papal Registers Relating to Great Britain and Ireland 1305–1342*, W. H. Bliss, ed., London, Eyre and Spottiswoode, 1895, p. 531.

43 W. H. Bliss and C. Johnson, eds, *Calendar of Entries in the Papal Registers Relating to Great Britain and Ireland 1342–1362*, Vol. III, London, Eyre and Spottiswoode, 1897, p. 605.

44 *Calendar of the Close Rolls, Edward III, 1349–1354*, op. cit., p. 230.

45 *Calendar of the Patent Rolls, Edward III, 1348–1350*, op. cit., p. 556.

46 *Calendar of the Close Rolls, Edward III, 1349–1354*, op. cit. pp. 267–8.

47 Ibid., pp. 273–274.

48 Nancy Lenz Harvey, *Elizabeth of York: The Mother of Henry VIII*, New York, Macmillan Publishing Co. Inc., 1973, p. 25.

49 Ronald Williamson, 'Medieval English Pilgrims and Pilgrimages,' in Lenz Kriss-Rettenbeck and Gerda Möhler, eds, *Wallfahrt Kennt Keine Grenzen*, Zürich, Verlag Schnell & Steiner München, 1984, p. 114.

50 James Gairdner, *The Paston Letters*, London, Chatto and Windus, 1904, Vol V, p. 112, No. 782.

51 Charles Lethbridge, ed., *The Stonor Letters and Papers 1290–1483*, Vols. I and II, London, Offices of the [Camden] Society, 1919, Vol. II, pp. 68–9. She goes on to ask him to remember what they discussed at her departure and to give money to her son from her first marriage. See also *Excerpta Historica, or Illustrations of English History*, London, Samuel Bentley, 1831, pp. 353–5.

52 *Calendar of the Patent Rolls, Edward III, 1327–1330*, op. cit. pp. 454–5.

53 Ibid., p. 70.

54 *Calendar of the Patent Rolls, Edward III, 1348–1350*, op. cit., p. 581.

55 Mary Anne Everett Wood, ed., *Letters of Royal and Illustrious Ladies of Great Britain*, Vol. I, London, Henry Colburn, 1846, p. 61.

56 Larry D. Benson, ed., *The Riverside Chaucer*, New York, Houghton Mifflin, 1987, p. 857.

57 Bliss 1895, op. cit., p. 278.

58 Storrs, op. cit., p. 59.

59 Jonathan Sumption, *Pilgrimage: An Image of Mediaeval Religion*, Totowa, NJ, Rowan and Littlefield, 1975, p. 292.

60 *Calendar of Entries in the Papal Registers Relating to Great Britain and Ireland 1447–1455*, J. A. Tremlow, ed., Hereford, The Hereford Times Limited, 1915, p. 252.

61 W. H. Bliss, ed., *Calendar of Entries in the Papal Registers Relating to Great Britain and Ireland 1305–1342*, London, Eyre and Spottiswoode, 1895, p. 531.

62 Bliss 1895, op. cit., p. 474.

63 Ibid., p. 494.

64 Bliss and Johnson 1897, op. cit., p. 17.

65 Bliss 1902, op. cit., pp. 388–9.

66 Ibid., p. 389.

67 Ibid., pp. 379, 325.

68 Tremlow 1915, op. cit., p. 123; *Calendar of Entries in the Papal Registers Relating to Great Britain and Ireland 1455–1464*, J. A. Tremlow, ed., London, His Majesty's Stationery Office, 1921, p. 520–1.

69 *Calendar of Entries in the Papal Registers Relating to Great Britain and Ireland 1458–1471*, J. A. Tremlow, ed., London, His Majesty's Stationery Office, 1933, p. 541.

70 *Calendar of Inquisitions Post Mortem and Other Analogous Documents Preserved in the Public Record Office*, M. C. B. Dawes, ed., London, Her Majesty's Stationery Office, 1970, Vol. XV, p. 187.

71 *Calendar of Inquisitions Post Mortem and Other Analogous Documents Preserved in the Public Record Office*, M. C. B. Dawes, ed., London, Her Majesty's Stationery Office, 1954, Vol. XIII, p. 266.

72 *Calendar of Inquisitions Post Mortem and Other Analogous Documents Preserved in the Public Record Office*, J. B. W. Chapman, ed., London, His Majesty's Stationery Office, 1952, Vol. XIV, pp. 247–8.

73 Richard Taylor, *Index Monasticus*, London, Richard and Arthur Taylor, 1821, p. xviii.

74 Ernest F. Jacob, ed., *The Register of Henry Chichele, Archbishop of Canterbury, 1414–1443*, Vol. 2, Oxford, Oxford University Press, 1937, pp. 280–281.

75 Quoted in Duffy 1992, op. cit., pp. 194–5. See Henry Harrod, 'Extracts from Early Wills in the Norwich Registries,' *Norfolk Archaeology* 4, 1855, pp. 317–39, 338, for the whole excerpt.

76 Duffy 1992, op. cit. p. 167, and Harrod, op. cit. p. 338, n1.

77 Richard Hart, 'The Shrines and Pilgrimages of the County of Norfolk,' *Norfolk Archaeology* 6, 1864, p. 277.

78 J. T. Fowler, ed., *Extracts from the Account Rolls of the Abbey of Durham*, Vol. II, Durham, Andrews & Co., 1899, p. 452.

79 See John Allen, 'Englishmen in Rome and the Hospice 1362–1474', *The English Hospice in Rome, The Venerabile* 21, 1962, pp. 61–8 for dozens of women's names.

80 Ibid., pp. 69–81.

81 Ibid., p. 71.

82 George Hay, 'Pilgrims and the Hospice', *The English Hospice in Rome, The Venerabile* 21, 1962, pp. 109–44.

83 Ibid., p. 7.

84 *Calendar of the Close Rolls, Edward III, 1349–1354*, op. cit., p. 206.

85 Ibid., p. 233.

86 *Calendar of the Patent Rolls, Edward III, 1367–1370*, op. cit., p. 212.

87 Ibid., p. 226.

88 Storrs, op. cit., pp. 65–6.

89 Myers, op. cit., p. 12.

90 *Calendar of the Patent Rolls, Richard II, 1388–1392*, prepared under the superintendence of the Deputy Keeper of the Records, London, His Majesty's Stationery Office, 1902, p. 390.

91 Ibid., p. 390.

92 Myers, op. cit., p. 18.

93 *Calendar of the Patent Rolls, Richard II, 1391–1396*, prepared under the superintendence of the Deputy Keeper of the Records, London, His Majesty's Stationery Office, 1905, p. 393.

94 In an earlier case, a French ship sailed from southern France for Damietta in 1250. Not including passengers who were knights, clerics or their retainers, over ten percent of the remaining 342 passengers were women. Fifteen travelled with their husbands, one travelled with her father, two with a brother and twenty-two travelled with no chaperon. One was presumably English as she is listed as the daughter of 'Rogerius Anglicus'. Anthony Luttrell, 'Englishwomen as Pilgrims to Jerusalem: Isolda Pare Wastell, 1365' in Julia B. Holloway, Constance C. Wright and Joan Bechtold, eds, *Equally in Gods Image: Women in the Middle Ages*, New York, Peter Lang, 1990, pp. 88–102, here, p. 186.

95 Andrew McCall, *The Medieval Underworld*, London, Hamish Hamilton, 1979, p. 35.

96 Storrs, op. cit., pp. 60, 63–4.

97 *Calendar of Close Rolls, Richard II, 1389–1392*, prepared under the superintendence of the Deputy Keeper of the Records, London, Mackie and Co., His Majesty's Stationery Office, 1922, pp. 255–6.

98 *Calendar of the Patent Rolls, Henry IV, 1399–1401*, prepared under the superintendence of the Deputy Keeper of the Records, London, His Majesty's Stationery Office, 1903, p. 46.

99 *Calendar of Close Rolls, Henry IV, 1399–1402*, prepared under the superintendence of the Deputy Keeper of the Records, London, Mackie and Co., His Majesty's Stationery Office, 1927, p. 170.

100 Storrs, op. cit., pp. 64–6.

101 *Calendar of the Patent Rolls, Edward III, 1374–1377*, prepared under the superintendence of the Deputy Keeper of the Records, London, His Majesty's Stationery Office, 1916, p. 312.

102 *Calendar of Close Rolls, Richard II, 1385–1389*, prepared under the superintendence of the Deputy Keeper of the Records, London, Mackie and Co., His Majesty's Stationery Office, 1921, p. 592. 'An ordinance of the council, traceable to 1376, required that none should cross the seas without the king's license (Cal. Pat. 50 Ed. III, 312). The statute 5 Ric. II, I, c.2, required a license of all travellers, except lords, well known merchants and soldiers. In 1389, pilgrims and other travellers to the Continent were restricted to the ports of Dover and Plymouth (Rot. Parl. iii, 25).' From I. S. Leadam and J. F. Baldwin, eds., *Select Cases Before the King's Council 1243–1482*, Cambridge, MA, The Harvard University Press, 1918, p. 85, n. 3. See above for texts.

103 *Calendar of Close Rolls, Henry VI, 1441–1447*, W. H. B. Bird, ed., prepared under the superintendence of the Deputy Keeper of the Records, London, Mackie and Co., His Majesty's Stationery Office, 1937, pp. 232–4.

104 Duby, op. cit., pp. 510–11.

105 Duby, op. cit., pp. 536–7.

106 Duby, op. cit., p. 510.

107 McCall, op. cit., p. 34.

108 Williamson, op. cit., p. 299. Duffy disagrees with some of his identifications.

109 Citations from Gairdner, op. cit., Vol. II, No. 105, p. 135.

110 *Chaucer's World*, compiled by Edith Rickert, edited by Clair C. Olson and Martin M. Crow, New York, Columbia University Press, 1948, p. 257. Summarized from Coram

Rege Roll 552, Rex, m. I d.

111 Book I, chapters 27, 42, 44, 46, 47.

112 Julia B. Holloway, trans., *Saint Bride and Her Book*, Newburyport, MA, Focus Texts, 1992, p. 14.

113 Horton and Marie-Hélène Davies, *Holy Days and Holidays, The Medieval Pilgrimage to Compostela*, Lewisburg, Bucknell University Press, 1982, p. 177.

114 John G. Bellamy, *Crime and Public Order in England in the Later Middle Ages*, London, Routledge & Kegan Paul, 1973, p. 65. See Rot. Parl., iv, 447b.

115 Davies, op. cit., p. 204.

116 F. M. Stenton, 'The Road System of Medieval England,' *The Economic History Review*, 1936, p. 15.

117 J. C. Dickinson, *The Shrine of Our Lady of Walsingham*, Cambridge, Cambridge University Press, p. 22. Quoted from *Calendar of the Patent Rolls, 1258–68*, op. cit., p. 182.

118 From *Materials Becket* i. 472–473 translated in R. C. van Caenegem, ed., *English Lawsuits from William I to Richard I*, London, Selden Society, 1990, Vol. 2, p. 501.

119 Jacques Rossiaud, *Medieval Prostitution*, Lydia G. Cochrane, trans., Oxford, Basil Blackwell, 1988, p. 33.

120 *Select Cases in the Court of King's Bench under Richard II, Henry IV and Henry V*, G. O. Sayles ed., Selden Society, Vol. VII, London, Bernard Quaritch, 1971, pp. 220–1. Sayles tells us that the Lady Hilary may possibly be the wife of Sir Roger Hilary; she was one of the Staffordshire Audleys and died 1410–11.

121 W. H. Bliss, ed., *Papal Petitions to the Pope 1342–1419*, Vol. I, London, Eyre and Spottiswoode, 1896, pp. 512–13.

122 Luttrell in Holloway, et al., op. cit., pp. 184–97.

123 McCall, op. cit., p. 33.

124 Bliss 1895, op. cit., p. 318; Storrs, op. cit., p. 61.

125 R. B. Dobson, *The Peasants' Revolt of 1381*, London, Macmillan, 1970, p. 133.

126 Ibid., p. 182.

127 Ibid., p. 323.

128 Ibid., p. 139.

129 Charles Zika, 'Hosts, Processions and Pilgrimages: Controlling the Sacred in Fifteenth-Century Germany,' *Past and Present* 118, 1988, pp. 25–64, here p. 57.

130 Ibid., p. 58.

131 Ibid., pp. 63–4.

132 Ibid., p. 62.

133 See Lynn Staley on Margery Kempe's dating of her text during the reign of Henry V and fears about disruption to the body politic, *Margery Kempe's Dissenting Fictions*, University Park, PA, The Pennsylvania State University Press, 1994, pp. 155–6.

134 *Calendar of Close Rolls, Edward IV, 1468–1476*, prepared under the superintendence of the Deputy Keeper of the Records, London, Mackie and Co., Her Majesty's Stationery Office, 1953, pp. 298–9.

135 André Vauchez, *Sainthood in the Later Middle Ages*, Jean Birrell, trans., Cambridge, Cambridge University Press, 1997, p. 395.

136 *Calendar of the Patent Rolls, Henry VII, 1485–1494*, prepared under the superintendence of the Deputy Keeper of the Records, London, His Majesty's Stationery Office, 1914, pp. 434–437.

137 Citations from Josiah Pratt, ed., *The Acts and Monuments of John Foxe*, 4th Edn, London, The Religious Tract Society, 1887, p. 268.

138 Sumption, op. cit., p. 196.

139 Anne Hudson, *The Premature Reformation: Wycliffite Texts and Lollard History*, Oxford, Clarendon Press, 1988, p. 279.

140 Ibid., p. 307.

141 G. R. Owst, *Literature and Pulpit in Medieval England*, Oxford, Basil Blackwell, 1966, pp. 147–8.

142 Edmund Waterton, *Pietas Mariana Britannica*, London, St Joseph's Catholic Library, 1897, p. 106. (From *The Repressor of over-much blaming of the Clergy*, Reginald Peacok, vol. i, p. 194. Rolls Edit.)

143 Hudson, op. cit., p. 114.

144 Ibid., p. 141.

145 Norman P. Tanner, ed., *Heresy Trials in the Diocese of Norwich*, 1428–31, London, Butler & Tanner Ltd, 1977, p. 14.

146 Ibid., pp. 7, 14, 26.

147 Ibid., p. 142.

148 Leonard E. Whatmore, *Highway to Walsingham*, Walsingham, The Pilgrim Bureau, 1973, p. 4.

149 Philadelphia, University of Pennsylvania Press, 1995, p. 94.

150 Ibid., p. 118.

151 Ibid., p. 101.

152 Ibid., p. 146.

153 Duffy 1992, op. cit., p. 141.

154 Philip M. Soergel, *Speculum* 69, 1994, pp. 766–8, here p. 768.

155 Storrs, pp. 69–71.

156 Toulmin Smith and Lucy Toulmin Smith, ed., *English Gilds*, London, Oxford University Press, 1924, pp. xxx, xxxvi. However, for evidence that English women were more restricted in guild activity than men see Erika Uitz, *Die Frau in der Mittelalterlichen Stadt*, Leipzig, Edition Leipzig, 1988, pp. 52–3; Eileen Power and M. M. Postan, eds, *Medieval Women*, Cambridge, Cambridge University Press, 1975, pp. 64–5; Margaret Wade Labarge, *A Small Sound of the Trumpet*, Boston, Beacon Press, 1986, p. 149.

157 Toulmin and Toulmin Smith, op. cit., pp. 157, 177, 180, 182, 84, 184, 231, 172–3.

158 Hudson, op. cit., pp. 508–9.

159 Ibid., pp. 134–6.

160 Ibid., p. 509.

161 Shannon McSheffrey, *Gender & Heresy: Women and Men in Lollard Communities 1420–1530*, Philadelphia, University of Pennsylvania Press, 1995, p. 144.

162 'Kempe did not need to visit Jerusalem to write an account of Margery's experience there; she could easily have drawn upon written accounts of journeys to the Holy Land, which were designed to simulate the immediacy of actual experience.' Later Staley discusses the 'fiction of Margery's final journey'. See Staley, op. cit., pp. 76–7, 169.

163 Sandford Brown Meech and Hope Emily Allen, eds, *The Book of Margery Kempe*, London, Oxford University Press/EETS, 1961, Book I, chapter 15, p. 22.

164 Ibid., p. 60.

165 Ibid., p. 25.

166 Ibid., Book I, chapter 15.

167 Ibid., Book I, chapter 11.

168 Ibid., Book I, chapter 27. See also *The Book of Margery Kempe*, B. A. Windeatt, trans., Harmondsworth, Penguin, 1985, pp. 311–12.

169 Meech and Allen 1961, p. 85.

170 Ibid., p. 106.

171 Meech and Allen, Book II, chapters 5 and 6.

172 Jennifer C. Ward, *English Noblewomen in the Later Middle Ages*, London, Longman, 1992, p. 6.

173 From Bliss 1896, op. cit., pp. 22–3; and Bliss and Johnson 1897, op. cit., p. 112.

174 Ward 1992, op. cit., pp. 146, 83, 88, 154. A biography of Elizabeth de Burgh by Frances Underhill was due to come out from St Martin's Press in the autumn of 1999. I did not have a chance to view it before this book went to press.

175 Jennifer C. Ward, trans. and ed., *Women of the English Nobility and Gentry 1066–1500*, Manchester, Manchester University Press, 1995, p. 188.

176 Ward 1995, op.cit. See, for example, pp. 220–1.

177 Ibid., p. 184.
178 *Calendar of the Patent Rolls, Edward III, 1343–1345,* op. cit., p. 350.
179 *Calendar of the Patent Rolls, Edward III, 1348–1350,* op. cit., p. 514.
180 Ward 1992, op. cit., pp. 32, 107.
181 Ward 1995, op. cit. p. 183.
182 Bliss 1896, op. cit., p. 287.
183 Ward 1995, op. cit., p. 82.
184 *Calendar of the Patent Rolls, Henry IV, 1401–1405,* prepared under the supervision of the Deputy Keeper of the Records, London, His Majesty's Stationery Office, 1905, p. 215.
185 Nancy Harvey, op. cit., pp. 169–70.
186 Merry Wiesner-Hanks and Melissa J. Martens, compilers, *Early Women's Literature: A Provisional Check List of Works in the Newberry Library Written By or About Women and Published Before 1700,* Chicago, The Newberry Library, 1993, number 013.
187 Nicholas Harris Nicolas, *Privy Purse Expenses of Elizabeth of York: Wardrobe Accounts of Edward the Fourth,* London, William Pickering, 1830/repr. New York, Barnes & Noble, 1972, pp. 6, 24, 26, 61.
188 Ibid., p. 76.
189 Ibid., pp. 52, 84.
190 Ibid., p. 91.
191 Ibid., p. 2.
192 Ibid., p. 89.
193 Ibid., pp. 53, 193.
194 Ibid., p. 1.
195 Ibid., p. 2.
196 For other offerings of the Queen on special feast days, see ibid., pp. 6, 10, 12, 14, 29, 31, 37, 38, 39, 50, 56, 64–5, 67, 77, 78, 81, 83–4, 87, 88, and 97. She also gives money to the friars of the monastery of Saint Katherine in Mount Sinai, ibid., p. 21, and also barrels of beer to the friars in Canterbury, ibid., p. 57.
197 Ibid., pp. 3, 215–216.
198 Ibid., pp. 3–4.
199 Ibid., p. 96.
200 R. N. Swanson, *Religion and Devotion in Europe, c. 1215–c. 1515,* Cambridge, Cambridge University Press, 1995, p. 320.
201 Nicolas, p. 37.
202 Ibid., p. 78.
203 Ibid., p. 197.
204 Gail McMurray Gibson, *The Theater of Devotion: East Anglian Drama and Society in the Late Middle Ages,* Chicago, The University of Chicago Press, 1989, pp. 63, 156, 157.

3   Gender, pilgrimage and medieval perceptions of space

This chapter explores theoretical issues of space, with particular emphasis on the factor of gender. Pilgrimage seems easily comprehensible in terms of space: the pilgrim leaves profane space, the home, for sacred space, the shrine or church or cathedral. But the divisions between sacred and profane are not necessarily easily distinguished. Pilgrimage confounds simple binaries as we have seen in the attempts to control pilgrimage. We can see this tension between the sacred and profane in art, specifically the pilgrimage stained glass window at York Cathedral.

Spatial practice

Numerous scholars have undertaken theoretical work concerning the meaning and representation of space. These scholars include Gaston Bachelard, Pierre Bourdieu, Michel de Certeau, Gilles Deleuze, Jill Dubisch, Alphonse Dupront, Félix Guattari, Roberta Gilchrist, David Harvey, Henri Lefebvre, Fatima Mernissi, Margaret Miles, Henrietta Moore, Pierre Nora, Edward Soja,[1] and Yi-Fu Tuan. They analyse the organisation of space as a culturally constructed text. These theoreticians have looked at societies as diverse as ancient Greece and the Marakwet of Kenya, some touching on medieval pilgrimage. Pilgrimage is movement, specifically movement through space to a site designated as especially holy or privileged. As Margaret Miles puts it, pilgrimage

> was a strong experiential reminder that the unpredictability of human life is not adequately represented by a sedentary lifestyle. Travel over dusty countrysides, steep and slippery mountain passes, through woods, and over hills and valleys was a more accurate representation of human life. Different geography created awareness of the diverse landscapes of the soul, the rocks, sunlight, green growth, and the dust of emotional life.[2]

As a ritual, a pilgrimage can be read as 'an instrument for establishing the fundamental contexts of time, space and authority within which social relations and political identity are enacted'.[3] Analysing the spatial practice of pilgrimage with particular attention to gender dynamics provides us with a better understanding of both the experience and representation of pilgrims in medieval culture.

Yi-Fu Tuan's work establishes the social meaning of space. He delineates between space and place in *Space and Place: The Perspective of Experience* by describing place as valued space, 'filled with meaning'.[4] The pilgrimage route functions as a 'place', just as a shrine does. 'As a result of habitual use [a habitually used] path itself acquires a density of meaning and a stability that are charecteric traits of place.'[5] A pilgrim may walk on a strange and foreign pilgrimage route for the first time, but because the route has a goal – to a particular relic or shrine – it attains meaning for the pilgrim. Additionally, pilgrimage shrines and churches along a pilgrimage route are sacred places, essential in defining the character of a particular route and in transforming a pilgrim's specific experience.

In his model of the Middle Ages in *Topophilia: A Study of Environmental Perception, Attitudes, and Values,* Tuan shows how the prevalence and importance of a calendar of festivals created a cosmic view which was highly stratified, one which he calls vertical. 'Man plays two roles, the social-profane and the mythical-sacred, the one bound to time, the other transcending it.'[6] A pilgrim plays two roles – that of his or her quotidian existence and that of the religious sojourner. This vertically charged medieval world Tuan sees symbolized in Gothic architecture.[7] The cathedral, and particularly the shrine, functioned as sacred spaces. Not only is this space sacred, but it has meaning as well. '[A]rchitecture "teaches" … [A]rchitecture is the key to comprehending reality.'[8] A statue, rood screen or stained-glass window creates its own meaning in the context of a specific pilgrimage route. Two identical statues, for example, would have differing meanings on different pilgrimage routes. As we have seen in Chapter 1, the architecture of and images in the churches along the route to the shrine at Walsingham create pilgrimage experiences specifically designed to be received by women pilgrims.

Michel de Certeau agrees with Tuan that a distinction must be made between space and place. While a place is stable, where 'elements are distributed in relationships of coexistence', a space is a 'practiced place'. A place is turned into space by the act of walkers.[9] We might see this in medieval maps which

> included only the rectilinear marking out of itineraries (performative indications chiefly concerning pilgrimages), along with the stops one was to make (cities which one was to pass through, spend the night in, pray at, etc.) and distances calculated in hours or in days, that is, in terms of the time it would take to cover them on foot. Each of these maps is a memorandum prescribing actions. The tour to be made is predominant in them.[10]

While space and place suggest the physical pilgrimage, we also need to examine the inward perception of or transformations fostered by pilgrimage. Pilgrims' perceptions of achieving an identical goal, a pilgrimage shrine, differ for each individual. Space exists in our experiences and perceptions of it. A thirty-mile pilgrimage might be a day's journey for an experienced walker and pilgrim, but a great trial for an ailing pilgrim or one unused to leaving home. Each pilgrimage journey would have differed enormously, depending on the length of the journey and the origin of travel. To come to a local shrine after an hour of walking on foot would have been a totally different spiritual experience from coming to the same shrine distant from one's home after two months on the road. The mundane facts of travel affected the pilgrimage undertaken and the experience it evoked for the pilgrim herself.

Alphonse Dupront analyses the phenomenon of pilgrimage in terms of psychology and space. The pilgrim walks elsewhere in need of an 'other' place, a sacred place in space which allows the rupture with the everyday.[11] Pilgrimage cannot exist without space, a space marked by the alterity of the sacred.[12] A static sacred space allows for the active gesture of pilgrimage through space and this act sacralizes space and time. Dupront reads the pilgrim costume and other signs of the pilgrim, such as the scallop shell which signifies St James, his shrine of Santiago de Compostela, and pilgrims in general, as proof of the space which make the pilgrim.[13] The sacred *locus* provides an opening giving access to the transcendent, with the fulfilment of the pilgrim realized at the sacred space. Here the pilgrim undergoes a kind of 'space therapy', by creating a new universe.[14] Dupront is careful to point out that this one place or site is ambiguous representing as it does both penitence and liberation. [15]

Ideally or classically, pilgrimage functions as a passage of space which enables the subject to become a stranger to himself.[16] In Dupront's paradigm, the pilgrim is a man who walks on foot through space, becoming 'other', transmuting both man and the space he passes through. The purpose of pilgrimage is to meet the other, and this alterity transmutes the pilgrim. Pilgrimage, then, is a metaphysical act. The act of pilgrimage transfigures the pilgrim to an other world and offers passage to that other world. The act of pilgrimage liberates the pilgrim from quotidian life and makes a rupture with the everyday.[17] When pilgrimage becomes a group activity or collective act, Dupront argues, it is characterized as the society of festival, hence the accusations of abuses which proliferated in the later Middle Ages. Dupront sums up his anthropology of pilgrimage with three rules. Sacred space is a fundamental aspect of pilgrimage, a space which differs from quotidian space.[18] Pilgrim faith receives and consecrates the sacralities of place.[19] And the pilgrim becomes a stranger to himself, discovering his 'other' thereby leading to communion with the 'Other', God.[20]

Dupront's analysis provides a useful paradigm for understanding pilgrimage and space, though without extensive delineation of the subtle differences among various pilgrimage routes which would, in turn, differentiate various pilgrimage experiences. Victor and Edith Turner, however, do explicate more thoroughly specific pilgrimage sites in their book *Image and Pilgrimage in Christian Culture: Anthropological Perspectives*. They use spatial imagery in describing pilgrims as marginalized or liminal, on the threshold, arguing that pilgrimage is a *rite de passage* which has three stages for the pilgrim: first, separation from society, second, being marginalized or liminal (on the threshold), and third, reaggregation or reintegration into the community with enhanced status due to the pilgrimage undertaken. Since pilgrimage is generally a voluntary activity the Turners call it quasi-liminal or liminoid.[21] Ritual subjects, in this case pilgrims, in a liminal phase are liminars and, as such, are ambiguous.[22] Among the attributes of liminality are the levelling of status and communitas or social antistructure.

It is a liminal phenomenon which combines the qualities of lowliness, sacredness, homogeneity, and comradeship ... The bonds of communitas ... liberates [identities] from conformity to general norms ... [I]t is a spring of pure possibility. It may be regarded by the guardians of structure as dangerous ... It has something magical about it. Those who experience communitas have a feeling of endless power ...[23]

They argue that '[p]ilgrimages are an expression of the *communitas* dimension of any society, the spontaneity of interrelatedness ... From the point of view of those who control and maintain the social structure, all manifestations of *communitas*, sacred or profane, are potentially subversive.'[24] In their view, then, pilgrimage is a potentially disruptive act, at least, it is perceived that way by the state.

John Eade and Michael J. Sallnow have situated the Turners' position as coming in opposition to earlier views which read pilgrimage as reflecting or reinforcing secular social structure. The Turners' influential ideas seductively suggest that the ritual space of pilgrimage liberates pilgrims from societal limitations, including those imposed by social class or gender. The Turnerian paradigm provides a structure for scholars who want to see women's behaviour as empowering and ultimately subversive of misogynist power structure. For example, Julia Bolton Holloway utilizes the Turners in her useful translation and edition of *Saint Bride and Her Book*, writing that '[m]any of Bride's relatives had made pilgrimages, participating in that liberating and liminal state outside of hierarchies'.[25] She also suggests that 'in eternity, in religion and on pilgrimage ... all could theologically be equal'.[26] The Turnerian paradigm is that of anti-structure, which, however, could be compromised by logistical and organizational imperatives. The Turners point out that, although '[o]n pilgrimage, social interaction is not governed by the old rules of social structure', once 'a pilgrimage system becomes established ... it operates like other social institutions'.[27]

The Turnerian paradigm has been subjected to a number of critiques, many of which point out that pilgrimage does not eliminate traditional social boundaries.[28] As Jill Dubisch has shown that 'social distinctions and hierarchies (class, caste, status, gender, occupation, local identity) are not dissolved during pilgrimage but continue to structure relationships and generate conflicts ... Pilgrimage may reflect and reinforce, as well as mask, social hierarchy and social difference.'[29] Social difference may also be seen in motivations for going on pilgrimage, which vary enormously. One pilgrimage site may have differing meanings for different groups of pilgrims, depending on social class, ethnicity and religious background.[30] Certainly medieval pilgrimage was *not* always liberating *nor* did it free one from hierarchies, particularly gender hierarchy. Gender was a fact of women pilgrims' experiences, both historically and in terms of how they were represented.[31] Caroline Walker Bynum, both in *Holy Feast and Holy Fast* and her book of essays, *Fragmentation and Redemption: Essays on Gender and the Human Body in Medieval Religion*, criticizes the Turners for not taking gender into consideration, since, once medieval women's experience is taken into account, modern theoreticians' paradigms clearly cannot be universally applied. 'Turner's ideas describe the stories and symbols of men better than those of women ... And when women recount their own lives, the themes are less climax, conversion, reintegration and triumph, the liminality of reversal or elevation, than continuity.'[32] Bynum points out the dangers in generalizing from the experience of one gender.

To what extent does pilgrimage *create* liminality and to what extent does it draw people who are *already liminal*, such as women? Bynum has suggested that medieval women were perceived as liminal in general, not only on pilgrimage.[33] In other words, what the Turners perceive as liberating liminality was in fact a culturally negative liminality, though one not necessarily acknowledged or recognized by women themselves. Dubisch suggests that 'pilgrimage may be a way of trying to overcome liminality, to connect, to identify oneself with the core symbolic structures of one's society. Liminality, like communitas … is not necessarily an inherent feature of pilgrimage … but is variable, situational, and fluctuating'.[34] Even the apparent liminality of a figure such as Margery Kempe has been questioned. Lynn Staley subtly argues that liminality for Margery Kempe is merely a ruse. 'Rather than the marginality that most scholars assign to Margery, I see Kempe as creating a figure whose liminal status is ultimately resolved, not by reintegration into the community, but by her rejection of its demands and practices.'[35] In Staley's reading, Kempe as author sets Margery the character up as marginal or liminal, in, for example, pilgrim society itself when her fellow pilgrims to the Holy Land reject her, place her low at table and force her to wear foolish clothing. Staley argues that the author 'creates a self whose social liminality is a necessary part of a literary fiction'.[36] Nevertheless, Staley's argument still argues for the perceived negative liminality of the female pilgrim.

Recent work on space by Henrietta L. Moore in *Space, Text and Gender: An Anthropological Study of the Marakwet of Kenya* is suggestive for work on gender and pilgrimage. If space can embody social meanings, then it can be treated as a kind of language, as de Certeau has also shown.[37] Moore points out that '[t]his "advanced" semiotic position dominates contemporary anthropological analyses of cultural forms'. Using Clifford Geertz and Paul Ricoeur, who call human activity a text, Moore reads space as a text. '… [A]ctual bodily movement through and action in ordered space are simultaneously both action and interpretation; they are therefore intelligible as an act of reading, where reading itself is understood as enjoined decoding and interpretation.' The actor moving through space is not without age, gender, or class, as the Turnerian model would suggest. 'Spatial representations express in their own logic the power relations between different groups; they are therefore active instruments in the production and reproduction of social order.'[38]

In other words, ordered space is not natural, it only appears to be. The spatial text 'reproduces the ideological forms which produce it and which make both these forms and itself appear "natural"'.[39] While the act of pilgrimage may seem natural or without form, in fact it reflects the social factors which produced it in the first place. Wandering on a path in the countryside en route to a shrine is no more liberating from gender roles, for example, than undergoing the rite of marriage in a church. Spatial practice, as Edward Dimendberg has put it, 'is *social* practice embodied in the modalities through which human beings live in space and produce and reproduce themselves within it'.[40]

Moore's model allows us to read space as a text in which age, gender and class *are* distinguishing factors. While the Turnerian model might be more utopic, Moore forces us to see how space reproduces hierarchies of the social order which cannot be erased in historical reality. Mary Ann Tétreault, in her discussion of ancient Greece, agrees with Moore's model. '[G]ender is a marker of a complex system of authority that grants or withholds status and therefore access to the primary arena within which those included compete for especially coveted resources ... [G]ender ... is an element in the religious and social tenets and practices that underpin hegemonic ideologies.'[41] Moore's and Tétreault's insistence on not neglecting gender as a crucial element in looking at space helps us to consider women pilgrims as experiencing pilgrimage differently from men.

Tuan points out that in the Middle Ages, though social hierarchy was rigid, orderly spatial expression did not exist in where people lived or how they moved.[42] He argues for socially specified perceptions of space,[43] which are modified by gender. 'In cultures of strongly differentiated sex roles, men and women will look at different aspects of the environment and acquire different attitudes toward them.'[44] How would a woman experience a pilgrimage differently from that of a man? In many ways, no doubt, the experience would be identical. Or the experience would differ from man to woman as much as it would from man to man or woman to woman. But some aspects of pilgrimage were only experienced by women as this book has discussed. For example, Chartres was famed for possessing a relic of the Virgin. Her veil or tunic was believed to ease labour pains for women in childbirth. Surely, then, a pregnant woman making the pilgrimage to Chartres in the Middle Ages would have a very different relationship with seeing or touching the Virgin's tunic since it would have an immediate impact upon her physical experience. Pilgrimage experiences can differ depending on gender.

But meaning is not only created by and for pilgrims, it is also imposed on pilgrims. The meaning in the performance of pilgrimage is received differently depending upon the actor and the audience of the performance. To see a pilgrim moving in space, from one space to another (sacred) space, differs depending on the pilgrim. Abstract perceptions of space affected how pilgrims were viewed in the Middle Ages, particularly with regard to gender.

Pierre Bourdieu in his study of Berber society argues that

> the opposition towards the fields or the market, towards the production and circulation of goods, and movement inwards, towards the accumulation and consumption of the products of work, corresponds symbolically to the opposition between the male body, self-enclosed and directed towards the outside world, and the female body, resembling the dark, damp, house, full of food, utensils and children.[45]

This essentialist view, associating male and female to categories of public and private, has been criticized. And, indeed, in our study of secular and religious literature of the late medieval period, we can see that, while there is a general *tendency* towards this alignment, it is far from universal.

In the Middle Ages, particularly in the later medieval period and in England, a woman pilgrim on the move was perceived spatially in a much different manner than a male pilgrim. A shift in perceptions of space in England followed the plague in the mid-fourteenth century with consequent anxiety about (fake) pilgrims and their

movements. Women pilgrims in secular literature functioned in part as symbols of
the socially mobile – and therefore threatening – labourer of late medieval England.
As we will see in the next chapter, the spatiality of medieval women pilgrims is the
story of their – perceived – power or lack of power. Women pilgrims, while they
perceived themselves as acting in a meaningful and culturally normative way, were
often received by secular literary authors as symbolically subversive. Their public
performance needed to be contained through the figure of the sexual and sometimes
ridiculous woman pilgrim figure, while in religious texts, women pilgrims were
perceived relatively uncritically.

While we have abundant evidence that women were well represented on pilgrimage,
they were not treated equally with male pilgrims at all shrines *spatially*. One text,
'Incypyt the Stacyons of Rome,' whose content, dating roughly 1440–5, puffs the
advantages of going to Rome as opposed to Santiago or Jerusalem for the best and
most convenient indulgences around. Male and female pilgrims are singled out. At St
Peter's, for example, you receive seven years' of pardon for every step and God's blessing,
'Man or wommon wheþur þou bee … To man or womman þat dedur come.'[46] But St
Peter's has one hundred altars, we are told, 'of þe holy crosse þe seuennyþ ys,/ In þe
whych no wommon cometh ywys.'[47] We are never told why the altar of the Holy
Cross is reserved for males and why both sexes are allowed into the other altars listed.
Relics in Rome include a shirt the Virgin made Christ, her milk and his foreskin. But
the Sancta Sanctorum likewise remains off limits to women.

> Ther ys a chapell of gret pardon
> And of mony synnis Remyssyon,
> Menne call hit sancta sanctorum;
> In þat chapell shall no womon com.
> Ther-yn ys A saluatowr
> To whom men don gret honour,
> The whyche was sent to our lady
> (Whyle þat she was her vs by)
> From her sone þat ys a-bouen,
> Aftur þe tyme of his ascencion.
> Ther may no wommon entre þor
> By-cause of her þat synned sore;
> She browyt vs alle to þe qwede
> Tyll cryste on crosse suffered dede:
> Euery day, seuen þowsand yere
> Of pardon þou may haue þere;
> And also, yyf þou wylt craue,
> Plener Remyssyon þou may haue.[48]

The work, although mentioning men and women pilgrims throughout, does seem
directed at a male audience. After all, it functions as a propaganda piece for pilgrimages to Rome based on the amazing number of years of pardon available there. The
Sancta Sanctorum is remarkable for its high remission rate, one option not available

to women. Furthermore, the reason for prohibition against women is due to Eve's sin, spoken of in the breath just after mentioning Mary who, according to Catholic dogma, redeemed the sin of Eve. In the *Stacyons of Rome*, the reader is informed of all the wonderful sights to see in the Holy City and how many years can be taken off purgatory. The narrator specifies two places where women are specifically forbidden to enter. Since the narrator can describe what lies within he must be a man (or a disobeying woman). The prohibition of women from these two spots precludes them from the 'bonus points' available at these two spots in terms of indulgences. John Capgrave also comments on women not being admitted to certain areas. He claims that the exclusion of women was attributed to 'many lewd causes to which I wil give no credens.' While Capgrave rejects women's sexual misbehaviour for this exclusion, he acknowledges the dangers for women who go to crowded pilgrimage sites.

> All those whech have be at Rome knowe well that the women there be passing desirous to goo on pilgrimage and to touch and kiss every holy relik. Now in very soothfastness these places which are forbode to them are rit smale ... And uphap some woman in the press, eithir for sikness or with child, be in grete perel there, and for this cause they were forbode the entre of these houses as I suppose.[49]

Paternalistic sentiments of protecting women govern Capgrave's interpretation of this practice of exclusion.

Rome was not the only location where women's access to sacred spots were limited. The architecture of Qalet Seman, the sixth-century Syrian shrine of the stylite Saint Simeon, suggests that the four basilicae were designated for different groups, including women. Cynthia Hahn shows how women were restricted from entering the shrine area from their allotted space.[50] Women were also not allowed into the feretory, or shrine area, of St Cuthbert in Durham, nor were they allowed within the area by the monastery. This prohibition was supported by a legend in which the king's daughter accused Cuthbert of having impregnated her. When confronted by the king, Cuthbert prays to God for a sign, whereupon 'suddenly, in the self-same place where the King's Daughter stood, the Earth (making a hissing noise) presently opened and swallow'd her up in the presence of all the beholders'. The king realizes his error, begs pardon, and asks for his daughter back,

> which petition the said holy Father granted, upon condition that no women after that time should have resort unto him. Whence it came, that the King did not suffer any Woman to enter into any Church dedicated to that Saint; which to this day is duely observed in all the Churches of the Picts, which were dedicated in the honour of that Holy man.[51]

Also told about Cuthbert is the story of Judith, the wife of Earl Tostig, who, when she tried to enter, was paralysed at the door.[52] Durham was not the only cathedral to boast prohibitions against women. The tomb of Gilbert of Sempringham also had some sort of gender separation. Finucane tells us how women were not allowed into the Cistercian house of Pontigny where St Edmund's bones were. His bones had to be carried out to the women at the gates.[53] Eventually, women who had travelled from England were allowed to enter to gain the indulgences granted to pilgrims.[54] Despite these restrictions, money from pilgrims of either sex was, needless to say, more than welcome.[55]

David Harvey has argued that we must look at space and social relations as processes which reinforce one another. Using his work, Daphne Spain argues that an exclusive space reserved for men, a 'gendered space', allows men to 'produce and reproduce power and privilege'.[56] She hypothesizes that, where men and women have different status in society, gendered spaces are created. This 'institutionalized spatial segregation then reinforces prevailing male advantages'.[57] There is a problem with shrine areas being reserved for men, excluding women. The control of space means the control of knowledge and power. In the case of the Sancta Sanctorum, men are allowed more indulgences than women by virtue of their sex. They are allowed to enter and receive pardon while women cannot. Additionally, men are granted the privilege of vision, viewing the holy altar or the Sancta Sanctorum. This increased knowledge permits male pilgrims to have an advantage over female pilgrims.

Late medieval Lollard criticisms of the efficacy of pilgrimage include many of the elements satirized by Chaucer and other writers: revelry dominating piety, money outweighing good works, and fetishism of probably fake relics over true love for God. But one aspect of these criticisms strikes at the very meaning of pilgrimage itself. Pilgrimage exists because a pilgrimage site is perceived by an individual or group as being special in some particular way. In Christian pilgrimage, a site evolves because it is seen as 'sacred', whether due to relics it possesses[58] or an event which took place at the site which is perceived as miraculous.[59] Perhaps the site is a commemorative spot of some event or person. As William Melczer has written concerning the desire to pilgrimage to the site where relics are present, '[t]he underlying notion was that the sacred consecrates its immediate environment: hence the need to share that environment, the need for an unmediated contact with the sacred'.[60] The reasons for the development of a pilgrimage site are numerous, including, at the most cynical level, the deliberate propagandizing of such a site by interested parties, whether clergy or merchants. This making of space as 'sacred' or 'blessed' was criticized by Lollard thinkers, who argued that, if place could save or redeem, then Eve would never have eaten the apple and Satan would not have fallen from heaven. As Sarah Beckwith points out, the Lollard view despised the 'idolatrous attachment to place', which profanely confined spirituality to 'a particular shrine, site of pilgrimage, relic or church'. The Wycliffite view held that true spirituality manifested 'itself most insistently in the soul of the good man or woman'.[61] Despite these criticisms, pilgrimage was a social activity deeply embedded in medieval society. While the Reformation would succeed in crumbling the ubiquitous presence of the activity of pilgrimage, the concepts of sacred as opposed to non-sacred space did not disappear.

Sacred and profane realms, however, were not always discrete. While Tuan and Dupront talk easily about the distinctions between perceived sacred and profane spaces, it has been pointed out recently that space cannot be so easily distinguished. Henri

Lefebvre in his book, *The Production of Space*, explores in part the spatial practice in the Middle Ages. Medieval spatial practice, writes Lefebvre

> embraced not only the network of local roads close to peasant communities, monasteries and castles, but also the main roads between towns and the great pilgrims' and crusaders' ways ... Thus the road to Santiago de Compostela was the equivalent, on the earth's surface, of the Way that led from Cancer to Capricorn on the vault of the heavens, a route otherwise known as the Milky Way – a trail of divine sperm where souls are born before following its downward trajectory and falling to earth, there to seek as best they may the path of redemption – namely, the pilgrimage that will bring them to Compostela ('the field of stars').[62]

In his look at Western culture, Lefebvre draws out paradigmatic shifts in social space, suggesting that each new period builds upon the traces of the old, each period leaving vestiges of itself out of which is produced the next space. Lefebvre suggests a shift in spatial modes takes place starting around the twelfth century when Western Europe experienced the emancipation from the crypt and from 'cryptic space'.[63] In the twelfth century, with this collapse of 'absolute space,' the space of holy or religious places, comes what Lefebvre calls historical space or the 'space of accumulation'.[64] Money and commodities were destined to bring with them a new culture and a new space. With this transition from feudal to capitalist space, varying types of spaces confront each other. 'Religious space did not disappear with the advent of commercial space ... Alongside religious space, and even within it, there were places, there was room, for other spaces – for the space of exchange, for the space of power.'[65] So for Lefebvre, religious space collides with, even appropriates, mercantile space.

This idea that sacred space is not pure can be seen in Jill Dubisch's work on a contemporary Greek Orthodox shrine on the island of Tinos. She writes that by its very nature pilgrimage,

> although centered around a specific place, violates notions of boundedness ... The boundaries of the pilgrimage site itself, which at first seem clearly to delineate a sacred space with a devotional focus, become blurred, and then dissolve, as pilgrims scatter and return to their homes, taking something of the pilgrimage site with them, spiritually and materially. The pilgrimage site is a web – at its center the object of devotion, but with strands spun outward both by the pilgrims and by other forces ... [A] pilgrimage site is connected in complex ways to the non-sacred world around it. It has economic, social, and political ramifications for the local community, the region, and even the nation.[66]

There exists no absolute division between the sacred and profane in pilgrimage, since everyday life may invade 'sacred' space. The boundaries between sacred and profane are fluid and dissolve.[67] To use a slightly different terminology, one could say that the sacred and profane interpenetrate.[68]

This fluidity has brought rise to suggestions that pilgrimage, as a topic, may in fact be the ideal 'postmodern' subject. Pilgrimage is increasingly being seen as a context in which meanings and interest are contested.[69] '[P]ilgrimage lends itself to an approach that regards ritual as process rather than as fixed structure, and that sees meaning not as fixed but as multiple and mutable and often contested ... In this sense, pilgrimage may constitute a perfect postmodern subject for the anthropologist.'[70] Pilgrimage read as a polymorphic phenomenon differs 'not only in form and meaning from one cultural setting to another, but also in its forms, motivations and meanings within a single context'.[71] Early discussions of pilgrimage shared 'structuralist foundations, with pilgrimage being seen as either supporting or subverting the established social order'. But Eade and Sallnow suggest that pilgrimage be viewed not only 'as a field of social relations, but as a *realm of competing discourses*'. A cult has a plethora of religious discourses which pilgrims impose on it. A cult is constituted by the varied, often conflicting, expectations and experiences brought to a shrine by different categories of pilgrims.[72] With gender taken as a crucial element in pilgrimage experience, we can see how it is a site of contesting images, as in, for example, secular and religious literature.

Figure 6 Pilgrims on their way to Canterbury from the Trinity Chapel Window, Canterbury Cathedral

Art: the sacred and the profane

One of the Trinity Chapel windows from the early thirteenth century shows pilgrims on their way to Thomas's shrine. A bearded man is riding a white horse. He is followed by a young man, a woman and another man walking with a crutch or staff. The woman is the furthest back dimensionally, situated behind the men. In a sense, this window symbolizes the state of research on women pilgrims so far. They exist, but are situated so far back they are barely noticed, obscured by the male pilgrims in the foreground. Yet women pilgrims appear often enough in art throughout Western Europe for us to conclude that women went on pilgrimage so frequently as to be easily identifiable as visual icons. Medieval artworks throughout England and Europe depict women pilgrims in a wide variety of media. The fluid shift between the secular and religious can be seen, not just in the act of pilgrimage itself, but in the art representing pilgrims. Medieval art representing women pilgrims reflects this contrast between the profane and sacred.

In one example, a group of pilgrims appear in a wood-carving in the Hospital del Rey in Burgos, one of thirty-two hospitals in Burgos and which was founded in the twelfth century by Alfonso VIII. In the fifteenth century wooden reliefs, carved to the left of the church portal, St James appears as an intercessor. Below him is a naked male pilgrim who is making a severe pilgrimage of expiation. To the right stands a group of pilgrims including a woman gazing lovingly at, and possibly suckling, her baby. Her husband stands next to her with a scallop shell on his hat and their son stands below them.[73] This and other [see previous note] varied late medieval and Reformation European examples of women pilgrims in art works show that they were normal and regular icons; that is, seeing them a viewer would recognize the attributes which identify them as a category: pilgrim, female.

The subject of the wall paintings in Eton College Chapel and in the Lady Chapel of Winchester Cathedral is the Miracles of the Virgin. The paintings, whitewashed in Elizabethan times, date from sometime between 1498 and 1524. Both sets of paintings contain a panel representing the Miracle of Mont S. Michel. In the Eton College Chapel it is to be found on the north wall, in the lower easternmost panel. In the Winchester Lady Chapel it is to be found in the centre lower panel on the south wall. While in the paintings the compositions are reversed, the same figures are depicted. The Virgin shelters a woman at her feet. Mont S. Michel towers behind and two pilgrim spectators watch. In the Winchester painting the woman holds a child and the inscription reads, '*Hic beata virgo mulierem inter undas parientem protexit et pluribus eam spectantibus a periculis liberavit.*' The story goes that the woman went into labour on her way to Mont S. Michel as the tide swiftly came in. Due to the Virgin's intervention, the woman was found alive with her baby after the tide receded.[74] Now, this is a miracle story and not a historical woman pilgrim who is depicted. But the presence of a woman pilgrim in Winchester, at the start of the Pilgrims' Way to Canterbury, suggests an acknowledgement of the presence of women pilgrims on this route. Furthermore, the pregnant or maternal state of women pilgrims is likewise recognized in these panels.

Figure 7 Matilda of Cologne from the Trinity Chapel Window, Canterbury Cathedral

Figure 8 The lame daughters of Godbold of Boxley from the Trinity Chapel Window, Canterbury Cathedral

Stained glass provides a mimesis of the pilgrimage culture in late medieval England. For example,

> [t]he representations of St William's Shrine in the St William Window at York provide one of the best glimpses of the pilgrim traffic. A group of sick and lame men and women is shown bathing in the water at the shrine, which is adorned with models of those parts of the body for which cures had been sought.[75]

Women pilgrims frequently show up in stained glass, such as those appearing in the Trinity Chapel windows of Canterbury Cathedral, seven of the original twelve windows surviving (one scene is at the Fogg Museum in Cambridge, Massachusetts). The miracles represented include those which took place 1171–3 and which were recorded in two different prose accounts of Thomas Becket's death, one by a monk named William and the other by the Prior of the Cathedral Priory, Benedict. The accounts were clearly used by the glaziers, working 1213–20, though the wording differs from both accounts.[76] Various women appear in these miracle windows, such as Petronilla of Polesworth, an epileptic nun. After she has a fit in front of her abbess, she is taken to Thomas' tomb in the crypt. Her feet are bathed in holy water and she is cured. In another panel, Juliana of Rochester is cured of blindness after visiting the tomb. The leper Richard Sunieve of Edgeworth is shown accompanied on his successful pilgrimage to Canterbury by his mother, master and mistress. Also shown is Matilda of Cologne, a madwoman who murdered her baby. Her two attendants are shown subduing her with cudgels, and later being thanked by her after she is cured at the tomb. In another set of panels, the story of Sir Jordan Fitzeisulf is depicted. He does not fulfil his vow to go on a pilgrimage to St Thomas after his son recovers from an illness. Among the members of the household shown are Sir Jordan's wife. In the depiction of Gilbert, son of William le Brun, his parents are shown delighted when he recovers from near death. Yet another window shows a mother calling on Thomas to rescue her child, who is saved from a fever only to have a wall topple onto his cradle during a storm.

These stained glass windows show the saint's efficacy pictorially. The scenes teach the pilgrim that praying to Thomas is a good idea since such a prayer has great power before God, that a pilgrimage to Canterbury is a proper way to show gratitude to Thomas for his aid, and that a thank offering would not be out of place.[77] Church glass and wall-paintings provided information for the unlettered about Scripture and histories of the saints.

> [A] representational work of visual art can carry an intrinsic code comprehensible within a relatively wide cultural tradition. A picture of a man or a woman, or even more specifically of a monk, priest, warrior, or bishop will be recognizable to anyone within a broad Christian tradition.[78]

In addition to what we might call 'normalized' depictions of women pilgrims, that is, depictions which show women pilgrims acting as they ideally should, we also have, as in literature, women connected with pilgrimage who somehow are at odds

Figure 9 Woman seizing the ear of a kneeling man in the Pilgrimage Window at York Minster, north aisle

with ideal Christian behaviour. The visual representation of women pilgrims is bifurcated between the 'sacred' woman pilgrim whose experience proves the efficacy of the saint being praised, and the 'profane' woman pilgrim in, for example, the Pilgrimage Window at York Minster. In the north aisle of the nave of York Minster, the third window from the east is called the Pilgrimage Window, dating from the fourteenth century. Structured much like a fourteenth-century illuminated manuscript page, with small medallions set into the grisaille panels,[79] some of the depictions in the glass are what you might expect: a knight on pilgrimage with a horse and banner, a lady with attendant on pilgrimage, St Peter holding the church, St John with Longinus and Stephaton, the Crucifixion, the Blessed Virgin with two companions, and so on. But the central medallion on top depicts a woman seizing the ear of a kneeling man. The borders on the bottom contain, in the left-most section, the parody of a funeral, possibly that of the Blessed Virgin, with monkeys carrying a coffin, a small monkey attached to the coffin, cross bearer, bell ringer, fox reading from lectern to cock; then in the centre a woman with distaff pursues a fox with a goose; also there are an archer and horse watched by a monkey and owl; and in the rightmost section is a hound chased by a stag, attacked by a smaller hound. In the left and right sides of the window are depicted squirrels, owls, monkeys and urinals. The tracery depicts Jesus between two angels of the passion.[80] How can we understand this pilgrimage window, consisting, as it does, of both the most sacred of images – Christ's Crucifixion – and the most profane – urinals and fighting?

Michael Camille in his book, *Image on the Edge: The Margins of Medieval Art*, discusses the cultural space of margins, most especially in manuscripts, but also in physical spaces, such as the monastery, cathedral, court and city. Why do the margins often contain wierd creatures or profane subjects? What is the point of these odd intrusions into the religious sphere? The further away from Jerusalem, the more deformed and alien things become. Outside time and space, God controls all. But the sacred centre radiates out into the profane edge.

> Although it lacked our predominant dichotomy of public versus private, the medieval organization of space was no less territorial ... This control and codification of space represented by the labelled territories of the centrifugal circular World Map created, of necessity, a space for ejecting the undesirable – the banished, outlawed, leprous, scaborous outcasts of society. If these edges were dangerous, they were also powerful places.[81]

Camille emphasizes the trouble with simple binary opposites, arguing that the profane is essential to the sacred. The central hegemony depends on margins for its continued existence.[82] In fact, medieval people enjoyed the ambiguity present in the confrontation between the sacred and profane. He contends that the margins are arenas of confrontation, where individuals often crossed social boundaries.

In terms of monkeys specifically, as in the York Minster window, Camille shows how the parody of religious activities in fact reinstates their very legitimacy. For example, the image of a nun suckling a monkey from a *Lancelot Romance* manuscript

> parodies the traditional type of the *Virgo lactans* ... Whereas the Virgin gave birth to Christ, this supposed virgin has give birth to a monstrous sign that, in its distortion of the human, points to her all-too-human sin. Such images work to reinstate the very models they oppose.'[83]

So the hegemony of the church and its hierarchies are underscored, not undermined, by these seemingly blasphemous and irreverent images.

In discussing monasteries and cathedrals, Camille points out that, unlike the cloister, the exterior of the church was not part of the sacred space, rather it was the junction with the world.[84] Furthermore, he says, an eruption of low-life squabbling and suffering could be found in the very spaces where churchmen complained a lot went on besides devotion.[85] The thirteenth-century French cleric Humbert of Romans complained that churches were not only for prayer but were locations where people 'indulge in idle chatter, do business transactions and secular work ... and some desecrate the church by doing physical violence there'.[86] Thus, the medallion in the Pilgrimage Window at York Minster showing two men wrestling is, perhaps, not that surprising. It illustrates 'fallen' behaviour and, by implication, proper Christian behaviour of turning the other cheek. In the midst of the sacred, the marginal world erupts. But the marginal, profane world is contained through this appropriation of it, neutralizing its potency. This we will see with the satirical works dealing with women pilgrims, who appear potent and sexually threatening on the page, but, through the medium of satire, are mocked.

Camille also addresses the issue of reception of these images, particularly by pilgrims.

> As well as articulating boundaries and limits for those existing within, those persons outside the Church were also addressed by these powerful images, notably pilgrims who had similarly renounced the world for a short period of wandering as they travelled towards the *stabilitas* of the sacred centre.[87]

The reader or viewer of a visual text like the Pilgrimage Window described above is confronted with two distinct aspects of medieval life, one sacred and other profane. The viewer is thus situated neither outside nor inside but in-between, on the edge. The pilgrims travelling to a pilgrimage site at a monastery or cathedral are still unstable in themselves, their existence highlighting the inherent instability of the quotidian world as contrasted with the eternal stability of God and his representative churches. Humbert of Romans argued against these pilgrims, particularly those addicted to its activities:

> 'There are others who move about, unable to remain in one place: they appear now here, now there, running to and fro without ceasing. These are like the people of whom it is said in Jeremiah 14, "They love to move about and never rest and the Lord is not pleased with them." Blessed Benedict calls them *gyrovagi*.'[88]

As we will see with the symbolism of the woman pilgrim figure in literature, pilgrimage is a potentially dangerous and subversive act since it defies being fixed. Its very nature is that of movement. Movement suggests change which suggests, in turn, the overturning of order.

Women pilgrims are depicted in imaginative secular works as unstable and unfixed. The profane women in the York Minster Pilgrimage Window, seizing the ear of a kneeling man or pursuing with her distaff the fox with the goose, seem to be active, vital women, free of the societal oppression based on gender. But Camille cautions us against reading such images as liberating or feminist.

> The margins, as we have often seen, represent things excluded from official discourse ... How [women] are pictured in the margins might at first seem to free them from this passive specular role of doll or icon. But this, too, is an illusion. The inversion and release of liminality works only for those in power, those who maintain the status quo and have something at stake in resisting change ... The margins are not the site of liberation for medieval women ... These are images made, for the most part, by and for men ... [W]omen are clearly the victims of a deep misogyny in medieval marginal art, which seals them into oppressive simulations of their social position ... Once again we are forced to see

overlaps and continuities in the cultural practices and spaces that we tend to separate, and to see how revealing are the edges of discourse, which always return us to the rules of the centre – where women, like peasants, servants and other subjected groups are, in the end, the ones who have to eat shit.[89]

So the Pilgrimage Window at York Minster functions in various ways. It shows one 'proper' female pilgrim: significantly a lady, a member of the upper class, accompanied and served by an attendant. The other women are profane and of a lower social class, depicted chasing a fox with a distaff in hand or behaving in a distinctly 'unladylike' way by seizing the ear of a man kneeling. By showing the man kneeling and being henpecked by his (presumed) wife, the medallion, this visual representation of profane and incorrect everyday behaviour, in fact asserts and proscribes the opposite form of behaviour. The borders or margins of the pilgrimage window reflect anxiety as to what pilgrimage activities in reality were feared to bring out: a parody or mockery of religious, sacred and proper behaviour. The interpenetration of sacred and profane in the act of pilgrimage is reflected in medieval art, which represents both sacred and secular modes of understanding women pilgrims. The next chapter follows another mode of expressing this bifurcation in an examination of the secular and sacred literature of late medieval England.

Notes

1   Edward Soja criticizes the hegemony of *temporality* in historicism as opposed to *spatiality* in understanding social life. He promotes seeing the 'lifeworld' in the 'construction of human geographies, the social production of space and the restless formation and reformation of geographical landscapes, social being actively emplaced in space *and* time in an explicitly historical *and* geographical contextualization'. Edward Soja, 'History, geography, modernity,' in Simon During, ed., *The Cultural Studies Reader*, Routledge, London, 1993, pp. 135–50, here p. 136. Soja also cites Foucault's linkage of space, knowledge and power and his suggestion that the history of spaces would be the history of powers. Ibid., p. 146.

2   Representations of women pilgrims adapted to, rather than questioned, existing perceptions of gender roles, reinforcing women's socialization. Margaret Miles, 'Pilgimage as Metaphor in a Nuclear Age,' *Theology Today*, 45, 1988, p. 169.

3   Charles Zika, 'Hosts, Processions and Pilgrimages: Controlling the Sacred in Fifteenth-Century Germany,' *Past and Present* 118, 1988, p. 26.

4   Minneapolis, MN, University of Minnesota Press, 1977, p. 199.

5   Ibid., p. 182.

6   Englewood Cliffs, NJ, Prentice-Hall, 1974, p. 129.

7   'The medieval cathedral was meant to be experienced; it was a dense text to be read with devout attention and not an architectural form to be merely seen.' Tuan 1974, op. cit., p. 137.

8   Tuan 1977, op. cit., p. 102.

9   Michel de Certeau, *The Practice of Everyday Life*, Steven F. Rendall, trans., Berkeley, University of California Press, 1984, p. 117.

10 Ibid., p. 120.

11 'Un autre espace, un autre lieu, autant de transmutations contraintes dans l'acte pèlerin où l'on se retrouve différent de son exister habituel et comme connaturellement autre, puisque tout est autre.' Alphonse Dupront, *Du Sacré: Croisades et pèlerinages: Images et language*, Paris, Gallimard, 1987, p. 49.

12 'Il n'y a pas de pèlerinage sans "lieu."' Ibid., p. 371.

13 Ibid., p. 374.

14 Robert Worth Frank, Jr., 'Pilgrimage and Sacral Power,' in Barbara N. Sargent-Baur, ed., *Journeys Toward God: Pilgrimage and Crusade*, Kalamazoo, MI, Medieval Institute Publications, 1992, pp. 31–43, here p. 33.

15 'Ambivalence donc essentielle, la pénitence et la libération; l'épreuve de cette double opération en un lieu, en fait un lieu marqué par l'accomplissement salvateur.' Dupront, op. cit., p. 318.

16 Ibid., p. 370.

17 'Pèlerinage et 'lieu sacré' s'inscrivent dès lors dans une dramatique d'accomplissement dont les protagonistes existentiels demeurent l'homme en son acte pèlerin, l'espace, réalités et puissances sacrales enfin. Pareille distinction analytique doit conduire l'approche d'une 'phénoménologie' du pèlerinage et des lieux sacrés – l'objet même de la présente étude —, selon trois temps organiques, la démarche d'aller, ou le corps à corps de l'homme avec l'espace; réception et création emmêlées du 'lieu' sacral; rencontre, au 'lieu sacral', avec ce qui, à travers le mystère sacral, demeure un 'au-delà'.' Ibid., p. 373.

18 'Le 'lieu sacré' est, dans l'expérience religieuse de l'espèce humaine, une nécessité.' Ibid., p. 412.

19 'Le pèlerinage est gest "extraordinaire" d'une quête humaine du sacral.' Ibid., p. 413.

20 'Le pèlerinage est volonté de puissance, collective ou individuelle … Puissance de se faire étranger à soi-même, jusqu'à découvrir "l'autre" en soi, et en faire puissance de communion en "l'Autre".' Ibid., p. 414.

21 Victor Turner and Edith Turner, *Image and Pilgrimage in Christian Culture*, Oxford, Basil Blackwell, 1978, p. 35.

22 Ibid., p. 249.

23 Ibid., pp. 250–1.

24 Ibid., p. 32. As Paul Strohm puts it in a somewhat different discourse, the pilgrimage 'offers a "processual" form, with challenges to the social order enacted in a series of dramas set in linear time', Paul Strohm, *Social Chaucer*, Cambridge, Harvard University Press, 1989, p. 152. For a Turnerian and Bakhtinian reading of *The Canterbury Tales* see Frederick B. Jonassen's 'The Inn, the Cathedral, and the Pilgrimage of *The Canterbury Tales*' in Susanna Greer Fein, David Raybin, and Peter C. Braeger, eds, *Rebels and Rivals: The Contestive Spirit in The Canterbury Tales*, Kalamazoo, MI, Medieval Institute Publications, 1991, pp. 1–35.

25 Julia B. Holloway trans., *Saint Bride and Her Book*, Newburyport, MA, Focus Texts 1992, p. 5. For more on the conjectured 'equality' of men and women on pilgrimage, see Julia B. Holloway, Constance S. Wright and Joan Bechtold, eds, *Equally in God's Image: Women in the Middle Ages*, New York, Peter Lang, 1990, pp. 167–8.

26 Holloway 1992, op. cit., p. 5.

27 Turner and Turner, op. cit., p. 31.

28 From 'Introduction', John Eade and Michael J. Sallnow, in *Contesting the Sacred: The Anthropology of Christian Pilgrimage*, London, Routledge, 1991, pp. 4–5.

29 Jill Dubisch, *In a Different Place: Pilgrimage, Gender, and Politics at a Greek Island Shrine*, Princeton, Princeton University Press, 1995, p. 43.

30 Ibid., p. 44.

31 Zika points out how in Corpus Christi processions in fifteenth-century Germany 'just as the women are designated a rear position in the Corpus Christi procession, they find little prominence in the social performance and communal structuring of Corpus Christi', op. cit., p. 45.

32 Carolyn Walker Bynum, *Fragmentation and Redemption: Essays on Gender and the Human Body in Medieval Religion*, New York, Zone Books, 1991, p. 32.

33 Ibid., pp. 47–8.

34 Dubisch, op. cit., pp. 95–7.

35 Lynn Staley, *Margery Kempe's Dissenting Fictions*, University Park, PA, The Pennsylvania State University Press, 1994, p. 40, fn2.
36 Ibid., p. 76.
37 de Certeau, op. cit., pp. 97–107.
38 Cambridge, Cambridge University Press, 1986, pp. 88–9.
39 Ibid., p. 85.
40 Edward Dimendberg, 'Henri Lefebvre on Abstract Space', in *Philosophy and Geography II: The Production of Public Space*, Andrew Light and Jonathan M. Smith, eds, Lanham, MD, Rowman and Littlefield, 1998, p. 20.
41 'Formal Politics, Meta-Space, and Construction of Civil Life,' in ibid., pp. 81–97, here pp. 81–2.
42 Tuan 1974, op. cit., p. 174.
43 Ibid., p. 34.
44 Ibid., pp. 53–4, here p. 61. See also Tuan 1977, op. cit., p. 13.
45 Bourdieu, quoted in Gillian R. Overing and Marijane Osborn, *Landscape of Desire: Partial Stories of the Medieval Scandinavian World*, Minneapolis, University of Minnesota Press, 1994, p. 45.
46 All citations from Frederick J. Furnivall, ed., *Political, Religious, and Love Poems*, London, K. Paul, Trench, Trübner & Co./Oxford, Oxford University Press, 1903/1965, p. 144, ll. 32, 36.
47 Ibid., p. 145, ll. 61–2.
48 Ibid., p. 159, ll. 460–77.
49 Jonathan Sumption, *Pilgrimage: An image of Mediaeval Religion*, Totowa, NJ, Rowman and Littlefield, 1975, p. 263.
50 Cynthia Hahn, 'Seeing and Believing: The Construction of Sanctity in Early-Medieval Saints' Shrines', *Speculum*, 72, 1997, p. 1090, fn 84.
51 This section is from *Of the coming of St Cuthbert into Scotland, taken forth of the Scottish History*. From J. Davis, ed., *The Ancient Rites, and Monuments of the Monastical and Cathedral Church of Durham*, London, W. Hensman, 1672, pp. 60–3.
52 Sumption, op. cit., p. 262.
53 Ronald C. Finucane, *Miracles and Pilgrims: Popular Beliefs in Medieval England*, London, Dent, 1977, p. 87.
54 André Vauchez, *Sainthood in the Later Middle Ages*, Jean Birrell, trans., Cambridge, Cambridge University Press, p. 125. See also p. 446.
55 Women were not always the ones barred from entry. Barbara H. Rosenwein discusses gendered restrictions in churches and at altars. Caesarius of Arles' (470–542) *Rule for Nuns* stipulated that men should not be permitted into the inner precincts of the monastery, with a few exceptions, such as the bishop. Generally, though, women 'were the polluters'. She cites Gregory of Tours (538–94) telling of a woman struck dead when she transgressed spatial restrictions to see the pillar of St Symeon. See Barbara H. Rosenwein, *Negotiating Space: Power, Restraint, and Privileges of Immunity in Early Medieval Europe*, Ithaca, Cornell University Press, 1999, p. 41. Rosenwein also discusses the convent of the Holy Cross at Poitiers founded by Queen Radegund, which claimed possession of a piece of the True Cross. 'This was a "woman's" relic. It had been discovered by Helena, mother of Constantine, and in the monastery of Radegund, where it joined a cache of other precious relics, it was off-limits to the public and even to most men.' Ibid., pp. 52ff., especially 56.
56 Daphne Spain, *Gendered Spaces*, Chapel Hill, The University of North Carolina Press, 1992, p. 3.
57 Ibid., p. 6.
58 Dubisch, op. cit., p. 233, suggests that increased veneration of relics contributed to the belief that material things and places could be sacred. Patrick Geary points out that '[i]n its new location [a stolen relic] became an important symbol only if the society made it one, and this symbolism was necessarily a product of that society … [R]elics are most

peculiar sorts of symbolic objects – symbols without intrinsic significance.' From *Furta Sacra, Thefts of Relics in the Central Middle Ages*, Princeton, Princeton University Press, 1978, pp. 7, 152.

59 Zika, op. cit., discusses bleeding hosts as relics of Christ's body and the pilgrimages and processions made in honour of them.

60 William Melczer, *The Pilgrims' Guide to Santiago de Compostela*, New York, Italica Press, 1993, p. 2.

61 Sarah Beckwith, *Christ's Body: Identity, Culture and Society in Late Medieval Writings*, London, Routledge, 1993, p. 24.

62 Henri Lefebvre, *The Production of Space*, Donald Nicholson-Smith, trans., Oxford, Blackwell, 1991, p. 45. Lefebvre distinguishes between spatial practice, representation of space, and the space of representation.

63 Ibid., p. 256.

64 Dimendberg, op. cit., p. 22–3; Lefebvre, p. 263. Patrick Geary argues how difficult it is to determine what kind of systems are used in the transference of goods in the Carolingian and post-Carolingian periods. Geary argues that rather than barter, gift and theft were the most basic forms of trade during this period, in Geary 1986, op. cit., pp. 169–74. 'When new political, social, religious, and economic systems began to develop in the twelfth century, the relative significance of relics in providing these services [thaumaturgic power, ability to substitute for public authority, protect and secure the community, determine the relative status of individuals and churches, and provide for the community's economic prosperity] was weakened,' ibid., p. 179.

65 Lefebvre, op. cit., p. 266.

66 Dubisch, op. cit., pp. 38–9.

67 Ibid., p. 257.

68 Beckwith argues that the imitation of Christ, particularly as it developed in the late Middle Ages, 'entails a different understanding of sacred-profane relations. The denial of any special place or person, church, priest, is also a denial of the very distinction between sacred and profane, and an affirmation of their interpenetration,' op. cit., p. 77. Badir uses Henre Lefebvre's discussions of space to analyse the performing body and archival representation in the early modern period. As Badir puts it, 'To Lefebvre social spaces, as produced by representational practices, "*interpenetrate one another and/or superimpose themselves upon one another*" (emphasis Lefebvre's). Social boundaries such as class, location, and gender, or visible boundaries such as walls and enclosures, give rise to "an appearance of separation between spaces where in fact what exists is an ambiguous continuity"', Patricia Badir, 'Playing Space: History, the Body, and Records of Early English Drama,' *Exemplaria* IX, 1997, p. 269. So, too, with pilgrimage, the conjunction of the sacred and profane is in 'ambiguous continuity'.

69 Dubisch, op. cit., p. 161.

70 Ibid., pp. 41–2.

71 Ibid., p. 46.

72 Eade and Sallnow, op. cit., pp. 5, 10.

73 Vera and Hellmut Hell, *The Great Pilgrimage of the Middle Ages: The Road to St James of Compostela*, London, Barie and Rockliff, 1964/1979, pp. 42, 46. In the Franciscan Chapel of Nancy, there exists a sculpture of Gerhart of Vaudemont wearing a pectoral cross and carrying a staff, indicating his pilgrim status. Behind him stands his wife, embracing him almost like the Virgin embraces Christ in scenes of the entombment like a Man of Sorrows. From a Warburg Institute art folder. See also *Warburg Journal* No. XXV, Pl. 30 fig. e. In Conques, on the Tympanum of the Church of St Foy, there is a section depicting the Last Judgment. It includes a procession of saints. The figures range from Mary, on the extreme right. Peter stands behind her. Others include abbots and founders, even the crowned Charlemagne, as well as a monk and pilgrims. A female pilgrim appears to stand at the extreme left next to a male pilgrim with staff. Hell, op. cit., pp. 100, 109. In Überlingen, the fifteenth-century frescoes in the Chapel of St Jocelyn depict a family in

Santiago, a father, mother and son, who are thanking St James for his intervention. The legend of this family tells how the landlord's daughter at an inn in Santo Domingo fell in love with the son, who didn't reciprocate her affection. While he is not looking, she plants a golden cup in his baggage. He is subsequently reported as a thief, whereupon the cup is discovered in his things and he is hanged. The parents continue on their journey to Santiago and implore St James to intercede. Upon the return trip they find their son on the gallows still living. After bringing the case before a magistrate who refuses to believe them, the judge points to some chickens being roasted for him and declares that 'they are more likely to return to life than the hanged thief', whereupon the chickens fly away! The fresco depicts the parents and the redeemed son thanking St James for his help. The mother is to the back and the left of her family. Hell, op. cit., pp. 180, 196–7. A detail from a Flemish altar picture, dating from around 1490, depicts three pilgrims seeking shelter. The hats of two of the pilgrims are adorned with pilgrim badges or shells, including that of the woman. Lenz Kriss-Rettenbeck and Gerda Möhler, eds, *Wallfahrt Kennt Keine Grenzen*, Zürich, Verlag Schnell & Steiner München, 1984, p. 205. Two women pilgrims appear in a group of about seven pilgrims in a painted panel by Hans Burgkmair from 1504 which was in a former cloister dedicated to Katherine in Augsburg. Ibid., p. 350. Winnenden lies a little northeast of Stuttgart and was a stopping place for pilgrims travelling from central Germany via Einsiedeln. The reliefs on the high altar of the castle church, dating from 1520, show a seated St James blessing two pilgrims, one man and one woman. Hell, op. cit., p. 197. One relief on the wing of an altarpiece in Tiffen depicts a pilgrim family sharing a bed in an inn. The woman is to the right in the picture. Kriss-Rettenbeck and Möhler, op. cit., p. 133. The Meister von Alkmaar in 1504 painted a series of panels. One shows a group of pilgrims receiving hospitality and a room for the night. They are gathered on a square and a woman is showing one of the pilgrims in. In the left foreground a woman pilgrim stands with her back to the viewer watching the scene. Ibid., p. 177. A copper engraving by Lucas of Leyden, dating from about 1508, shows three pilgrims. An older bearded male pilgrim is on the path, walking by use of his staff. Under the trees by the side of the road sit a husband and wife. The man, seated upright, is carving a pear. The woman is likewise seated, though she is leaning over on her elbow, looking at the fruit eagerly. They both have the scallop shell emblem on their hats, indicating that they are on their way to or from Santiago, as well as the 'vera icon' or true image – the veil of Veronica which retained the image of Christ's face after he wiped it on her veil on his way to Calvary. Hell, op. cit., pp. 60, 75. Also Thomas Raff, ed., *Wallfahrt Kennt Keine Grenzen (Katalog der Ausstellung im Bayerischen Nationalmuseum, München, 1984)*, München, C. Wolf & Sohn, 1984, p. 19. A coloured woodcut by Hans Burgkmair from 1508 depicts a pilgrim group of four, two men, a woman and a child. All are clad in pilgrim outfits and carry staves. The woodcut illustrates a section of a sermon about pilgrimage given by Johannes Geiler (1445–1510). The beginning of the text is printed beneath the picture and begins, 'Unser pilgershaft solln wir volbrinen mit geistlichen fröden in dem lob gots and in haltung seiner gebot …' (Our pilgrimage we should carry out with spiritual joy in the praise of God and in keeping with his commandment …). Ibid., pp. 24–5. Other artwork depicting women pilgrims includes a pair of silver drinking mugs which are painted, dating from after the Reformation. One mug is shaped like a man and the other like a woman. They are depicted with the usual attributes of pilgrims, a doubled knobbed staff, rosary, broad-brimmed hat and shoulder drapery to which shells and mementos are attached. Ibid., pp. 22–3. A copper engraving from about 1580, by Raphael Sadeler after designs by Johannes Stradanus, depicts the personification of Pietas as a kneeling-at-prayer woman pilgrim. She has the staff and rosary, in addition to the shells on her hat and cape, all typical attributes of a pilgrim. Ibid., pp. 26–7.

74 M. R. James and E. W. Tristram, *The Wall Paintings in Eton College Chapel and in the Lady Chapel of Winchester Cathedral*, Oxford, Oxford University Press, 1929, pp. 14–15, 29, 33, 35–7.

75 Sarah Crewe, *Stained Glass in England 1180–1540*, London, Her Majesty's Stationery Office, 1987, p. 78.

76 Jonathan Alexander and Paul Binski, eds, *Age of Chivalry: Art in Plantagenet England 1200–1400*, London, Weidenfeld and Nicolson, 1987, p. 211.

77 D. Ingram Hill, *The New Bell's Cathedral Guides Canterbury Cathedral*, Bell & Hyman Limited, 1986, p. 107. See also pp. 105, 109, 111, 113–14 and Sarah Brown, *Stained Glass in Canterbury Cathedral*, London, Cathedral Gifts Ltd, 1991.

78 See Geary 1978, op. cit., p. 6.

79 Crewe, op. cit., p. 54.

80 John Toy, ed., *A Guide and Index to the Windows of York Minster*, ed. John Toy, Dean & Chapter of York, York, 1985, p. 17.

81 London, Reaktion Books, 1992, p. 16.

82 Ibid., pp. 9–10.

83 Ibid., pp. 30.

84 Ibid., p. 72.

85 Ibid., pp. 82–3.

86 Ibid., p. 91.

87 Ibid., p. 56.

88 Ibid., p. 137.

89 Ibid., pp. 126–7.

4 Secular and religious literary depictions of women pilgrims

We have seen how political controls and the figuring of pilgrimage as, potentially, false and, thereby, threatening, were forms of power exerted in late medieval England. But power exercised in the realm of representation can be as important as actual material or legal power. David Harvey suggests that '[a]ny system of representation, in fact, is a spatialization of sorts which automatically freezes the flow of experience and in so doing distorts what it strives to represent'.[1] Rodney Hilton looking at the preoccupation with the figure of the ploughman in late medieval England, points out that

> [S]ymbols are chosen because of their contemporary resonance. It is no accident that the ploughman appears so powerfully, whether as himself or as a symbol in the last century and a half of the middle ages. He had become a *disturbing* figure.[2]

Like the ploughman, the woman pilgrim becomes a figure which proliferates in late medieval English texts. She became a symbol not unconnected from the ploughman. In terms of pilgrims and representation, the literature of post-plague England is littered with characters who disguise themselves as pilgrims, thereby casting the sincerity of all pilgrims, signed visibly by the pilgrim costume, into question. This post-plague period is when this topos of the disorderly and sexual female pilgrim becomes prevalent in English secular literature. Fears and anxieties about social disorder become displaced in secular literature most typically onto the female pilgrim figure.

Natalie Zemon Davis has argued for how gender politics can stand in for matters of the political and social order.[3] Similarly Lynn Staley has shown with Margery Kempe that gender is a displacement for concern with the social order in terms of both spiritual and civil authority.[4] The disorderly woman is a multivalent image.[5] While anthropologists generally agree that rites and ceremonies of role reversal, where the disorderly woman is 'on top', 'are ultimately sources of order and stability in a hierarchical society', Davis suggests that such disorder could, in fact, 'undermine as well as reinforce' that hierarchy. Davis speculates that 'the ambiguous woman-on-top of the world of play made the unruly option a more conceivable one within the family'.[6] This book argues, similarly, that the secular, sexual, disorderly female pilgrim figure works both for reinforcing social order and undermining it. This figure, presented as sexual and disruptive, stems from a misogynist tradition, but signifies much beyond mere sexism. The female pilgrim figure represents social disorder – or anxieties about potential disorder – through its displacement into 'sexual disorder'. Ultimately, though, this figure is controlled through satire and irony, reinscribing social order.

Women pilgrims in secular literature: disguise, lying, sexuality

In the mid-twelfth century, Suger, Abbot of St-Denis, compiled a retrospective account of his renovations and enlargement of the Abbey Church of St-Denis, justifying the expensive endeavour. He argued that transferring relics from the narrow crypt above to a conspicuous display in the new choir would help prevent the rioting of unruly crowds of pilgrims. Enlarging and amplifying the church was necessary, particularly on feast days, he writes in *De Administratione*, 'for the narrowness of the place forced the women to run toward the altar upon the heads of the men as upon a pavement with much anguish and noisy confusion'.[7] Not only did Bishops and Archbishops attend the inspection of Charles the Bald's relics, but 'also an innumerable crowd of people of both sexes'.[8] Suger specifically singles out women in his description of the crowd. In *De Consecratione* he observes

> Often on feast days, completely filled, [the original church] disgorged through all its doors the excess of the crowds as they moved in opposite directions, and the outward pressure of the foremost ones not only prevented those attempting to enter from entering but also expelled those who had already entered. At times you could see, a marvel to behold, that the crowded multitude offered so much resistance to those who strove to flock in to worship and kiss the holy relics, the Nail and Crown of the Lord, that no one among the countless thousands of people because of their very density could move a foot; that no one, because of their very congestion, could [do] anything but stand like a marble statue, stay benumbed or, as a last resort, scream. The distress of the women, however, was so great and so intolerable that you could see with horror how they, squeezed in by the mass of strong men as in a winepress, exhibited bloodless faces as in imagined death; how they cried out horribly as though in labour; how several of them, miserably trodden underfoot [but then] lifted by the pious assistance of men above the heads of the crowd, marched forward as though upon a pavement; and how many others, gasping with their last breath, panted in the cloisters of the brethren to the despair of everyone.[9]

In the *Ordinatio*, Suger describes how the *Sancti Sanctorum* was

> so much cramped by [the] narrowness [of the lower church or crypt] that, on the hour of the Holy Sacrifice, the brethren partaking of the most Holy Eucharist could not stay there, and that they were oftentimes unable to withstand the unruly crowd of visiting pilgrims without great danger. You could see how people grievously trod down one another; how – what many would not believe – eager little women struggled to advance toward the altar marching upon the heads of men as upon a pavement; how at times, pushed back and forth and almost half-

dead, they escaped in the nick of time into the cloisters with the aid of merciful men, and stayed there gasping almost with their last breath.[10]

Suger's vivid comments are illustrative of the descriptions of pilgrims one encounters in later medieval writings. Pilgrims, in Suger's view, are an unruly crowd, an intolerable magnitude, and a threat to the brethren. Suger's description depicts crowds of pilgrims trapped in a eulogized,[11] sacred space. Suger's distaste for them is evident and he wishes to disgorge and purge them from his artistic masterpiece. Suger's response to the crowds of pilgrims is not to get rid of pilgrimage, but to enlarge the religious space they flock to, a space which is filled with light and renders formerly 'crypted'[12] objects and religious images visible. Suger describes the howls of the crushed women as if they were in labour, giving birth to a messy confusion and racket. While pilgrims in general are unruly, he uses the wholly sexual simile of birth and labour applicable only to women, a characteristic one encounters in late medieval English secular writings about women pilgrims.[13] Like the screams of a woman in labour which cease only once she has given birth, the tainting of his cathedral space will be pure only after the pilgrims are ejected from the boundaries of the building.

Reminiscent of Suger, Jean Gerson likewise perceives women's spirituality as excessive. In a 1415 treatise, *De probatione spirituum*, meant to help theologians determine the authenticity of visionaries, Gerson is particularly suspicious of Bridget of Sweden. He argues that women purporting to be inspired are suspect, their religious ardour 'overheated, versatile, [and] unbridled'. Such women need to be watched, given as they are to uncontrolled speech.

> There is hardly any other calamity more apt to do harm or that is more incurable. If its only consequence were the immense loss of time, this would already be sufficient for the devil. But you must know that there is something else to it: the insatiable itch to see and to speak, not to mention … the itch to touch.[14]

The use of the word itch suggests a kind of repulsion on Gerson's part for both women's speech and women's bodies, as Carolyn Dinshaw has pointed out.[15] But, further, the act of pilgrimage is implicated. The desire of women to see and touch the actual sights of Christ's life and of importance to saints was as repulsive to Gerson as women's own bodies in the weightiness of their physical presence. It is as though women touching holy sights would infect those sacred spots with a scaly disease. The unruly crowd of pilgrims of both sexes in Suger's description of St-Denis is a topos in English secular literature. Women pilgrims, however, are virtually always singled out for sexual impropriety.

The unruly pilgrim is figured as lying or being in disguise, as in the English translation of the *Roman de la Rose*, ascribed to Chaucer. When Fals-Semblant and Dame Abstynaunce-Streyned try to decide how to dress themselves while travelling to Wikkid-Tonge, 'Whether it to done were/ To maken hem be knowen there,/ Or elles walken forth disgised./ But at the laste they devysed/ That they wolde gon in tapinage,/ As it were in a pilgrimage,/ Lyke good and hooly folk unfeyned' (RR 7357– 64).[16] *Tapinage* rhymes with *pilgrimage*, yoking the two concepts. *Tapin* is a concealed or disguised person and *tapinage*, a word which entered Middle English in the fourteenth century, means place of concealment or disguise.[17] Gower uses it in his *Confessio Amantis* (II. 187) 'This newe tapinage of lollardie'. Here the disruptive activities of lollardy have been linked with the impression of hiding or disguise. Disguise is an integral element of pilgrimage as seen in another Chaucerian text. In Book V of *Troilus and Criseyde*, Troilus thinks to disguise himself as a pilgrim to try to see Criseyde in the Greek camp, but he is too well known.

> And ofte tyme he was in purpos grete
> Hymselven lik a pilgrym to desgise
> To seen hire; but he may nat contrefete
> To ben unknowen of folk that weren wise,
> Ne fynde excuse aright that may suffise
> If he among the Grekis knowen were;
> For which he wep ful ofte and many a tere.
> (V, 1576–1582).[18]

False pilgrims are also present in the English *Roman de la Rose*, where Dame Abstinence dresses like a Beguine. Her pilgrim's staff is 'of Thefte' (7401) and her scrip is 'of Faynt Distresse' (7403). Fals-Sembland dresses as a friar. Another example of pilgrimage being used as an excuse for travel appears in Chaucer's *The Legend of Good Women*. In the *Legend of Philomela*, Philomela weaves a cloth which describes how she was raped by Tereus and how he then cut her tongue out and imprisoned her. He sends this cloth to her sister, Tereus's wife Progne.

> And whan that Progne hath this thing beholde,
> No word she spak, for sorwe and ek for rage,
> But feynede hire to gon on pilgrymage
> To Bacus temple; and in a litel stounde
> Hire dombe sister sittynge hath she founde,
> Wepynge in the castel, here alone.
> (LGW 2373–78)

In this case, feigning a pilgrimage is not criticized in the text since it is the means by which Progne can rescue her sister. Additionally, it is a pagan pilgrimage and not a Christian one.

Two lesser-known English works contain as elements women in disguise either as pilgrims or on pilgrimage. The first is an intriguing fragment of the fifteenth-century English romance *Pierre (or Peare) de Provence*.[19] The story is a romance in which the lovers, Peare and Maguelone, are tragically separated only to be reunited in amazing circumstances. They live and Maguelone bears a bouncing boy who becomes the King of Naples. One plot twist occurs immediately after they separate. Hiding herself in the woods on a road to Rome, Maguelone 'saw folk going and coming, and among them a pilgrimess, whom she persuaded to change clothes with her. In pilgrim's garb she reacht Rome'.[20] She eventually ends up in Peare's home country of Provence (en aigues mortes). The French version makes 'a pilgrimess kind to Maguelone, who then builds a small hospital at a Saracen port near there, and nurses the sick'.[21] In the English version she goes to

> the dukes place, & ther [in the hospital, was put where a pilgrim] or a pore body shuld be, & logid ther that nyhtt. & on the morowe she spake vn-to the hospetlere, & prayd that she myht be hir servaunt, 'ffor y am wery of the world'.

After the master of the hospital dies, Maguelone 'was made hospetlere; & she contenvid ffulle welle & vertuously in this hospitale, so muche that the people said that she was sum seint; & she was called 'the holy hospetlere'; & alle country came thiddir'.[22] Through a bizarre turn of events, the Sultan, whom Peare has been serving for three years, allows him to return home, giving him three barrels of gold, which Maguelone miraculously receives and with which she builds a new hospital and church. Peare, meanwhile, is ill and taken to Maguelone's hospital to be cured. Naturally they don't recognize each other, she washes his feet and hands and kisses them as was the custom. At last she recognizes him, puts royal robes on under her nun's garments. Then 'she tells Peare she is his love, throws off her nun's dress, and lets her fair hair fall to the ground'.[23] This story is clearly a Greek-style romance and the unrealistic turn of events unlikely. What is of interest for us is the ease with which Maguelone takes over the pilgrim hospice and becomes a nun without, apparently, having taken orders since she marries with no problem. We see the trick of pilgrim clothes as disguise.

The other work which likewise utilizes pilgrimage disguise as an element is a ballad dealing with Walsingham, found in a manuscript dating from after 1650. However, the editor presumes that *Gentle Herdsman* 'must have been written, if not before the dissolution of the monasteries, yet while the remembrance of them was fresh in the minds of the people.'[24] In this ballad, *Gentle heardsman, tell to me*,[25] disguise is crucial to the woman pilgrim's journey. She is in dialogue with a shepherd and asks the way to Walsingham.

> "Gentle heardsman, tell to me,
> Of curtesy I thee pray,
> Unto the town of Walsingham
> Which is the right and ready way."

> "Unto the towne of Walsingham   (5)
> The way is hard for to be gon;
> And verry crooked are those pathes
> For you to find out all alone."

> "Weere the miles doubled thrise,
> And the way never soe ill,   (10)
> Itt were not enough for mine offence;
> Itt is soe grievous and soe ill."

"Thy yeeares are young, thy face is faire,
Thy witts are weake, thy thoughts are greene;
Time hath not give thee leave, as yett, (15)
For to committ so great a sinne."

"Yes, Heardsman, yes, soe woldest thou say,
If thou knewest soe much as I;
My witts, and thoughts, and all the rest,
Have well deserved for to dye." (20)

"I am not what I seeme to bee,
My clothes and sexe doe differ farr:
I am a woman, woe is me!
Born[26] to greeffe and irksome care."

This poem shows that women pilgrims could and perhaps did travel dressed as men. Undoubtedly the dangers of kidnapping and rape caused women, particularly those travelling alone, to dress as men and thus stave off, though not wholly prevent, attraction. In this poem the female pilgrim is undergoing penance for the sin of pride in refusing her lover's entreates. One wonders if she likewise would have gone on pilgrimage had she given in to the sin of lust, in which case she could have been criticized for her loose sexuality.

By the late fourteenth century in England, pilgrimage was associated not only with religious activity, not only disguise, but also with subterfuge, lying and disorder. William Langland comments on the mendacity of pilgrims in the opening lines of *Piers Plowman*:

Pilgrymes and palmeres plighten hem togidere
To seken Seint Jame and seintes in Rome;
Wenten forth in hire wey with many wise tales,
And hadden leve to lyen al hire lif after.
I seigh somme that seiden thei hadde ysought seintes:
To ech a tale that thei tolde hire tonge was tempred to lye
Moore than to seye sooth, it semed bi hire speche.
(Prologue, 46–52)[27]

The doctor of divinity later confirms this by saying 'for pilgrymes konne wel lye' (XIII. 179). For women pilgrims, such subterfuge was additionally suspected to take the form of sexual misbehaviour. In *Piers Plowman*, a pardoner decides to join Piers and others on the pilgrimage to Truth. 'Bi Seint Poul!' quod a pardoner, 'paraventure I be noght knowe there;/ I wol go fecche my box with my brevettes and a bulle with bisshopes lettres' (V. 639–40). The pardoner clearly is satirized for wanting to making money on unsuspecting pilgrims. But the response to his exclamation comes from a woman. '"By Crist!" quod a commune womman, "thi compaignie wol I folwe./ Thow shalt seye I am thi suster." I ne woot where thei bicome' (V. 641–2). While the duplicity of the pardoner lies in the connection between finances and spirituality, hers lies in the connection between coin and sex. Furthermore, her faked familial connection with him disguises a potentially illicit sexual connection. Likewise in the Prologue, 'Heremytes on an heep with hoked staves/ Wenten to Walsyngham – and hire wenches after:/ Grete lobies and long that lothe were to swynke/ Clothed hem in copes to ben knowen from othere,/ And shopen hem heremytes hire ese to have' (53–7). The male pilgrims are in disguise and not true pilgrims. And they are implicated in sexual impropriety. But the women are defined solely by their sexuality; we are not even told if they are in disguise as pilgrims, though they go to Walsingham. For women pilgrims generally in late medieval English secular literature, disorder was suspected to take the form of sexual impropriety and so they become victim to traditional misogynist satire and critique.

Henri Lefebvre has looked at medieval perceptions of space which may help to explain this difference in how men and women were figured sexually as pilgrims, wherein sexuality impropriety is defining for women and merely incidental for men. He argues that Greek space restricted woman's station. Her realm is the household, around the hearth and shrine, in a closed and fixed space. 'Women's social status was restricted just as their symbolic and practical status was – indeed, these two aspects were inseparable so far as spatiality (spatial practice) was concerned.'[28] Christian space is inherited from antique conceptions of space, including this view of woman. Once the shrine is no longer in the home where women can go, a woman pilgrim inevitably will be criticized since she is no longer in a fixed or closed space. Shannon McSheffrey reminds us that in examining historical gender roles we should not simply equate the male with public sphere and the female with the domestic or private. Class and marital status affected both sexes ability to perform publicly. However, 'there can be no doubt that late medieval society regarded certain activities as more appropriate for a man than a woman … A "public" woman was in some ways an unchaste woman.'[29] As Margaret Miles points out in her discussion of *The Pilgrim's Progress*, the metaphor of pilgrimage adapts to, rather than questions, existing gender roles. It reinforces women's socialization.[30] In secular literary works, physical disguise or deceit in language is displaced in female pilgrim figures onto the realm of the sexual. The sexual female pilgrim is a figure of disruption and danger, evoked by artists who then carefully control her through irony or satire. The power of representation to distort and fix social relations is realized in the topos of the sexual woman pilgrim.

There is a long tradition of satirical works which appropriate pilgrimage as a metaphor for figurative female waywardness, predating Chaucer's Wife of Bath. Ovid in *The Art of Love* satirically refers to the pagan temple as a place to pick up a lover. 'Say she worships Egyptian Isis,/ And goes where no watchful male/ May follow, clashing her sistrum? What about the Good Goddess,/ Banning men from her temple (except her own/ Chosen adherents)?'[31] *De Coniuge Non Ducenda (Against Marrying)*, which dates from 1222–50, argues satirically against marriage as a kind of hell on earth. One of the speakers warns a prospective groom, 'The wicked wife seeks leave to ride/ To pilgrims' abbeys far and wide;/ The brothels offer more delights/ Than visiting the holy sites.'[32] In John Lydgate's *The Pain and Sorrow of Evil Marriage*,[33] the narrator warns young men against marriage which he himself has happily escaped.

Wyves been bestes very vnstable/In ther desires, which may not chaunged be;/
Like a swalowe which is insaciable,/ Like perilous Caribdis of the trouble see,/ A
wave calme, full of aduersite,/ Whoes blandisshyng medled with myschaunce—
/Callid Syrenes ay full of variaunce.

They hem reioise to see and to be sayne,/ And to seke sondry pilgremages;/
At grete gaderynges to walken vpon the playne,/ And at staracles to sitte on hie
stages;/ If they be ffaire, to shewe ther visages;/ If they be ffowle of look or
countenaunce,/ They can amend it with plesaunt daliaunce.

Of ther nature they gretly hem delite,/ With holy fface fayned for the nones,/
In seyntuaries ther ffrendes to visite,/ More than for relikkes/ or any seyntis
bones,/ Though they be closed vnder precious stones;/ To gete hem pardoun,
like there olde vsages,/ To kys no shrynes, but lusty yong images.

(459–60, 92–112)

Lydgate is clearly sceptical of the women pilgrims. In this poem, well established in
the long tradition of poems warning against marriage by such authors as Juvenal
through Chaucer (*The Merchant's Tale*), women go on pilgrimages to show themselves
off and have sexual dalliances.

A Middle English lyric in the voice of a woman shows how she appropriates
pilgrimage as her excuse for her pregnancy.

> *A, dere God, what I am fayn,*
> *For I am madyn now gane!*
>
> This enther day I mete a clerke,
> And he was wily in his werke;
> He prayd me with him to herke,
>   And his counsel for to layne.
>
> I trow he coud of gramery;
> I shall now telle a good skill why:
> For what I hade siccurly,
>   To warne his will had I no mayn.
>
> Whan he and me brout un us the schete,
> Of all his will I him lete;
> Now will not my girdil met –
>   A, dere God, what shall I sayn?
>
> I shall sey to man and page
> That I have bene of pilgrimage.
> Now will I not lete for no rage
>   With a clerk for to pleyn.[34]

Pilgrimage becomes for the pregnant maiden the excuse for her state. Sexual looseness is displaced into a realm labelled pilgrimage. Pilgrimage is the explanation, if not excuse, for moral laxity.

The Fifteen Joys of Marriage,[35] a composition which dates between the late-fourteenth and mid-fifteeth centuries, illustrates the activities of a few female pilgrims who sorely lack religious and spiritual aims. Women use the excuse of pilgrimage to entertain their lovers. A parody of the fifteen joys of the Virgin Mary, this work comtemplates the miseries of married life for men. In the eighth joy,[36] the wife makes a pilgrimage to Le Puy as a sort of vacation from domestic responsibilities, succeeding in almost driving her husband mad. While in childbirth she vows herself to Our Lady of Puy in Auvergne and of Roc-Amadour. Thereafter,

> [s]pring draweth near, and virtues are stirred by the influence of the elements and the planets. 'Tis then the time to frolic in the fields. Then make [the gossips] ready to go on a pilgrimage ... [T]hey have devised this pilgrimage, because they cannot do as they will in their own homes.

The wife pretends that the baby is ill and reminds the husband of her vow when in labour. She makes him suffer until he agrees that she may go on pilgrimage. Of course, she must be accompanied by her fellow gossips and sometimes 'a certain gallant that will gladly do her pleasure and service on the way, of his honest meaning and courtesy'. If no gallant attends her, her husband is her unlucky escort. '[I]t would have been better for him, whatsoever his estate may be, that he had stayed at home, for he shall carry mill-stones about his neck daily.' She scolds him and makes demands.

> Now come they painfully to Puy in Auvergne, and achieve their pilgrimage, and God knoweth the goodman is sore trampled and crowded in the press to make a way for his wife; then she giveth him her girdle and her rosary to touch the relics of the Holy Image of Our Lady with the same; and God knoweth he is sorely hurried and elbowed and buffeted. And in their company are divers rich dames, damosels and citizens' wives, that buy rosaries of coral, of jet, of amber, enamels and other the like trinkets. And then must his wife have them as handsome as the rest; and peradventure the goodman is none too rich, but nathless he must get them for her.

After they return home she longs to be travelling again, they have more children and 'ever she will scold and become mistress of all. Then is the goodman firmly shut in the trap, with groans and dolour that he holdeth for joys; wherein he shall always dwell and end his days in misery.'

In the Eleventh Joy,[37] an older woman advises a young woman who has become pregnant by a man who will or cannot marry her on how to ensnare another gallant. The young woman flirts with the unsuspecting swain and proposes that a group of them go on a 'pilgrimage to Our Lady of such a place'. On the pilgrimage she rides behind the young man, clasping him against her body. 'Now make they this pilgrimage right devoutly, God wot! They return home to dine, for the pilgrimage is devised only to bring on the other. And ever the gallant is nigh the wench.' The young woman manages to entice him into marriage by making him besotted with her. Only a few months after the marriage the wife gives birth. They are doomed to a loveless life. 'But nathless he is in the trap, where-from he shall ne'er escape, but shall languish ever therein and end his days in misery.'

In the Twelfth Joy[38] we encounter the archetypal henpecked husband, one, moreover, who acquiesces to his torturer. She may blatantly deceive him.

> If she would be about any privy matter, she doth compel him to rise up at midnight, putteth him in mind of some task he must perform, or doth dispatch him upon a pilgrimage she hath vowed, because, forsooth! she hath a pain in her side; and, rain or hail, he shall go.

Here pilgrimage is used as a means to rid the house of the bothersome husband who hinders the wife's infidelity. This husband, like all the others in *The Fifteen Joys of Marriage*, 'languisheth out his life in grief and sadness and shall end his days in misery'. Katharina M. Wilson and Elizabeth M. Makowski read *The Fifteen Joys of Marriage*, along with the *Wife of Bath's Prologue*, another text with a pilgrimaging female, as examples of what they call 'general misogamy', works which promote wifelessness as the ideal state.[39] A work in this same tradition includes another example of this topos. In the 93rd tale of *Les Cent Nouvelles Nouvelles* (1461), the wife tells her husband she has gone on a pilgrimage so that she can keep a rendezvous with the village priest.[40]

Le Mesnagier [or Ménagier] de Paris[41] is a text ostensibly written by an older husband for his young wife of fifteen. In discussing the subject of love, the husband relates the tale of a woman who runs away from her husband for a younger lover, who then abandons her. She is forced to live as a prostitute in Avignon. The husband finds out about her adulterous behaviour and subsequent plight. He is not the only one to hear tell of this and rumours in the village fly, whereupon he gets her brothers to go to her.

> They were to clothe her in coarse cloth and cockle shells like pilgrims coming from St James, have her adequately mounted, and send her to him when she was one day away from Paris ... The wise man let it be known publicly that he was overjoyed that his wife was returning home in good health from the place where he had sent her, he said that he had long ago sent her to St James of Compostela on a pilgrimage with which his father, on his deathbed, had charged him.

The brothers do as the husband suggests, dressing her as a Compostela pilgrim and bringing her home with her virtue unblemished. 'Thus the good man restored and preserved his wife's honor.'[42] This story suggests the fluid relationship between the holy and the sexual. The mere sign of pilgrimage, in the clothing of a Compostela pilgrim, transforms the wife from whore to virtuous pilgrim in the eyes of her townspeople, even though in reality she remains a (forgiven) adulterer.

The Book of the Knight of Latour Landry was originally compiled by Geoffroy de la Tour-Landry in the second half of the fourteenth century for his three daughters, wherein the author attempts to give edifying moral lessons to his motherless children.

The book became very popular, with almost a dozen copies of the original text existing in manuscript. Translated into German as *Der Ritter vom Turn*, it was translated from the original French into English and printed by Caxton in 1484. An even earlier English translation from the reign of Henry VI also exists in the British Museum. The work includes an example of a woman who says she is going on a pilgrimage but in fact is trying to meet her lover. Since her trusting husband suspects nothing, he fully endorses her desire to go on pilgrimage

> to a place that was of oure lady. And thei thought they were wel atte ease, that they might haue her foly speche and communicacion togedre, in whiche they delited them more thanne to saie praieres or seruice to God, or to haue ani deuocion in her pilgrimage.[43]

Her lascivious motive, hidden by a sacred excuse, is confounded by the intervention of divine presences. She is unable to fulfill her lustful desires when she falls sick and has visions of her parents, a pit of fire and the Virgin. She confesses all to a priest who interprets her visions. His glosses include a reading of the image of Virgin which she saw.

> All thei that gone on pilgrimage to a place for foule plesaunce more thanne deuocion of the place that thei go to, and couerithe thaire goinge with seruice of God, fowlithe and scornithe God and oure lady, and the place that thei goo to, as dede the squier whanne he come to that place, and that ye hadde more plesaunce in hym thanne ye hadd of the plesaunce of God, or on the pilgrimage that ye yede to.

After listening to the priest, the woman is cured and reforms. The squire visits her a half-year later and remarks on her transformation, whereupon she tells him she will love only her husband. The narrative concludes:

> And therfor here is an exaumple that no body shulde go in holy pilgrimages for to fulfell no foly, plesaunce, nor the worlde, nor flesshely delite. But their shulde go enterly with herte to serue God; and also that it is good to praie for fader and moder, and for other frendes that ben dede, for thei impetrithe grace for hem that be alyue. And also it is good to yeue almesse, as ye haue herde before.

As in *Le Mesnagier [or Ménagier] de Paris*, there is a fluid relationship between the holy and sexual. Pilgrimage is a permeable arena for both modes of discourse.

Recognizing the conflation of pilgrimage with the sexual, Christine de Pizan in her book, *A Medieval Woman's Mirror of Honor: The Treasure of the City of Ladies*,[44] gives advice to different classes of women on how to conduct their lives. The personified allegories of Reason, Rectitude and Justice command the narrator, Christine, to write their advice. In extolling the quality of patience in noble women, they say, 'The princess trying to amass virtue upon virtue should remember that Saint Paul says: "Whoever has all the other virtues, prays unceasingly, goes on pilgrimages, fasts at length, and does all good, but has no charity, profits in nothing.'"[45] While the three ladies make this qualification about going on pilgrimage with false spiritual emotions, at the same time they state that '[n]o lady is so important that it is shameful or unsuitable for her to go devoutly and humbly to pardons or to visit churches or holy places'.[46] In other words, a high-born lady need not disdain the activity of pilgrimage when it is done genuinely. But city women with property should be particularly careful of entering illicit spaces.

> Some women travel on pilgrimages away from town in order to frolic and kick up their heels in jolly company. But this is only sin and folly. It is a sin to use God as excuse and shelter for frivolity. Such pilgrimages are entirely without merit. Nor should a young woman go trotting about town, as is the custom – on Monday to St Avoye; on Tuesday, to who knows where; on Friday to St Catherine, and elsewhere on the other days ... [T]he surest thing for the soul's profit and the body's honor is to avoid the habit of trotting here and there.[47]

The artisan's wife should also control herself. 'Neither is it good for her to go to so many gatherings across town, nor to go travelling off needlessly on pilgrimages, which invariably would cause unnecessary expense.'[48] The fact that Christine cites pilgrimage and recommends that women avoid pilgrimage to prevent false rumours about character from starting, indicates that female pilgrims had a dodgy reputation or else Christine would not have warned her female readers away from such activities.

The numerous examples above illustrate the generally dubious position of women pilgrims in secular literature. In Chapter 2 we saw how there were attempts to control pilgrims' movements. How does this play out in literature? To illustrate how one might undertake a spatial analysis of literary texts taking gender into consideration, I'll look at the *General Prologue* of *The Canterbury Tales*. The opening eighteen lines evoke in the reader an expectation of a national poem for all of England and all Englishmen and women. Words like 'every' (ll. 3, 6, 15) and the plurality of actors – 'smale foweles' (l. 9), 'folk' (l. 12), 'palmeres' (l. 13), 'they' (ll. 16, 18) – create a sense of communality, unity and totality. Pilgrims come from 'every shires ende/Of Engelond' (ll. 15–16). All of England is penetrated with a sense of desire to go on pilgrimage, to far off shrines and most especially to a peculiarly English martyr who remains nameless, but needs no introduction.

With lines nineteen and following, the *General Prologue* fragments into individuality. A first-person narrator tells of separate pilgrims in the well-known portraits. Place names in the Knight's portrait are woven to create the edges of Western Christendom (ll. 51–66). With the Squire, we head westward to easily accessible places on the Continent ('In Flaundres, in Artoys, and Pycardie,' l. 86). The Prioress returns us to England, close to London: 'And Frenssh she spak ful faire and fetisly,/ After the scole of Stratford atte Bowe,/ For Frenssh of Parys was to hire unknowe' (ll. 124–6). Thereafter, most of the portraits mention a specific physical place in England.[49] When we are presented with individual portraits, the picture of England is likewise individualized and fragmented into specific place names.

Two portraits are significantly non-specified. We meet the ideal 'Persoun of a toun' (l. 478), a town which remains unnamed, and his brother, the equally ideal ploughman. The cosmic picture of England we encountered in the opening of the *General Prologue* is echoed here. Just as people from all over England come to Canterbury, the good parson visits everywhere, to the farthest reaches of his parish, and everyone, high or low. The Parson, an ideal cleric, comes from a town, every town. The ambiguity of the Parson's town suggests its placelessness and ideal nature, whereas the narrow geographical specificity of the named cities and locales in the other portraits indicates the fallen nature of those pilgrims.[50] Chaucer's poem is set in a fallen, historical time, penetrated with flashes of ideal behaviour, as in the opening eighteen lines of the *General Prologue*, and with the Parson and Ploughman.

One pilgrim is indelibly linked by readers with a place: the Wife of Bath. In fact, the name given to us in the *Prologue* is not the Wife of Bath, but the 'Wif...of biside Bathe' (l. 445). She comes from just outside Bath, beyond its borders, setting up in the reader a sense of dislocation in connection with the only secular woman on pilgrimage in Chaucer's work. This sense of dislocation is maintained with the assertion 'She koude muchel of wandrynge by the weye' (l. 467). Wandering evokes a sense of goallessness or being lost, of not being pinpointed geographically. The pilgrimage shrines she has visited are specifiable; she had been three times 'at Jerusalem', and had also been 'At Rome ... at Boloigne,/ In Galice at Seint-Jame, and at Coloigne' (ll. 463–6), all the conventional big-name pilgrimage goals. The prepositions 'at' and 'in' make her destinations specific and fixed, while she herself and her activities are less definite in space, being 'of biside Bathe' and 'wandrynge' between her home and those pilgrimage sites.

Why does Chaucer include the Wife of Bath in the frame tale of *The Canterbury Tales*, a woman pilgrim of the merchant class who is apparently not hunting for wealth? From our documentary evidence, we could see that women from various

Figure 10 The Wife of Bath, as depicted in the Ellesmere Manuscript

classes travelled (abroad), some travelling modestly, alone and without a horse, and some travelling with an entire retinue and in luxury, attended with courtiers and horses for company and protection. Chaucer includes Alison since she fits into the class made fun of in the genre of misogynist literature which satirizes women pilgrims. The women of that genre are, while not necessarily wealthy, well-fixed enough to contemplate leaving home and surviving financially during that time. This misogynist literature almost invariably mentions other bad habits of the wives, such as over-spending on luxury items and demanding material goods beyond the desire – and sometimes means – of the hen-pecked husband. Alison emerges from this genre.[51] As for the wealthy woman pilgrim, the prioress fulfills that class role with her being attended by numerous religious. Her hypocrisy is apparent not only materially – the brooch, for example – but spiritually in her anti-semitism.

But why not a poor woman pilgrim? Chaucer in his corpus typically displays a compassion for those poverty-stricken. Those of a certain wealth are depicted as having the luxury of hypocrisy, as it were. Only the Parson and the Ploughman in the *General Prologue* are allotted the privilege of honesty which the poor are perceived as fulfilling. In the *Friar's Tale*, the poor widow is preyed upon by the summoner and she eventually triumphs due to her righteous anger. Constance in the *Man of Law's Tale* is also to be pitied for her lack of possessions. All she possesses is a boat and faith in God. Griselda and Janicula in the *Clerk's Tale* are the humblest of the poor until her marriage to Walter, a state she returns to at one point in the tale. The mother in the *Prioress's Tale* is also unwealthy and pitiable. The poor but genuine woman pilgrim, whom we shall examine at the end of this chapter, enters Chaucer's text only obliquely. She exists, in transformed guise, in his tales. She cannot appear in the frame tale since she generically belongs to saints' legends and hagiography, not the estates satire of the *General Prologue*. And she enters not as a pilgrim figure, but as a figure from hagiography or haloed in religious imagery.

Women pilgrim figures in religious literature

Despite the strong tradition in which women pilgrims are seen as literally and figuratively wayward, exemplified most famously in the Wife of Bath, a competing view of women pilgrims lies in religious works. Saints' legends, such as those in *The South-English Legendary* or Osbern Bokenham's *A Legend of Holy Women*, endorse women pilgrims to validate the sanctity of the holy figure in question, such as Mary Magdalene and Lucy. Various versions of the miracle in the legend of Mary Magdelene feature a woman on pilgrimage (see *The South-English Legendary*, *A Legend of Holy Women* and the *Golden Legend*).[52] After Christ's death, Mary, and her siblings Lazarus and Martha, go to Marseilles where they preach. While there, a man and his wife who have had no children are converted by Mary and then conceive. The husband plans to go on a pilgrimage to Rome and the pregnant wife insists on accompanying him. During the trip, a tempest blows up and the wife gives birth and dies. The husband, distraught, leaves the wife on a nearby island with the baby whom he assumes will die since the wife cannot give suck, being dead. He goes to Rome and then the

Holy Land for two years. Upon his return he sees the child playing on the island and his wife alive. She tells him,

> [N]ow I have returned and have finished the voyage you have, and the same pilgrimage. For just as Saint Peter led you to Jerusalem and showed you every place where Christ preached to our frailty, where he died and rose and passed hence, so blessed Magdalen led me with you and showed me everything, and I've learned it well.[53]

Hereafter they destroy pagan temples and Magdalen continues her conversion of France. A Book of Hours depicts this miracle as well as there being wallpaintings of it in the crypt of Rochester Cathedral.

The *Liber Celestis* of St Bridget of Sweden (1303–1373; canonized 1391) falls into the literary category featuring religious women pilgrims, even though it tells the story of an almost contemporary historical figure. In Archbishop Gregersson's *Officium Sanctae Birgittae*, we are told how she convinces her husband to go on pilgrimage to Saint James in Compostela. Her husband then becomes ill in France, whereupon St Dines comes to her and shows her great marvels: 'howe þat sho suld wende to Rome and to Jerusalem, and how þat sho suld passe out of þis werld'.[54] Thereafter Christ appears to her and tells her to go to Rome and Jerusalem. Her revelations include seeing the nativity and the birth of Christ. St Bridget went on pilgrimage to Assisi, Trondheim, Compostela, Bari, Monte Gargano, Jerusalem, and Rome. She founded an order for women dedicated to the Virgin and a Bridgettine house was founded in Syon in Middlesex in 1415 by Henry V. Her revelations were dictated by her in Old Swedish, transcribed in Latin by her spiritual mentors and then checked by her. These visions were translated later into several Middle English versions.[55]

We know that this text belongs to the sacred category, not only because it is a hagiography, but also in the details of how it uses pilgrimage. Christ

> likened hymselfe to a pilgrame þat had ben ferr and comyn agayn to hys awn cuntre wyth ioy ... I ame þis lord, þat went in pilgramage when I toke mankynd and come into þe world, all if I were in heuen euer in my godehede, and in erth.[56]

Certainly anything Christ does is sanctioned and Bridget's replication of Christ's pilgrim status elevates her. God the Father speaks to Bridget and tells her of the five virtuous places in Jerusalem where pilgrims should visit to 'be made clene vnto my wirshipe'[57]: those places are where Mary was born, where Christ was born, Calvary, the sepulchre and the Mount of Olives. Mary appears to Bridget telling her how a soul which is guilty of sloth may avoid purgatory:

> in going to þe kirke: in seking of perdone; and in seking of holi places ... seke pilgramage for his saule, and also send þe offering to places of hali saintes for his saule; rewarde him for his trauaile þat gose for him.[58]

Christ appears and tells her how one of his treasures on earth are the bodies of the saints who loved him. 'And I sall rewarde þame þat visites þaire places þat þai are wirshiped in eftir þaire wille and þaire trauaile.'[59] He also bids her go to Jerusalem:

> Criste apperid to Saint Bride in Rome, and bad hir ordeine hir to Jerusalem to visit þe sepulcre and oþir holi places, and þat sho suld wende when he warned hir … Criste bad þe spouse þat sho suld wende to Jerusalem, and þat sho suld noȝt lete for eld, for he was maker of kinde, and he mai gif hele als him liste, and he suld strengþe hir and hirs and puruai for þame and bringe againe to Rome.[60]

Pilgrimage is a means for Bridget to show her obedience to Christ, particularly since her advanced age is emphasized. We also see how she is specially blessed by him through the revelations she experiences at blessed sites on her pilgrimage, such as seeing the Virgin give birth and suckle the Christ child. Her pilgrim status makes her both a chosen Christian for God and a replica of him as pilgrim.

In another hagiographical work, the legend of St Lucy, we are told of a pilgrimage she and her mother, Eutice, make to Catania, where St Agatha was freshly martyred, in hopes of curing Eutice of dysentery which she had been inflicted with for four years. Agatha comes to Lucy in a dream, whereafter the mother is cured and both of them give away Lucy's patrimony as alms. Lucy's betrothed is bothered by her depleting her fortune and complains to the consul. She is questioned and Paschasius, the consul, upon hearing her harsh condemnatory words against him for defying God's law, accuses her of speaking like a strumpet. She is even taken to a brothel to be defiled but her body miraculously becomes heavy and she cannot be taken there. After great tortures, during which she can still speak, she dies, martyred after receiving the sacrament.[61] The accusation of speaking like a strumpet falsely allies God's word spoken by a woman with loose and lascivious sexualized speech. The sacred and erotic are mistakenly allied with each other. Like the woman pilgrim figure, who is textualized as either sacred – in religious works – or erotic – in secular works, the truthtelling saint is likewise seen as the site of both discourses, but in a positive way.

John Lydgate's translation of 'Ave Maria!' offers a positive view of pilgrimage and a woman pilgrim figure as it is a religious poem.

> Hayle! glorious lady and heuenly quene,/ Crownyd & regnyng in þy blys full cage,/ Helpe vs pylgryms in erthely tene,/ In worshyp of all þy pylgremage;/ Thy holy concepcion was they furst pylgremage/ *Cuius honore tu nobis faue,*/ And here we knelyng before thyne Image/ *Tibi concepte dicimus Aue.*
>
> Hayle! glemeryng sterre now in þy byrthe,/ To all þis world thow spredyst þy lyght,/ Thy ioy full name yeueth vs myrthe./ Now blessyd be he þat Mary þe hyght,/ For thorow all þe worlde þow yevest þy lyght,/ *O maris stella domina pia,*/ With all oure hert and all oure might/ *Tibi clamamus* Aue Maria…
>
> (280, 1–16)[62]

Lydgate commences with the conventional allusion to us on earth as pilgrims seeking salvation. Elsewhere he refers to the Vigin as the 'loodsterre'.[63] The concept of life being a pilgrimage in our search for God is an old conceit. Lydgate stretches the meaning of pilgrimage here. We on our earthly pilgrimage worship the Blessed Virgin for all of her pilgrimages, the immaculate conception being the first of her pilgrimages. The concept of conception constituting a pilgrimage in itself lends validity to the pregnancy not only of Mary, but of ordinary women themselves, such as the pregnant speaker in the lyric 'This enther day …' It is as though an *imitatia Mariae*, through pregnancy, could constitute a type of pilgrimage comparable to the *imitatio Christi* of pilgrims to the Holy Land. In scenes depicting the Annunciation, Mary is typically depicted in an interior space or some kind of architectural shelter or structure. Margaret Hallissy points out that

> Mary, as ever a symbol of womanly perfection, is depicted as enclosed. According to one homilist, Mary, 'whenne the angel come to hure and fonde hure [was] inne a pryvy chambre and nou3t stondynge ne walkynge by stretys.' No gadabout Mary. She stays at home, in her chamber.[64]

Yet Lydgate envisions Mary's conception as pilgrimage. How can we understand these conflicting representations of women pilgrims in secular and religious works?

Binary opposites

We have seen how medieval women pilgrims, by moving publicly through space, came to symbolize a threatening politicized figure. While it was more 'normal' for men in the Middle Ages to be public and visible, women more typically should have been private and concealed. Limits and prohibitions define movement. A pilgrimage route is established through these boundaries and limits. In the spatial model set up by Gilles Deleuze and Félix Guattari, they contrast 'state space' with 'nomad space'. Briefly put, 'state space' is represented by limited movement along preset paths. It is hierarchical, homogenous, centred, uniform, always controlled, and closed. 'Nomad space', on the other hand, is open-ended, enterable at any point, acentered, anti-hierarchical, multiple, open, without borders and in marginalized areas. In a sense, ideal pilgrimage is constituted in state space, with the Church reading and controlling the concept and activities of pilgrimage. But nomad space informs the sexual woman pilgrim of secular literature, who belongs to space with no limits or borders, the space of in-between.

> A path is always between two points, but the in-between has taken on all the consistency and enjoys both an autonomy and a direction of its own … [T]he nomadic trajectory … does not fulfill the function of the sedentary road, which is to *parcel out a closed space to people* … The nomadic trajectory does the opposite: it *distributes people (or animals) in an open space* … a space without borders or enclosures … [I]t stands in opposition to the law or the *polis*, as the backcountry, a mountainside, or the vague expanse around a city.[65]

To use a different paradigm, we could see state space as the sacred and nomad space as the profane. As Sarah Beckwith points out, the sacred can only be understood in terms of its opposite, the profane. 'Profanation threatens the sacred as it empowers it.' In her discussion of Christ's body, Beckwith shows how

> bodily margins are where the bounded system is both created and destroyed, made powerful and vulnerable. But in displaying the very outlines of that body (through dislocation, rupture, entry, exit or traverse), and by so revealing the demarcations of the bounded system, that outline is made available for redrawing.[66]

Similarly with state and nomad space, the nomad space defines and justifies state space, but threatens whenever nomad space strays into state space.

While pious women pilgrims are figured as literally sticking to the straight and narrow, as part of the state space embodied in the Church, the Wife of Bath, for example, is figured on the outskirts of Bath, 'wandering by the weye'.[67] These examples of women pilgrims in English literature suggest the tendency in secular literature to question women's chastity while on pilgrimage and for religious genres to endorse pilgrimage for women. While male pilgrims could be depicted as incontinent in literary works, biology dictates that only women pilgrims could be publicly signed and visualized as sexually loose through their pregnant bodies.

The contradictory views of women pilgrims reflect shifting understandings of space. The overdetermined figure of the woman pilgrim suggests the irreconcilability of the two views and a fundamental division in medieval discourse and society. Movement lying in the authoritative structure of church doctrine through sanctioned pilgrimage simultaneously allows the opportunity for individuals to act out illicit desires. Yet the very act of representing women pilgrims as sexual remains under the authoritative control of the satirical poet, neutralizing their disorder.

Representational spaces, from Mary's womb to the womblike shrine at Walsingham which replicated the house of the Annunciation, interpret cosmological represent-ations. The spatial practice of pilgrimage renders these spaces as redemptive and represents a lingering ideological moment which is eroding starting in the fourteenth century. In late-medieval England, with the theatrical reenactment of Old and New Testament moments in religious plays and the mimetic nature of religious symbols, images are freed from their cryptic spaces into a public and accessible realm. But this commodification of sacred space in the fifteenth century, which attempts to unify the sacred and profane, remains a mediation doomed to unravel with the Reformation.

The sexual woman pilgrim constitutes history's -- or fiction's -- nostalgic attempt to remember and control a past hierarchical system. To use Henri Lefebvre's term-inology, the religious woman pilgrim belongs to the absolute space and the secular woman pilgrim to historical space, which is marked by social differences including gender.[68] Sexual women pilgrim figures belong to the realm of history, a reconstructed element. Pious women pilgrims in saints' legends are themselves *lieux de mémoire*[69] of the (imagined) memory of pure, undefiled pilgrimage. Binary oppositions structure the symbolic domain of geographic space. The pious woman pilgrim depicted as literally remaining on a controlled and limited path contrasts with the immoral one who transgresses borders. Each figure is structured by its opposite. Pilgrimage as a spatial system functions as a site of actual and symbolic struggle[70] between binary opposites. These opposites symbolize both conflicting modes of discourse (religious and secular, pious and immoral) and conflicting modes of space, which, in turn, reflect the social order. The immoral woman pilgrim symbolizes not only lustful female desires, not only Eve and her legacy, but also non-gendered social disorder, unruly class struggle and, in her sexual commodification, nascent capitalism or Lefebvre's 'space of accumulation' or historical space.[71] The socially peripheral sexual woman pilgrim is symbolically central to the imagination of post-plague England.[72]

Notes

1 David Harvey, *The Condition of Postmodernity*, Cambridge, MA, Blackwell, 1989, p. 206.

2 Rodney Hilton, *Class Conflict and the Crisis of Feudalism: Essays in Medieval Social History*, London, The Hambledon Press, 1985, p. 248.

3 Natalie Zemon Davies, *Society and Culture in Early Modern France*, Stanford, Stanford University Press, 1975, p. 127.

4 Lynn Staley, *Margery Kempe's Dissenting Fictions*, University Park, PA, The Pennsylvania State University Press, 1994, p. 177. 'The challenge to existing hierarchies [Kempe] dramatizes in Margery's life is based on cultural assumptions about gender categories, but gender is, finally, the means of expressing what are radical ideas about spiritual dominion,' ibid., p. 126.

5 Davis, op. cit., pp. 130–1.

6 Ibid., p. 145.

7 All quotes from Suger come from Erwin Panofsky, ed., trans., *Abbot Suger on the Abbey Church of St-Denis and its Art Treasures*, 2nd Edn, Gerda Panofsky-Soergel, ed., Princeton, Princeton University Press, 1979, p. 43.

8 Ibid., p. 69.

9 Ibid., pp. 87–9.

10 Ibid., p. 135.

11 Gaston Bachelard, *The Poetics of Space*, Maria Jolas, trans., foreward by Etienne Gilson, Boston, Beacon Press, 1964, p. xxxi.

12 Henri Lefebvre, *The Production of Space*, Donald Nicholson-Smith, trans., Oxford, Blackwell, 1991, p. 256.

13 Late medieval spatial organization reflected 'a confused overlapping of economic, political, and legal obligations and rights'. From David Harvey, op. cit., p. 241.

14 Quoted by Barbara Obrist, 'The Swedish Visionary Saint Bridget,' Katharina M. Wilson, ed., in *Medieval Women Writers*, Athens, GA, The University of Georgia Press, 1984, p. 236.

15 *Chaucer's Sexual Poetics*, Madison, The University of Wisconsin Press, 1989, p. 20.

16 All quotes from *The Riverside Chaucer*, Larry D. Benson, ed., New York, Houghton Mifflin, 1987.

17 The word *tapin/age* appears in early French/Provençal poetry. The linkage of sexuality, disguise, and pilgrimage appears in the bizarre 'cat scratch song' of Duke William IX of Aquitaine, Count VII of Poitiers, 'Farai un vers, pos mi sonelh.' Here the narrator has to have sex with two ladies. They twice call him 'sir pilgrim' (l.20). In calling him pilgrim they use the Provençal word *Tapin*. Gerald A. Bond, ed., *The Poetry of William VI, Count of Poitiers, IX Duke of Aquitaine*, New York, Garland, 1982, No. 5.

18 The disguise of a pilgrim was frequently used in wartime in both historical and literary examples. See Francis P. Magoun, '*Hymselven lik a pilgrym to desgise: Troilus* V, 1577,' *Modern Language Notes* 59, 1944, pp. 176–8 and B. J. Whiting, 'Troilus and Pilgrims in Wartime,' *Modern Language Notes* 60, 1945, pp. 47–9.

19 All citations from *Political, Religious, and Love Poems*, Frederick J. Furnivall, ed., London, Oxford University Press, 1965. Only two leaves and two narrow strips of two other leaves of the romance exist, and the editor completed the story from the 1845 Paris edition.

20 Ibid., p. 297.

21 Ibid., p. 297, n. 1.

22 Ibid., pp. 297–8.

23 Ibid., p. 300.

24 Thomas Percy, original editor; Henry B. Wheatley, ed., *Reliques of Ancient English Poetry*, New York, Dover Publishing, 1966, Vol. II, pp. 101–2.

25 Ibid., pp. 89–91.

26 'This poem is printed from a copy in the Editor's folio MS. which had greatly suffered by the hand of time; but vestiges of several of the lines remaining, some conjectural supplements have been attempted, which, for greater exactness, are in this one ballad distinguished by italics,' ibid., p. 87.

27 William Langland, *The Vision of Piers Plowman (B-Text)*, A. V. C. Schmidt, ed., London, J. M. Dent, 1995. All references are to the B-text unless otherwise noted.

28 Lefebvre, op. cit., p. 248.

29 Shannon McSheffrey, *Gender & Heresy: Women and Men in Lollard Communities 1420–1530*, Philadelphia, University of Pennsylvania Press, 1995, pp. 48, 65.

30 Margaret Miles, 'Pilgrimage as Metaphor in a Nuclear Age,' *Theology Today* 45, 1988, pp. 166–79.

31 Quoted in Alcuin Blamires, ed., *Woman Defamed and Woman Defended, An Anthology of Medieval Texts*, Oxford, Clarendon Press, 1992, p. 21.

32 Ibid., p. 126. See also Jehan Le Fèvre's *The Lamentations of Matheolus*, c. 1371–2, lines 947ff. and 2145–54.

33 Poem quoted from *The Minor Poems of John Lydgate*, Volume II, Secular Poems, Henry N. MacCracken, ed., London, Oxford University Press/Early English Text Society, 1934, pp. 459–60.

34 No. 83 in Maxwell S. Luria and Richard L. Hoffman, eds, *Middle English Lyrics*, New York, W. W. Norton & Company, 1974, p. 82.

35 Richard Aldington, trans., London, George Routledge and Sons Ltd, 1925; see also *Les Quinze Joyes de Mariage*, Joan Crow, ed., Oxford, 1969. Wynkyn de Worde translated it in 1509.

36 See Aldington, op. cit., pp. 157–63.

37 Ibid., pp. 185–95.

38 Ibid., pp. 199–204.

39 See Katharina M. Wilson and Elizabeth M. Makowski, *Wykked Wyves and the Woes of Marriage: Misogamous Literature from Juvenal to Chaucer*, Albany, SUNY Press, 1990, Chapter 4, esp. pp. 142–9. See also Joan Crow, 'A Little-Known Manuscript of the *Quinze Joyes de Mariage*,' *Studies in Medieval French*, E. A. Frances, ed., Oxford, Clarendon Press, 1961, pp. 121–49.

40 Pierre Champion, ed., Paris, 1928, 2 vols.

41 Tania Bayard, ed. and trans., *A Medieval Home Companion: Housekeeping in the Fourteenth Century*, New York, HarperPerennial, 1991. Bayard translates only a quarter of the original text. Eileen Power also translated this work publishing it in 1928 under the title of *The Goodman of Paris*, London, Routledge. See also Baron Jérôme Pichon, *Le Ménagier de Paris, Traité de morale et d'économie domestique composé vers 1393 par un bourgeois Parisien*, 2 vols. 1846, reprint. Geneva, Slatkin, 1966; and Georgine E. Brereton and Janet M. Ferrier, *Le Ménagier de Paris*, Oxford, Oxford University Press, 1981.

42 Bayard, op. cit., pp. 57–8.
43 All quotes from Thomas Wright, ed., *The Book of the Knight of La Tour-Landry*, New York, Greenwood Press, 1906/Early English Text Society, 1969, pp. 47–51.
44 Charity Cannon Willard, trans., Madeleine Pelner Cosman, ed., New York, Persea Books, 1989.
45 Ibid., p. 84. In addressing ladies of the court and admonishing them about their envy, the three ladies say, '[I]f another has more of Fortune's gifts in this world – which is only a brief journey, like a pilgrimage – why should you complain or grieve about it?' p. 160. Here Christine makes reference to the common image of life or the life of the soul resembling in metaphor a pilgrimage, which was fully executed by Guillaume de Deguileville in his allegory from the first half of the fourteenth century, *Le pèlerinage de la vie humaine*. She continues with this metaphor shortly thereafter while pointing out that everyone has faults. 'Sins hidden from the world are known to God, who alone knows who is a good pilgrim', p. 167. Near the conclusion of the book, the reader is told that '[t]he good pilgrim's true steadfastness is not really known until the end of the pilgrimage', p. 217.
46 Ibid., p. 88.
47 Ibid., p. 193.
48 Ibid., p. 210.
49 The Merchant is concerned with safety in the sea between the Dutch port of 'Middelburgh' and the Suffolk port of 'Orewell' (l. 277). The Clerk is famously of 'Oxenford' (l. 285), and the Sargeant of Law had often been at the 'Parvys' (l. 310), or the porch of St Paul's Cathedral. The Guildsmen most probably come from London and their Cook definitely knows London ale. The Shipman is of 'Dertemouthe' (l. 389). The Reeve is of 'Northfolk' (l. 619), from 'Biside a toun men clepen Baldeswell' (l. 620). The Pardoner is 'Of Rouncivale' (l. 670), a hospital at Charing Cross. The Host's inn is in Southwerk, just over the river from London.
50 We are told that 'A bettre preest I trowe that nowher noon ys' (l. 524). That a better priest exists nowhere suggests the lack of geographical specificity necessary for an ideal.
51 See Jill Mann's *Chaucer and Medieval Estates Satire: The Literature of Social Classes and the General Prologue to the Canterbury Tales*, Cambridge, Cambridge University Press, 1973.
52 *A Legend of Holy Women: Osbern Bokenham Legends of Holy Women*, Sheila Delany, trans., Notre Dame, University of Notre Dame Press, 1992, p. 121. See also Mary Serjeantson, ed., *Legendys of Hooly Wummen by Osbern Bokenham*, London, Oxford University Press/Early English Text Society, 1938, p. 167; *The South English Legendary*, Charlotte D'Evelyn and Anna J. Mill, eds., Vol. I, London, EETS, 1956, p. 311; Jacobus de Voragine, *The Golden Legend: Readings on the Saints*, William Granger Ryan, trans., Vol. I, Princeton, NJ, Princeton UP, 1993, p. 379. The story also appears in Theodor Erbe, ed., *Mirk's Festial: A Collection of Homilies*, London, Kegan Paul, Trench, Trübner & Co. Ltd., 1905, p. 207.
53 Delany, op. cit., p. 121.
54 *The Liber Celestis of St Bridget of Sweden*, Roger Ellis, ed., Vol. 1, Oxford, Early English Text Society/Oxford University Press, 1987, p. 2.
55 Alexandra Barratt, *Women's Writing in Middle English*, London, Longman, 1992, pp. 84–94. See also Julia B. Holloway, trans., *Saint Bride and Her Book*, Newburyport, MA, Focus Texts, 1992.
56 Ellis, pp. 301–2.
57 Ibid., p. 396.
58 Ibid., p. 404.
59 Ibid., p. 471.
60 Ibid., p. 475.
61 See Delany, op. cit., pp. 167–74.

62 Henry Noble McCracken, ed., *The Minor Poems of John Lydgate*, Vol. I, Oxford, Oxford University Press, 1911/1962, p. 280, ll. 1–16.

63 See both 'To Mary, the Queen of Heaven,' MS Bodley Tanner 110, leaf 244, B version, and 'Stella celi Extirpauit (1)', MS Harley 2255, leaves 103 and back, in MacCracken, op. cit. Vol. I, p. 284, No. 54, l. 2 and p. 294, No. 59, l. 1.

64 Margaret Hallissy, *Clean Maids, True Wives, Steadfast Widows: Chaucer's Women and Medieval Codes of Conduct*, Westport, CT, Greenwood Press, 1993, p. 96.

65 Gilles Deleuze and Félix Guattari, *A Thousand Plateaus: Capitalism and Schizophrenia*, Brian Massumi, trans., Minneapolis, University of Minnesota Press, 1987, p. 380.

66 Beckwith, op. cit., p. 56.

67 Ambiguously meaning wandering during her journey and wandering beside her path.

68 Neil Smith, 'Antinomies of Space and Nature', in Andrew Light and Jonathan M. Smith, eds., *Philosophy and Geography II: The Production of Public Space*, Lanham, MD, Rowman & Littlefield Publishers, 1998, pp. 49–69, here p. 57.

69 See Chapter 5 on Pierre Nora and the role of memory and history.

70 As in revisionist views of Bakhtinian carnival in *The Politics and Poetics of Transgression*, Peter Stallybrass and Allon White, Ithaca, Cornell University Press, 1986, p. 14.

71 See Lefebvre, op. cit., p. 263, and Edward Dimendberg, 'Henri Lefebvre on Abstract Space,' in Light and Smith, op. cit., pp. 17–47, here p. 23.

72 Stallybrass and White, op. cit., p. 5.

5 Performing Margery Kempe

Kempe's use of literary topoi

One work unites the opposing visions of women pilgrims as seen in secular and religious literature. *The Book of Margery Kempe* is a touchstone for the problematic of medieval perceptions of space and the role women pilgrims play in it. The genre of the *Book* melds hagiography – the influence of Bridget's revelations is evident throughout the work – autobiography, and visions. However, it contains so many topoi of imaginative secular and religious works which include women pilgrims, that it is impossible to imagine the author being unaware of the conventions in dealing with such figures. The author constructs a reader who is very aware of such topoi so that the *Book* can consciously acknowledge these topoi, only to deny some and accept others. The *Book* distills three major aspects of women pilgrim figures, both historical and literary, as we have encountered them so far. Women pilgrim figures are erotic, sacred, and threatening. Her use of these topoi means that Kempe, the author, is deliberately crafting her work.

The *Book* opens *in medias res*. While there is little introduction to the creature, she does manage to transmit her age, social status and marital status. The action is the result of erotic play: childbirth and Kempe's subsequent madness. Immediately, sex is the arena for troubled faith and spirit. Soon after Kempe also admits her temptation by a man in her church who, when she finally agrees to transgress with him, rejects her cruelly. Kempe tells us that she and her husband enjoy their sexual life very much. But she finally manages to abandon lust in the famous scene where she makes a deal with her husband that she will eat with him and pay his debts if he will stop sleeping with her. Money becomes the means by which she affects this deal. Just as a vowed pilgrimage could be avoided by paying a fine, so, too, her sexual debt is paid by coin.

As in many secular works featuring women pilgrims, Kempe is proud of herself and decks herself out in a gaudy way. Like many literary women pilgrims, Kempe is accused of not having actually gone on pilgrimage. In Beverley she is arrested and her accusers 'seydyn sche had [nowt] ben at Ierusalem ne in þe Holy Lond ne on oþer pilgrimage, liche as sche had ben in trewth' (132).[1] Even when she goes on pilgrimage with her husband, she is the focus of suspicion. '[M]any euyl folke…demtyn & seydyn þat þei went raþar to woodys, grouys, er valeys to vsyn þe lust of her bodijs þat þe pepil xuld not aspyin it ne wetyn it' (180). In order to test her devoutness, two priests take her on a pilgrimage.

[A]s þei cam homward a-geyn, þei mett women wyth childeryn in her armys, & þe forseyd creatur askyd ȝyf þer wer any man-childe a-mongys hem, & þe women seyd, 'Nay.' Þan was þe mende so raueschyd in-to þe childhod of Crist for desir þat sche had for to see hym þat sche mith not beryn it but fel downe & wept & cryid so sor þat it was meruayl to her it. (200)

The priests believe in her religiosity after this test. Kempe's doubters, who litter the text, function as sceptical readers, much like the narrators of satirical works poking fun at women pilgrims. They find it impossible to believe in her faith and the way she expresses it. She must be faking it or mad.

This scepticism confronting Kempe is present in another genre the *Book* is often identified with: hagiography. In hagiographical texts, the virgin martyrs speak boldly and publicly about their faith. They will be spared if they worship idols or apologize to pagan authorities. But they refuse. Often they are accused of speaking boldly, an accusation which frequently is tinged with the sexual. St Lucy is accused of speaking like a 'strumpet',[2] when in fact she is uttering the truth as the genre defines it. She is endorsed and sanctified for this public, bold and brazen speech. Similarly, female pilgrims of religious literature publicly proclaim their faith by the sign of going on pilgrimage. Public movement is like public speech – both function as declarations of faith. Public movement functions as a speech act of motion or space. In religious texts, devout women pilgrims are sanctioned for their pilgrimage activity. The public speech act of Lucy is eroticized since the accusation comes from a faulty interpreter. Being accused of speaking like a strumpet merely insures Lucy's martyrdom, just as publicly walking on pilgrimage assures women pilgrims in religious texts their cure and the proof of a saint's efficacy. In secular texts, however, public declamation, speaking boldly, is questionable, as when the Friar in *The Canterbury Tales* accuses the Wife of Bath of preaching.

In secular works, the speech act of going on pilgrimage by women is a public declaration and is questionable because of its very public nature. In Kempe's work we see the topos of the sexualized woman pilgrim, whose body, moving through public space, becomes the property of viewers, a body open to interpretation. Even the bodies of virgins and post-menopausal women are public bodies. Margery Kempe causes great anxiety and antagonism while wearing white clothes which signify a virgin, something she no longer was. But that such apparel was understood reveals the public display of costume. Clothing functions as a metonymy for the sexual state of one's body, one made public knowledge. When she goes to Germany when she is about sixty, and presumably past childbearing age, she believes that she is seen sexually. Priests accuse her of being an Englishwoman with a tail, an old term of abuse for the English, and they speak lewd words and give her dirty looks. She fears that she will be raped (236–7). While her companions remove their clothes to pick off lice, she refuses out of fear. Presumably this fear is one of violation. The public speech act of pilgrimage is eroticized in a negative way; hence the topos of the woman pilgrim in secular satirical works as a lascivious creature, hiding her true motives for going on pilgrimage. Kempe picks up on this, utilizing the topos to reveal how inaccurate it, in fact, is in the case of a sincere woman pilgrim like herself.

The Book of Margery Kempe utilizes these literary topoi deliberately. Public movement like public speech – or crying in Kempe's case – constitute speech acts of faith in Kempe's view. Pilgrimage is like weeping since both are public expressions of her belief in God. But, like the authors and readers of satirical works, these public expressions are criticized, a criticism which takes the form of eroticized expression. She is accused of being lustful and of feigning her tears. As Staley has pointed out, the *Book* uses the sceptical male scribe figure as a stand-in for the sceptical reader; since the scribe converts to believing in Kempe, so should we. In a sense, the *Book* starts off in the genre of satirical woman pilgrim's literature and converts to that of religious sacred works.

We can see Kempe's devout relationship to space when the *Book* utilizes religious literary topoi, as opposed to the secular literary topoi. Ellen Ross has offered a feminist interpretation of the spatial dimension of women's experience of the Divine in the Christian tradition, offering six types of these experiences, several of which can be seen in Kempe's life. In one type, historical place is recognized and experienced as a sacred presence. A geographical location gains recognition due to its association with particular historical events in the Christian tradition. Like early Christian women such as Paula, Melania, and Egeria, Kempe visits actual places from the Bible so she can nourish her own faith. Places are not merely historical but sacred spots where the pilgrim can experience Scripture. She locates herself in the historical, concrete, and physical world where the narratives took place. In Kempe's experiences in the Holy Land, we can see how this type of spatial experience helps her to come into touch with the divine, such as when she actually seems to witness the crucifixion. Another way to experience the divine spatially is in created space. Ecclesiastical structures are invested with sacrality through ritual tradition. We can see this in Kempe's life when she reacts strongly to seeing the Host, for example. These humanly created spaces, such as churches, become power centres where the Divine manifests itself regularly and with authority. Finally, nature becomes both a means to prove Kempe's connection with the Divine, such as when she prays for rain to put out a fire and it subsequently snows, and as a metaphorical vehicle to describe dimensions of the relationship between God and human beings.[3]

Of all women pilgrim figures, Kempe is about the most threatening one could name aside from the Wife of Bath, who has been found to be threatening by numerous critics in the past, as well as her fellow travellers. Kempe screams, is out of the control – sexually, physically, and financially – of her husband, and seems odd, not only to modern sensibilities, but also to medieval ones, at least according to Kempe herself. Most of all, though, she wanders throughout England and the Continent. The wandering woman is like the 'wandering womb' of Greek and medical theory, which threatens by its ability to stray.[4] The Mayor of Leicester finds her threatening not only because she wears white clothes, signalling an absent virginity and/or her adherence to the Flagellants, but because of his belief that 'þow art comyn hedyr to han a-wey owr wyuys fro us & ledyn hem wyth þe' (116). Her disruptive nature could inspire other women to be equally as transgressive.

The *Book* uses genres typical of those which feature women pilgrim figures, and switches from one genre to another, ultimately endorsing and situating itself in the

religious genre. While the *Book* opens in her domestic sphere, a secular and potentially satirizable place, it concludes with her on her knees in church. It plays with
perceptions of space, beginning in the proper domestic sphere which Margery denies
and leaves, and concludes in the enclosed and sanctioned religious confines of a church.
Daphne Spain argues that both men and women collude in accepting spatial hierarchies. Men do so because they are advantaged that way, women because they cannot
see a way beyond such stratifications, even if they disadvantage them. Kempe moves
herself into occupying the space of power and knowledge. As Vauchez has pointed
out, mystical sanctity was fundamentally elitist, 'claiming the high ground … [T]he
mystics … addressed themselves exclusively to political and religious leaders.'[5] In
writing herself into a spatially privileged space, Kempe demands acceptance by religious
authorities. The *Book* opens with her not totally confessing and by slandering others;
it concludes in prayer. While both scenes take place in enclosed spaces, they could
not be more dissimilar, the first one of total chaos, the last one of control.

Margery Kempe: the audience and the performer

The fluidity of the sacred and profane in the spatial practice of pilgrimage has given
rise to treating its study as a 'postmodern' subject. Another such aspect to pilgrimage
has been suggested by Turner who has called attention in his work to performance,
an emphasis which calls attention to 'the "postmodern turn" in anthropology'. With
performance becoming central to anthropological observation, 'postmodern theory
would see in the very flaws, hesitations, personal factors, incomplete, elliptical, context-
dependent, situational components of performance, clues to the very nature of human
process itself'.[6] In reading space as a text, as Moore suggests, we can also see culture as
the 'performance of a text'. Performance 'does the structuring of the structure of text',
as Edward M. Bruner puts it. But performance itself is a text to be read and interpreted.

> A postmodern anthropology views culture not as existing beyond and independent
> of – and hence 'expressed' in – such things as spatial arrangements, ritual, and
> other phenomena to which we and the actors assign meaning. Rather, it is these
> things by which culture itself is constituted. They are not 'expression'; they *are*
> culture.[7]

The 'text' consists of many parts. The pilgrimage shrine is both a set of material
objects[8] and a way of organizing space, both of which are the product and producers
of meaning and can be considered part of the text. The church containing a shrine, as
organized space, is another part of the text. The pilgrims themselves make up the
text, reading, rewriting and constituting the text. In this way, meaning, constantly
created, negotiated, contested, variable, emergent,[9] 'resides for the pilgrims in practice,
is produced by practice, and is both cause and consequence of their pilgrimage to the
shrine'.[10]

As we will see in the case of Margery Kempe, her *Book* functions as a script
performed by the author. By becoming a public spectacle and performer, she threatens
the society she acts before. Her tears and crying are subversive and exemplary for all

women pilgrims, real and literary, in that they carve out for her a public, though contested, space. Pilgrimage confounds discrete binaries in terms of space and performance. In the case of Margery Kempe, another binary crumbles, wherein the distinctions between performer and audience are not always discernible.

Although her book deals with twentieth-century women pilgrims to a Greek Orthodox shrine on the island of Tinos in the Cycladic Islands, the work of Jill Dubisch in *In a Different Place: Pilgrimage, Gender, and Politics at a Greek Island Shrine* is valuable for illuminating the situation of medieval women pilgrims. By using her theoretical framework, I am not suggesting that there is an essentialist element to the pilgrimages to women; but Dubisch's points about these specific women pilgrims apply to many of Kempe's activities as a pilgrim. The theoretical template Dubisch provides helps us to read Kempe's script. Dubisch discusses 'performance' itself as a general characteristic of social interaction since it presents 'the socially constructed self before others …'[11] Performances are transformative, not merely expressive, and constitute creative endeavours on the part of the performer. Furthermore, ways in which gender status is culturally constituted and performed may be used to make 'statements and claims – and even provide an idiom of resistance – in everyday context of social life'.[12] Pilgrimage is an especially important forum for performances.

> [R]eligious activities provide a 'space' for women's performances. Visiting the cemetery, attending a liturgy at a country church, going on a pilgrimage – these are all legitimate ways for women to move through public space and to socialize with other women … Our category of 'public' must thus be broadened to include not only the world of men but also the world of women, even when they do not gather in what is conventionally designated as 'public' space … That is, *women* may provide the 'public' audience for other women's performances (as well as the critical commentary that determines how such performances will be evaluated) … [W]omen's own stories about themselves can be seen as another type of female performance … Such accounts are not simply 'personal' – they position the teller in relation to her cultural and social world.[13]

Now, not all of Dubisch's comments apply unproblematically to Margery Kempe. That women's activities in the religious sphere give them legitimate reasons to move through public space is not, as we have already seen, necessarily true for medieval women pilgrims. Kempe performs in public and receives censure for it. But her performance is a way to establish herself in position to society and to place herself within public space.

Kempe's performances are situated in diverse spatial places and temporal moments. Kempe is sometimes a participant in what I will call 'Gospel Time', that is, she is a spectator to and/or participant in events taking place during Christ's life or crucifixion. For example, she listens to St John and Mary.[14] These events occur in 'Gospel Time' and her weeping in response to these events takes place within this time. The audience to her weeping consists likewise of members of 'Gospel Time' – Jesus, Mary, Joseph, an angel. On occasions when she encounters or sees members of Gospel

Time, the description of her viewing them consistently distinguishes between what she calls her spiritual eye and her bodily eye. She sees something with her spiritual eye as though with her bodily eye. Thus her 'bodily eye' is functioning, but sees with the spiritual eye. By perceiving in this way, she becomes the spectator of a religious drama.[15] For example, in Jerusalem,

> & þe forseyd creatur wept & sobbyd so plentyvowsly as þow sche had seyn owyr Lord wyth hir bodyly ey sufferyng hys Passyon at þat tyme. Befor hir in hyr sowle sche saw hym veryly be contemplacyon … Beforn hir face sche herd and saw in hir gostly sygth þe mornyng of owyr Lady, of Sen John & Mary Mawdelyn, and of many oþer þat louyd owyr Lord. (68)

Later at Mount Calvary, '[s]che had so very contemplacyon in þe sygth of hir s[owle] as yf Crist had hangyn befor hir bodily eye in hys manhode' (70).[16] Sometimes Kempe translates 'real' things that she sees into Gospel time. At Leicester Abbey, she sees the Abbot and brethren. 'Whan sche sey hem comyn, a-non in hir sowle sche beheld owr Lord comyng wyth hys apostelys, & sche was so raueschyd in-to contemplacyon wyth swetnes & deuocyon þat sche myth [not] stondyn a-geyns her comyng as curtesy wolde but lenyd hir to a peler in þe chirche & held hir strongly þerby for dred of fallyng …' (117). This reconfiguring in her mind continues, such as when she sees sick people. If she sees a sick man, especially one with wounds, she cries as though she has seen the battered Christ (176).[17] Often, this 'translation', as it were, takes place due to her memory. One time, on Good Friday, when she sees priests kneeling and others worshipping,

> be-for hir syght sodeynly ocupijd þe hert of þis creatur, drawyng hir mende al holy in-to þe Passyon of owr Lord Crist Ihesu, whom sche behelde wyth hir gostly eye in þe syght of hir sowle as verily as þei sche had seyn hys precyows body betyn, scorgyd, & crucifyed wyth hir bodily eye, whech syght & gostly beheldyng wrowt be grace so feruently in hir mende, wowndyng hir wyth pite & compassyon, þat sche sobbyd, roryd, & cryed …. (139–40)

In the Prior's Chapel, 'sche had so gret mende of þe Passyon of owr Lord Ihesu Crist & of hys precyows wowndys & how dere he bowt hir þat sche cryed & roryd wondirfully …' (164). During a sickness, she 'wept & sobbyd in þe mend of owr Lordys Passyon as thow sche sey hym wyth hir bodily eye sufferyng peyne & passyon be-forn hir' (138).

Karma Lochrie in her book, *Margery Kempe and Translations of the Flesh*, discusses the role of memory for meditation. Through the imaginary reconstruction of Biblical events and the locations where they occured, either through actual pilgrimage or reading or hearing about holy places, the Christian's affections are moved to imitate Christ mystically. Lochrie clearly shows how remembering Christ's life through one's imitation of Him relies on the incorporation of images into one's memory.[18] Anne Middleton also writes of the importance of images for identity formation. Margery Kempe creates her life in the image of a holy woman and images provide a source for Kempe's mystical authority.

If graven images were profoundly suspect, those that formed spontaneously in the individual memory and imagination steeped in direct assimilation of canonical texts of scripture and the lives of the saints – metonymies or images of equivalence that suggested themselves to Margery Kempe in daily domestic life – were fundamentally trustworthy, because their syntax of relation was implicit in a customary grammar of living.[19]

By enacting authoritative texts, Kempe establishes her public identity and interior subjectivity.

The work of Pierre Nora can help us read the role of memory in Kempe's entry into Gospel Time. In his introduction to his history of French collective memory, *Les Lieux de Mémoire*,[20] Pierre Nora sets up memory and history as opposing modes of understanding the past. As Natalie Zemon Davis and Randolph Starn understand Nora, we distinguish *lieux de mémoire*

> because we no longer live in a world suffused with memory or fully committed to overarching ideological narratives ... Memory could be sensed practically everywhere in a thoroughly traditional society; it would be hard to find anywhere in a consistently postmodern culture where all past moments would be equidistant, equally available and remote, from the present.[21]

Such a 'traditional' society could be seen in the Christian Middle Ages, where Christ's birth and death function as perpetually resurrected memories. Memory, for Nora, is in a continual state of evolution, a 'perpetually actual phenomenon', while history is always a reconstruction of the past, a representation which suppresses and destroys memory.[22]

> Memory installs remembrance within sacred; history, always prosaic, releases it again ... [M]emory is by nature multiple and yet specific; collective, plural, and yet individual. History, on the other hand, belongs to everyone and to no one, whence its claim to universal authority. Memory takes root in the concrete, in spaces, gestures, images, and objects; history binds itself strictly to temporal continuities, to progressions and to relations between things.[23]

Lieux de mémoire are remains or traces, 'the ultimate embodiments of a memorial consciousness that has barely survived in a history age'. Among these markers of another age or these illusions of eternity are festivals, museums, archives, monuments and sanctuaries.[24] These *lieux de mémoire* are fixed on the boundary between memory and history.

Memory is voluntary and spontaneous, not the duty or deliberate mode of history. Nora sets up a dichotomy between memory and history.

> Modern memory is, above all, archival. It relies entirely on the materiality of the trace, the immediacy of the recording, the visibility of the image ... The less memory is experienced from the inside the more it exists only through its exterior scaffolding and outward signs.[25]

Memory is site dependent, while history is event dependent. But some *lieux de mémoire* are not necessary wed to topographical space. Memory-sites, like statues or monuments to the dead, 'owe their meaning to their intrinsic existence; even though their location is far from arbitrary, one could justify relocation without altering their meaning'.[26] This is clear in establishing pilgrimage routes; the translation of relics suggests the mobility of 'memory-sites'; the operative element is the relic itself, not where the martyr actually fell. But other sorts of *lieux de mémoire* include 'places of refuge, sanctuaries of spontaneous devotion and silent pilgrimage, where one finds the living heart of memory'.[27] For Kempe, then, remembering Christ's life and death is realized in her present time. Her time becomes Gospel time. She lives in the memory of Gospel Time. The historical events of Christ's birth and death exist in Kempe memory. They are *lieux de mémoire* to the memory of Christ and Gospel Time is a *lieu de mémoire* in which Kempe performs. These moments become 'real', like dramas perpetually played out on the stage of her soul for her spiritual eye to witness. She is initially the audience of a religious drama, not a similacrum of Gospel events as in the miracle plays, but as a spectator in the real time of the Gospel.

But because of this reality as spectator in Gospel time, she inevitably becomes an actor as well through her reaction. Her acting reveals itself in the form of tears, roaring, and crying. Through this acting, she becomes a spectacle herself. The audience of visions, Kempe, becomes the performer. The spectator becomes the spectacle. Her drama of tears appropriates public space. She acts in 'public space', appropriating it for her drama. She performs her own play. Initially acting as an audience member who cries at witnessing a scene from the Gospel, her passive role as witness becomes the active role of actor in crying and weeping at the scene she views. And this spectacle of the actor Kempe inevitably draws an audience which either condemns her or endorses her 'drama', accusing her or supporting her performance.

How does Kempe explain the tears to herself? As we have seen above, she cries many times while carried into Gospel time. She cries, weeps and roars, falling down to the ground, 'so feruently þe fyer of lofe brent in hir hert' (147). Christ Himself tells her he causes her to cry. '[I]t is my-self, al-mythy God, þat make þe to wepyn euery day for thyn owyn synnes' (159). He makes her cry as a token of His love (183). But she is often maltreated for crying.[28] The accusations range somewhat, from people questioning her motivations to simply being irritated by her. For example, some believe she can turn on and off the tears without trouble and call her a hypocrite. In Canterbury, 'sche was gretly despysed & repreuyd for cawse sche wept so fast' (27), by both monks, priests, and lay people. Even her husband pretends not to know her. Her pilgrimage party in Constance wants the legate there to tell her she cannot accompany them unless she eats meat and stops weeping and speaking of holiness, though he defends her, saying her tears come from the Holy Ghost.[29] In Jerusalem, Rome and England her tears also cause much anger and suspicion (69, 83, 105). She continues to cry throughout her life. In Germany a monk is furious with her and calls her a hypocrite (235). Margery's tears can cause her audience to condemn her severely.

The negative reaction she provokes has been read in terms of a mystic's method to achieving the sacred. After tracing how in the Middle Ages the feminine came to be identified with fissured flesh and the loss of boundaries, Lochrie concludes that women mystics transgress in order to achieve divine union and knowledge.[30] Kempe's roarings and tears function, as does laughter, as a comment on society and her marginalized position in it. They allow her to carve out a privileged space for herself by subverting culturally sanctioned public speech.[31] For example, the Grey Friar banishes her from his church because her roarings silence *him*, the purveyor of approved public speaking. By appropriating the public space for her tears, Kempe questions the patriarchal language of the Church. As Dhira B. Mahoney suggests, her tears, which authenticate her experience, function as a language, replacing, and thereby subverting, patriarchal language. Her tears are a sign of her power.[32]

There are some who support her 'performance' of tears. In Jersalem '[o]þer gostly men louyd hir & fauowrd hir þe mor' (69). A priest in Rome 'beleuyd fully þat it was þe werkyng of þe Holy Gost & neiþyr feynyng ne ypocrise of hir owyn self' (84). Thomas Marchale is transformed by her and moved so that he cries and weeps and repents.[33] Although a friar excludes her from his sermon, other clerks allow her to remain during their sermons. '& ʒet þei suffyrd it ful paciently, & summe whech had spikyn wyth hir be-forn & haddyn knowlach of hir maner of leuyng excusyd hir to þe pepil whan þei herdyn any rumowr er grutchyng a-ʒens hir' (151–2). One Master Custawns decides not to despise her but to comfort her once he hears of Marie d'Oignies, a woman similarly expressive and inspirational to Kempe.[34] Ultimately one of her greatest supporters is her scribe, who initially decided never to believe her until he hears of others who cried for God. In fact, he bears witness to his support by crying as well. '[H]e þat was hir writer cowde not sumtyme kepyn hym-self fro wepyng' (219). In other words, he appropriates her language for his own. He, the representative of 'patriarchal language', a priest learned in the father tongue of Latin, utilizes her tears as a form of communication. He witnesses the drama of her life as a spectator, but, as Kempe does when she witnesses and enters Gospel Time, likewise becomes a spectacle and actor in writing down her life.

As a pilgrim, Kempe is an actor. She performs her pilgrimages, enacting her spirituality. Her text includes the language of tears. But she can appropriate her rival language, that of the 'patriarchy'. She is able to wield the language of the Church, albeit in the vernacular and not in Latin. Not only can she dictate coherently, but the end of the *Book* is a prayer, 'the sentences rhetorically and syntactically formed'.[35] She masters the language of power, the language of the Church, at crucial moments in her history, such as when she is questioned by the Archbishop in private. She is able to 'codeshift' from language to language, depending upon the situation. In the public sphere, such as a church when she hears a sermon, she uses the language of tears, the anti-patriarchal tongue which is beyond language, which subverts both the Latin and privileged speech of the priest. Her tears are a publicly disruptive discourse. But in the private chambers of the Archbishop or of other officials who question her, she is able to switch into their language and successfully use it against them to defend herself. Making a public spectacle of herself by use of the language of tears would be useless and, indeed, detrimental to her power in the private space of the practitioners of power.

This 'translation' of her speech from the screams of the public space to the 'rational' vernacular in the private world of male Church power is paralleled in her *Book* at the very start. We hear about her initial clerk who writes the book in a weird English-German which a second scribe claims only those with special grace can understand. He is fearful and refrains from copying it out in a more comprehensible form for four years. She prays and gains grace for him whereupon he can read and copy the book. Like her cries, the incomprehensible mixed language of the first scribe is threatening to the second scribe. But, like her cries, this language is comprehensible to those who believe in her and thereby have grace. Those who support her in her weeping are described as especially spiritual or are God Himself. The priest who struggles with the incomprehensible copy is granted God's grace. Thus the *Book* sets up at the very start a paradigm to be followed throughout the next pages: those with grace read her incomprehensible cries properly, that is, with God's grace. And her book appropriates public speech, that is, rhetorically comprehensible speech, thus carving out a place for itself in the public space. But as a public text it is threatening and subversive of official power since it privileges the chaotic language of tears and cries.

By crying publicly, Kempe performs the role of pilgrim-sufferer. Dubisch points out that the western view of emotion has traditionally been to see it as womanly, childish, weak, nonverbal, inchoate and chaotic, marginal. It has been seen as 'natural'. Kempe's crying and tears have been read as the language of mystics or as her simply being a bit odd, yet naturally so. But recent analysis has moved from viewing emotions as 'natural' to viewing emotions as 'cultural constructs ... part of the construction of culture itself and of relationship of the individual to culture'.[36] Dubisch argues for an anthropology of the practice and performance of emotions.

Suffering, she argues, may serve as basis for women's identification with other women, with laments as a form of female performance. But performance requires an audience, which for the pilgrim may vary from accompanying family members, friends, villagers to other pilgrims.[37] Emotion is not simply the expression of an internal state, but represents a person's relationship with the world, and, most especially, problems in that relationship. Suffering 'can be seen as expression of social identity and connection, as well as validation of the performance of social roles'. Through public suffering, women 'can demonstrate to and remind others of the difficulties inherent in performance of their roles'.[38]

By performing, the pilgrim separates herself as an actor from the audience, which may include fellow pilgrim-actors and regular members of the congregation. 'Through religious ritual women can detach themselves from their normal social contexts and create performative space for themselves ... [P]ilgrimage also provides performative and emotional space ...'[39]

These 'emotion-laden dramas' are then creative acts of the performer/sufferer/actor. The naturalistic view of emotion sees it as womanly and weak, chaotic and even threatening. Emotion is disorderly and anti-structure. Emotions can be used or can represent the opposition between pilgrims and the formal institution of the church. Much of women's mourning takes place outside of church, since the entry of a priest into a church creates disciplinary space and silence.[40] The church is where 'the emotional content of pilgrimage is appropriated and rationalized, the 'chaos' created by pilgrims is controlled and ordered, and the feminization of pilgrimage is obscured'.[41] The church is a contested space between pilgrims and church officials.[42] For women, then, suffering is a part of the politics of emotion, which is the strategy of the marginal and disempowered. We can read Margery Kempe as an actor of suffering, a performer of emotion.

Patricia Badir, in her analysis of the performing body in the late medieval and early modern periods, argues that '[t]he acting figure on stage, as framed, ordered, and disciplined by theatrical conventions, becomes a primary indicator of what subjects can and cannot do; its movement becomes a paradigmatic standard for the construction of boundaries and prohibitions.'[43] Kempe's emotions are culturally constructed and illustrate her relationship with the society of which she is a member. In drawing on the work of such medievalists as Sarah Beckwith, Miri Rubin, and Ruth Evans, Badir argues that

> the local preoccupation with the public display of the body by means of pageant, dress, and procession produced a functional sense of place within the immediate communities of towns which excluded the disenfranchised: the homeless, foreigners, women, and children. In other words, the imaginatively conceived boundaries of the body politic effectively incorporated behaviour and restricted physical movement according to hierarchical (and patriarchal) principles of order and civility. The boundaries of the community were drawn, within these acts, so as to separate insiders from outsiders and citizens from rogues ...[44]

Kempe scripts herself as performing her spirituality as a social outsider or, to use Badir's terminology, 'rogue'. Kempe uses this marginality to incorporate herself within sanctioned spiritual – and thus social – boundaries. Pilgrimage provides her performative and emotional spaces, which express themselves in cries and screams and tears, languages which threaten the religious order and which empower Kempe. Kempe's story is exemplary for the negative literary depictions of women pilgrims we have come across. Her *Book* distills the topoi dealing with women pilgrims of secular literature, from sexuality, such as those who cannot believe she is chaste with her husband, to suspected hypocrisy. Her *Book* exposes the social threat of the woman pilgrim in late medieval society. Her ability to codeshift from public wailing in shrines and churches to normative discourse in the private rooms of the Archbishop reveals changes in her self-presentation to construct an authoritative site for herself. These performances are modes along a spectrum, a spectrum which medieval women pilgrims peopled. By carving a socially sanctioned space for her spiritually, Kempe redeems or overthrows the topoi used against women pilgrim figures to empower herself. Kempe seems 'liminal', not only because she is a woman. Her behaviour renders her marginal in her culture – this is how she wants us to read her – though ultimately this very marginality translates into her absolute orthodoxy.

In Dubisch's analysis of her pilgrim group, she notes that women pilgrims often make public spectacles of themselves and, in doing so, by behaving in a way inappropriate to their own gender, these women were placed in the category of the opposite gender,[45] hence their perceived threat to society. This suggests that the categories of male and female break down. Pilgrimage allows a woman to leave her daily home life and domestic performance. Pilgrimage renders pilgrims 'equal' because they become public performers. But public performers 'should' be male. Clothed as women, female pilgrims threaten societal expectations, though in performing her pilgrimage, the woman pilgrim often fulfils those very roles she left behind. For example, a mother may travel without her children, but for the sake of her children. Pilgrimage, while seemingly liberating, can simply replicate the quotidian restrictions on one's life.

Kempe's position of authority remains ambiguous, both in the text itself and its critical reception. Her aberrant behaviour demands interpretation. Even her most sympathetic critics feel compelled to understand and rationalize her and her behaviour. They need to use normative discourse, like that she uses with the Archbishop, to explicate her. They translate her incoherence into coherence. This essay is yet another example in that genre. Something about Kempe forces us, the reader-audience, to become actors ourselves. In order not to feel marginalized by her text, we, as Kempe does with society, fight to establish our space *vis-à-vis* her text. Only then can we integrate ourselves with the text and establish our authority as reader-interpreters. But in doing so we neutralize Kempe's power. We 'perform' our endorsement of Kempe to render her comprehensible, but by doing so we strip her of her threat, the danger that we cannot understand her.

Notes

1 All citations noted parenthetically from *The Book of Margery Kempe*, Sandford Brown and Hope Emily Allen, eds, London Oxford University Press/Early English Text Society, 1961.

2 Sheila Delany, *Impolitic Bodies: Poetry, Saints and Society in Fifteenth-Century England: The Work of Osbern Bokenham*, New York, Oxford University Press, 1998, p. 171. See also *The Golden Legend*.

3 Ellen Ross, 'Diversities of Divine Presence: Women's Geography in the Christian Tradition,' in *Sacred Places and Profane Spaces: Essays in the Geographics of Judaism, Christianity, and Islam*, Jamie Scott and Paul Simpson-Housley, eds, New York, Greenwood Press, 1991, pp. 93–114, esp. pp. 94–5, 99–103, 107–8. 'God is present through the land, but now figuratively; the natural world provides a primary simile for describing the Divine's interaction with human persons,' ibid., p. 108.

4 Clarissa Atkinson, *The Oldest Vocation: Christian Motherhood in the Middle Ages*, Ithaca, Cornell University Press, 1991, p. 28.

5 André Vauchez, *Sainthood in the Later Middle Ages*, Jean Birrell, trans., Cambridge, Cambridge University Press, p. 411.

6 Turner quoted in Jill Dubisch, *In a Different Place: Pilgrimage, Gender and Politics at a Greek Island Shrine*, Princeton, Princeton University Press, 199, p. 45.

7 Dubisch, op. cit., pp. 158–9.

8 Michael Kimmelman counters Walter Benjamin's famous argument concerning mechanical reproduction, which would, as Kimmelman puts it, 'eradicate the aura of the original art object for the masses'. Rather, Kimmelman argues that 'in the next millennium, the allure of the original will *increase*, not decline … We have lost something, as Benjamin noticed, but it is not a craving for the original. It is an appreciation, one might say, for the virtues of pilgrimage. This comes to mind here [in Colmar, France] at what may be the ultimate pilgrimage site in Western art,' the site of Grünewald's Isenheim altarpiece. 'In the end, it turns out, one doesn't have to visit Colmar to realize the singular value of an isolated work of art. But it's probably as close as we can come today to a revelation.' From 'No Substitute for the Real Thing,' *The Sunday New York Times*, Arts and Leisure, February 22, 1998, p. 41.

9　Dubisch, op. cit., pp. 161–3. See also John Eade and Michael J. Sallnow, *Contesting the Sacred: the Anthropology of Christian Pilgrimage*, London, Routledge, 1991, pp. 1–9, who argue for a triad of person, place- and text-centred sacredness.

10　Dubisch, op. cit., pp. 163–4.

11　Ibid., pp. 203–4.

12　Ibid., p. 206.

13　Ibid., pp. 211–2.

14　Book I, Chapter 81.

15　Beckwith discusses the use of 'ghostli' and 'bodily' in Nicholas Love's *Mirrour of the Blessyd Life of Jesu Christ*, a fifteenth-century translation of a late thirteenth-century work. 'In Love's translation the interaction of 'ghostli' things and bodily things provoked by the imagining of Christ's life in such concretely literal terms instils an anxiety that is as much social as it is doctrinal … But this imagining must not confuse what is spiritual with what is bodily…That the operations with which he is engaging are very destabilizing ones is something Love appears acutely aware of. Rather than the porousness of categories – symbolic and social – licensed by incarnational practice, he insists, contrarily, on a hierarchical model which erects a ladder of social and linguistic condescension … [A]s there is no difference for [Margery Kempe] between the sights of her soul and her bodily eye, so graphic are her imaginings, so there is no difference between a crucifix and the object of its memorial signification.' Sarah Beckwith, *Christ's Body: Identity, Culture and Society in Late Medieval Writings*, London, Routledge, 1993, pp. 65–6, 81.

16　There are many such examples. When they go to the grave where Christ was buried, it was as though 'sche had seyn owyr Lord berijd euen befor hir. Þan sche thowt sche saw owyr Lady in hir sowle, how sche mornyd & how sche wept hir Sonys deth' (71). Once she is in Rome, her confessor is Saint John the Evangelist. '& he seyd "Dominus" verily in hir sowle þat sche saw hym & herd hym in hire gostly vndirstondyng as sche xuld a do an-oþer preste be hir bodily wittys' (81). At a church in Rome where Jerome is buried she similarly experiences a 'vision'. '[T]o þis creaturys gostly sygth aperyng, Seynt Ierom seyd to hir sowle, "Blissed art þow, dowtyr, in þe wepyng þat þu wepyst for þe peplys synnes, for many xal be sauyd þerby"' (99). One Holy Thursday, 'as þe sayd creatur went processyon wyth oþer pepil, sche saw in hir sowle owr Lady, Seynt Mary Mawdelyn, & þe xij apostelys. And þan sche be-held wyth hir gostly eye how owr [Lady] toke hir leue of hir blysful Sone, Crist Ihesu, how he kyssed hir & alle hys apostelys & also hys trewe louer, Mary Mawdelyn…Whan sche beheld þis sygth in hir sowle, sche fel down in þe feld a-mong þe pepil' (174). At home, she would cry out during the mass, 'for hir thowt þat sche saw owr Lord Crist Ihesu as verily in hir sowle wyth hir gostly eye as sche had seyn be-forn þe Crucifixe wyth hir bodily eye' (187). 'An-oþer tyme, as þe creatur lay in hir contempplacyon in a chapel of owr Lady, hir mynde was ocupijd in þe Passyon of owr Lord Ihesu Crist, & hyr thowt verily þat [she] saw owr Lord aperyn to hir gostly sygth in hys manhod wyth hys wowndys bledyng as fresch as þow he had ben scorgyd be-forn hir' (207). Once, while she is in the choir, 'sche saw wyth hir gostly eye owr Lordys body lying be-forn hir' (208). Christ himself confirms the legitimacy of her spiritual over her bodily eye. '… [n]o-thyng is so sekyr to þe in erthe þat þu maist se wyth þi bodily eye' (218).

17　Regularly on Palm Sunday she responds to the liturgy in Gospel time. '[I]t semyd to hir gostly sygth as þei sche had ben þat tyme in Ierusalem & seen owr Lord in hys manhod receyuyd of þe pepil as he was whil he went her in erth…Sche had many an holy thowt of owr Lordys Passyon & beheld hym in hir gostly syght as verily as he had ben a-forn hir in hir bodily syght' (184–5).

18　Philadelphia, University of Pennsylvania Press, 1991, pp. 28–30.

19　Anne Middleton, 'William Langland's "Kynde Name": Authorial Signature and Social Identity in Late Fourteenth-Century England,' in Lee Patterson, ed., *Literary Practice and Social Change in Britain, 1380–1530*, Berkeley, University of California Press, 1990, pp. 15–82, here p. 75.

20 Paris, Editions Gallimar, 1984.
21 'Introduction', *Representations* 26, 1989, pp. 1–6, here p. 3.
22 Nora, 'Between Memory and History, *Les Lieux de Mémoire*,' Marc Roudebush, trans., *Representations* 26, 1989, pp. 7–25, here pp. 8–9.
23 Ibid., p. 9. Alphonse Dupront likewise finds memory crucial, arguing that the religious imagination of a place or time is inscribed onto a pilgrimage space. 'Cet espace pèlerin, n'apparaît-il pas comme le tableau où s'inscrit, dans une extraversion du secret ou de la ferveur des croyances, la figure d'une attente et donc l'imaginaire religieux d'un milieu ou d'un temps? La confession du tropisme s'inscrit dans la geste du chemin. Ces chemins qui, même au temps des autoroutes, demeurent si profondément inscrits sinon dans la mémoire, du moins dans la sensibilité collective,' *Du Sacré: Croisades et pèlerinages: Images et language*, Paris, Gallimard, 1987, p. 54.
24 Nora 1989, op. cit., p. 12.
25 Ibid., p. 13.
26 Ibid., p. 22.
27 Ibid., p. 23.
28 As Beckwith points out, while tears and cries are the 'legitimizing symptoms of her compassion with Christ and the stages of her becoming Christ, they are also and simultaneously the signs of a rampantly competitive and quantified display', op. cit., p. 88.
29 Book I, Chapter 27.
30 Lochrie, op. cit., p. 46.
31 'Kempe's bodily movings and boisterous tears, then, are not only imitations or assumptions of the Virgin's sorrow, they are proclamations of her own privileged reading of Christ's body ... [H]er tears intrude upon the clerical prerogatives of reading and interpreting the word of God. She arrogates to herself these prerogatives while remaining outside the sites of their practice, the cloister, the pulpit, the anchorage ... Kempe removes tears from the domain of private devotion ... When she takes her tears on the road and into parish churches, she radically alters a tradition which had been previously confined to the oratory and to private prayer. Holy tears in the public marketplace and parish church are quite different from private weeping, insofar as the context for that weeping changes. Kempe's tears become a public spectacle ...' Ibid., pp. 194, 196.
32 Sandra J. McEntire, ed., *Margery Kempe, A Book of Essays*, New York, Garland Publishing, 1992, p. xiv; Mahoney's article, 'Margery Kempe's Tears and the Power over Language,' pp. 37–50.
33 Book I, Chapter 45.
34 Book I, Chapter 68.
35 McEntire, op. cit., p. xiv.
36 Dubisch, op. cit., p. 213.
37 Ibid., p. 216.
38 Ibid., p. 217.
39 Ibid., p. 218.
40 Ibid., p. 220.
41 Ibid., p. 222.
42 Ibid., p. 221.
43 Patricia Badir, 'Playing Space: History, the Body, and Records of Early English Drama,' *Exemplaria* IX, 1997, p. 260.
44 Ibid., p. 268.
45 Dubisch, op. cit., pp. 195–7.

6 Contextualizing female, male and child pilgrims

While this book could not be an exhaustive treatment of women pilgrims, I hope it has opened up some avenues for research. There are many pilgrimage routes beyond that of Walsingham to be examined in terms of gender by investigating the material cultural artifacts of myriad pilgrimage routes. For example, ampullae would be sold to Jewish pilgrims to Jerusalem, identical to Christian ones except for being decorated with a seven-branched candlestick instead of a cross.[1] How did Christian, Jewish, and Muslim pilgrims interact with each other and how did gender affect that interplay? More historical documentation of women pilgrims undoubtedly exists and needs to be made known to scholars so they can better reconstruct the lives of women and pilgrims in late medieval England. I could not cover all literary works connected with pilgrimage in this volume which may need analysis in terms of gender and pilgrimage. And the *Book of Margery Kempe* is so rich, that its potential for uncovering insight into late medieval women and pilgrimage seems inexhaustible. In literary works, pilgrimage can be mere incident, it can be a plot device, it can define the central character's activities, or it can control that figure's activities. Variations of its use in literature suggest how present it was in everyday life of late medieval England, so present as to remain almost unremarkable, special but normal, like a birthday or business trip today. Pilgrimage literature exists as a multifaceted genre. We would more accurately refer to pilgrimage 'literatures'.

While my theoretical interest has been with spatial perceptions throughout this book, I believe that the research here ultimately leads to a different arena which needs further investigation: the family. Family came up repeatedly in my research into women pilgrims. Sometimes it was incidental, in, for example, a letter of protection covering a husband and wife. Other times it appeared as the motivation for a pilgrimage; for example, Margaret Paston and her mother having pilgrimage activities taken for the health of John Paston. In hagiographical works, as Ronald Finucane has demonstrated, familial love was frequently a motivation for pilgrimage. From material cultural evidence, I have argued that women pilgrims would have been highly concerned with their motherhood on the pilgrimage to Walsingham. One might well ask: where are the families in the secular literature?

Familial relationships in term of parenthood can be found in secular literature. One poem, *The good wyfe wold a pylgremage* (Porkington MS, No. 10, leaf 135, back, circa 1460–1470),[2] narrated by a mother about to set off on pilgrimage, voices her advice to her daughter on how to behave while she is gone.

> The good wyf wold a pylgremage
> Vnto þe holly londe:
>   Sche sayd, 'my dere doȝttur,
> þou most vndor'-stonde
>   For to gowerne well this hous,
> And saue thy selfe frow schond.
>   For to do as I þe teche,
> I charge the þou fonde.
>   Witt an O & a ny,
> syd hit ys full ȝore,
>   that lothe chylde lore be-howytt,
> And leove chyld moche more.
>
> When I am out of þe toune,
>   loke that [thou] be wyse,
> And rene þou not fro hous to house
>   lyke a nantyny goat;
> For þe yonge men cheres the,
>   they wyll sey þou art nyce,
> And euery boy wyll wex bold
>   to stere þe to lovd wysse ...
>
>   (39, 1–20)

The poem continues with good standard parental advice, sort of the female version of Polonius advising Laertes. The mother tells the daughter not to show off to attract men's notice, not to hang her girdle too low on holy days, to hide her white legs and not to show her stockings or drawers like a butcher selling his meat. She should not indulge in light laughter or looks, tap her hands or feet, sit alone with men or talk too much. She is told not to change friends too often or swear pledges too hastily. She should not slander and should keep a steadfast mind. She shouldn't gad about in taverns if she wants to remain a maid nor should she drink or eat too much or spend more than she earns.

The poem concludes with some well-chosen words:

> Far-well douȝttur, far-well nowe!
>   I go vn-to my pylgremage;
> Kepe þe wel on my blessynge
>   tyl þou be more of a[ge],
> let no merth ner' Iollyte
>   þis lesson frowe þe swage;
> Then þou shalt have þe blys of heyvyn
>   to thy errytage.

Witt a O & a I,
   doʒttur, pray for me;
A schort prayer wynnythe heyvyn,
   the patter noster and ave. Amen.
                          (43, 157–68)

This poem reveals that women went on pilgrimage despite being mothers. In this case it seems the daughter is not an infant or even young child, since the advice deals with how to treat young men. She seems to be pubescent, at least if one takes the content of the advice into consideration. And this mother pilgrim does not seem to be frivolous or on pilgrimage for sexual adventures, if we assume that her advice to her daughter applies to herself as well.

But other women pilgrim figures do not appear to be concerned with their own motherhood – they are much more concerned with the marital tie rather than their parental identity. The Wife of Bath eerily prefigures Margery Kempe in terms of class, though not, apparently, in religious sincerity. For both, children are rarely or never an issue.[3] Alison never mentions having children and Kempe mentions her children only in Chapter 1 with her post-partum breakdown. Even then we hear nothing about the child. Only in Book Two of *The Book of Margery Kempe* do we get details about her grown son. Yet we know she had fourteen children. Historical women and women in saints' legends frequently went on pilgrimage with or for children. Why this difference with Kempe and Alison? Why does Chaucer not invoke motherhood for the Wife of Bath? He could have made her a funny – perhaps awfully so in being overbearing – mother. And Kempe is obsessed by Christ's birth and childhood, by Mary's motherhood, yet she cannot transpose that importance to her own situation. Why?

The issue comes down to genre. As seen in Chaucer, motherhood is a factor for hagiographical or quasi-hagiographical texts. Sincere motherhood is twinned for him with religious sincerity, and echoes Mary's maternal power.[4] There are a few mothers elsewhere in his works, as in the mother of Malyne in the *Reeve's Tale* who is raped by John and made ludicrous by the Reeve in the slapstick fight at the end of the tale, beating her own husband by mistake. Funny children do not pervade Chaucer's world. The baby in the *Reeve's Tale* functions as a (sick) plot device in that the placement of his cradle is crucial for the rape of the Miller's wife. But other babies or children – the boy in the *Prioress's Tale*, Constance's son Maurice in the *Man of Law's Tale*, Virginia the sacrificed daughter in the *Physician's Tale*, the daughter and son in the *Clerk's Tale* – are piteous and pitiable, not the fodder for mockery.

On the pilgrimage itself in the *General Prologue*, there is only one child – the Squire, and he is full-grown. Where is the Knight's wife or lover, the mother of the Squire? No mention is made of her. There are two brothers, the Parson and the Plowman, but one at least is childless and unmarried. The guild members, the Merchant, and the Miller are all married but travel without their wives. No family unit save the father-and-son duo of the Knight and Squire participant on the pilgrimage. This does not reflect historical documents or saints' legends, which, while not historical documents, do represent participants on pilgrimage in a wholly different way. Why not in secular literature?

The family as a functioning entity with father, mother, child[ren] and extended members such as grandparents, siblings, cousins does not seem of interest to Chaucer. He depicts few 'complete' families in his stories. Constance has a son but they are separated from her husband and his father for virtually the entire tale. The *Physician's Tale* has an exceedingly dysfunctional family with a homicidal father. The *Reeve's Tale* has a family due to its genre, the *fabliau*, alone. The *Clerk's Tale* has a father, mother, and two children, but the latter are separated from the parents and one would hardly call Walter's 'House of Lombardy' a happy family. Only the *Tale of Melibee* presents a family unit – with the mother providing the moral centre and stability, much like suffering mothers in hagiographical works.

The Knight's missing wife or lover, the Squire's mother, the erasure of Alison's children – these 'gaps' are necessitated by Chaucer's generic interests, but also are deliberate inclusions to expose the artifice of the frame tale. We as readers react positively to the General Prologue because it is so 'real'. The figures 'come to life'. Yet, in terms of the historical reality of pilgrimage, *The Canterbury Tales* reflect the artifice of estates satire with the various classes and stations of late fourteenth-century England. Babies, children, married women with children, like the missing spouse/lover of the Knight, are obliterated since Chaucer is not trying to depict a historically accurate painting of pilgrimage, but a literary exercise in genre which he tests and explodes. The family unit of at least two generations does not seem to concern Chaucer. The dynamics of married people fascinate him in part because of the rich literary material he can draw on: parodies, satires, and idealized portraits. The domination of one gender over another – Walter over Griselda, Virginius over Virginia, Alison over most of her husbands, cuckolded husbands defeated by crafty wives – *that* interests Chaucer. But the familial dynamics of more than one bond or tie horizontally or vertically is not of prime concern for him. Only (quasi-)hagiographical works, especially the *Clerk's Tale*, allow the exploration of such feelings and dynamics. And the *General Prologue* is anything but hagiographical, save in its descriptions of the Parson and the Plowman. Satire suggests that pilgrimage functioned as a means or venue to escape family and familial responsibilities, whereas in reality – from letters and hospital provisions, for example – pilgrimage crystallized familial duties, loves, and obligations. One path of further research would be into the family in Chaucer. He displaces the familial element of pilgrimage from the frametale to the tales themselves. We could try to reread tales in terms of family. The *Knight's Tale* with its Amazon sisters, Ypolita and Emelye, could be viewed as a sisterly text. Such a reading might expose as yet unknown dynamics in the Chaucerian canon. We could also read the *Reeve's Tale* and the *Clerk's Tale* looking at the brother-and-sister dynamics and what they signify. And the *Tale of Melibee* might be regularly assigned to students.

What is even more surprising is not that Chaucer includes few mothers, since his generic interests can allow them only in (quasi-)hagiographical works, but that Kempe does not. And here we see how the *Book of Margery Kempe* initially places itself generically in the tradition of secular pilgrimage literature, when Kempe's sincerity as a pilgrim is overtly questioned. It later transforms itself into a (quasi-)hagiography by its conclusion, when, not coincidentally, Kempe's motherhood is foregrounded by the inclusion of her eldest son, a rather unpleasant figure. In fact, Margery suffers due to her son's ill-treatment of her. While Margery Kempe starts out apparently uninterested in family save her husband, she ends her *Book* with an intense relationship with her son and daughter-in-law. As in the secular pilgrimage genre which the *Book* initially situates itself in, children are a minor factor. Kempe's son and her status as physical mother appear in relief only once the text has shifted into the genre of sacred pilgrimage where familial relationships abound.[5]

Although *The Book of Margery Kempe* seems to be more like Chaucer's *Canterbury Tales*, with its emphasis on her marital relationship rather than her relationship to her children, in fact, the work is saturated with family imagery. Rather than being concerned with her physical children, however, her role as mother is displaced into the spiritual realm, into her performances in 'Gospel Time'. For example, while meditating she sees

> Seynt Anne gret wyth chylde, and þan sche preyd Seynt Anne to be hir mayden & hir seruawnt. & anon ower Lady was born, & þan sche besyde hir to take þe chyld to hir & kepe it tyl it wer twelve ʒer of age wyth good mete & drynke, wyth fayr whyte clothys & whyte kerchys ... Þan went þei forth to Elysabeth, Seynt Iohn Baptystys modir, &, whan þei mettyn to-gyder, eyþyr of hem worshepyd oþer, & so þei wonyd to-gedyr wyth gret grace and gladnesse xij wokys. (18–19)

Thereafter Margery arranges for bedding for Mary once Jesus is born; Margery swaddles him and then accompanies Mary and Joseph and the baby into Egypt. Margery feeds and nurses the Virgin.[6] She interprets 'reality' in terms of the Gospel. She has a similar reaction to seeing children when she was in Rome. When she sees women with children (200), she immediately thinks of Christ's childhood and weeps.

> Sche was so meche affectyd to þe manhode of Crist þat whan sche sey women in Rome beryn children in her armys, ʒyf sche myth wetyn þat þei wer ony men children, sche schuld þan cryin, roryn, & wepyn as þei sche had seyn Crist in hys childhode. And, yf sche myth an had hir wille, oftyn-tymes sche wolde a takyn þe childeryn owt of þe moderys armys & a kyssed hem in þe stede of Criste. (86)

Margery visits a poor woman in Rome who suckles her little boy-child. 'Þan þis creatur brast al in-to wepyng, as þei sche had seyn owr Lady & hir sone in tyme of hys Passyon, & had so many of holy thowtys þat sche myth neuyr tellyn þe haluendel ...' (94). Motherhood and children are important for Kempe, just as they were for many medieval women pilgrims.

Future research on pilgrimage, exploring the roles of men, women, and children, can build on the recognition that no one can be autonomous in any society. The woman pilgrim rarely exists in literature and history except in terms of family, whether as wife, mother, or sister. Some might argue that this restricts our understanding of women to the confines of the family, not being viewed as independent beings. But children are necessarily read in terms of family, as in Finucane's exploration of the role of children who proliferate in saints' legends.[7] We might also look at children in these hagiographical tales from the specific vantage of pilgrimage; for example, do older children make vows along with their parents? Do differences exist between girl pilgrims and boy pilgrims? Finucane's work on medieval miracles has also opened up a way for us to reconsider the male pilgrim in terms of family as well.[8]

We should privilege *Piers Plowman* over the *Canterbury Tales* when we seek to understand the familial dynamics of medieval pilgrimage. In Langland's poem, the family unit is of major importance. Langland's empty pilgrim in Passus V, a mere purveyor of signs in the form of pilgrim badges, represents a trace of the satirical tradition in pilgrimage literature. But the pilgrim in search of St Truth, Will, exists in a familial construct. M. Teresa Tavormina has looked at marriage and the family in *Piers Plowman*. In building on her work, we see how pilgrimage is integrally tied into both familial and social space. Langland's use of family metaphors for spiritual truths and abstractions, presented in naturalistic family images or scenes, both touches the audience and reveals his sense of the social dynamics of spiritual life. Tavormina shows how for Langland individuals are grounded in familial experience. When the individuals do break free from societal structures, like the family, they generally end up leading 'disorderly' lives – as minstrels, wanderers or beggars.[9] Tavormina does not cite pilgrims in among the disorderly here since the picture of the pilgrim in *Piers Plowman* is more complex than that of mere condemnation or praise. Pilgrimage is both spiritual journey and the way one leads one's life, including family ties. In the C-Text, Actif protests that he cannot go on the pilgrimage to Truth because of his marital status and the distractions it affords.

> Thenne was oen hihte Actif, an hosbande he semede:
> 'Y haue wedded a wyf, wel wantowen of maneres;
> Were y seuen nyhte fro here syhte, sighen she wolde
> And loure on me and lihtly chyde and sygge y louede another.
> Forthy, Peres the plouhman, y preye the telle hit Treuthe
> I may nat come for a Kitte so a cleueth on me...'
>
>   (VII. 299–304a)[10]

Here it seems Actif uses his demanding (and sexualized) wife as an excuse not to go on pilgrimage. Elsewhere in *Piers*, familial duties and ties penetrate pilgrimage. Covetousness goes on pilgrimage with his wife as part of a family endeavour: 'Ac I swere now (so thee Ik!) that synne wol I lete,/ And nevere wikkedly weye ne wikked chaffare use,/ But wenden to Walsyngham, and my wif also,/ And bidde the Roode of Bromholm bryng me out of dette' (V. 224–7). Piers and Will fulfil their familial responsibilities and participate in pilgrimage, albeit somewhat differently. When the bells of Easter are rung, Will tells us

> ... I wakede,
> And callede Kytte my wif and Calote my doghter:
> 'Ariseth and go reverenceth Goddes resurexion,

And crepeth to the cros on knees, and kisseth it for a juwel!
For Goddes blissede body it bar for oure boote,
And it afereth the fend – for swich is the myghte,
May no grisly goost glide there it shadweth!'

(XVIII. 427–33)

Tavormina reads this as Will's finally taking on his proper role in guiding his family in their religious life.[11] Will's pilgrimage is one not devoid of family ties. While Will is distracted by family and everyday life, in the end his family's salvation – symbolized through their participation in the Easter liturgy (though significantly not his since he falls asleep) – rests on his ultimate understanding God and his own role as a Christian soul. For Piers, as Tavormina points out, '[e]ven the call to spiritual perfection does not eliminate certain family responsibilities.' Piers says, 'For now I am old and hoor and have of myn owene,/ To penaunce and to pilgrimage I wol passe with thise othere;/ Forthi I wole er I wende do write my biqueste' (VI. 83–5).

Only after making his will, of which his wife is executrix, settling his debts, and sowing and reaping the harvest, 'can he set out on pilgrimage … [H]is insolicitude for worldly meat need only affect himself, as would also have been the case had the pilgrimage to Truth actually taken place.'[12] Actif, Will, and Piers as successful or failed pilgrim figures show how family and kin ties are woven into the pilgrimage endeavour. Men and women in the Middle Ages, whether historically extant or imaginatively constructed, do not exist in a spiritual vacuum on pilgrimage. Social ties of marriage and parenthood bind them in their activities, but also can provide the structure for inner freedom and spiritual salvation.

Notes

1 Lionel Casson, *Travel in the Ancient World*, Baltimore, The Johns Hopkins University Press, 1994, see Chapter 19, To the Holy Lands, 300–29.

2 All citations from F. J. Furnivall, ed., *Queene Elizabethes Achademy*, London, N. Trübner & Co., 1869.

3 'The point about the Wife of Bath, of course, is that she simultaneously is and is not Margery Kempe. She shares in some of the same attitudes as Kempe and the beguines and others on whom Kempe modeled her life – pilgrimage, and direct access to the Bible and religious truth, in particular. Yet the hallmark of the lay-woman with religious leanings is the attempt at avoiding marriage and sublimating sexuality into religious devotion. Chaucerian comedy here, in other words, is at least by extension Pseudo-Dionysian, affirming Alice of Bath's nature of lay-religious with one hand while denying it with the other.' Robert Boenig, *Chaucer and the Mystics: The Canterbury Tales and the Genre of Devotional Prose*, Lewisburg, Bucknell University Press, 1995, p. 37.

4 'Nowhere, moreover, are Chaucer's Pseudo-Dionysian themes of control, silence, and fragmentation presented in a more metaphysical light than in his *Canterbury Tales* about good women. They partake in many ways of the kind of lives the women mystics led, they present women who are vulnerable, righteous, and long-suffering, women almost completely without control over their surroundings in a worldly sense. They suffer silently and lead fragmented lives, yet they exert a spiritual control that ultimately reveals a God who is in rigorous, absolute control of things.' Ibid., pp. 102–3.

5 However, see Liz Herbert McAvoy's 'Motherhood: *The Book of Margery Kempe*', in *Medieval Feminist Newsletter* 24, 1997, pp. 23–6, where she argues for the centrality of Margery's motherhood.

6 Book I, Chapter 81.

7 Also, see Richard Flynn's article on the emergent field of childhood studies. 'The Intersection of Children's Literature and Childhood Studies', *Children's Literature Association Quarterly* 22/3, 1997, pp. 143–5. See also Susan S. Morrison, 'Introduction, Medieval Children's Literature', *Children's Literature Association Quarterly* 23, 1998, pp. 2–6.

8 Finucane suggests several paths for further research of medieval children, including a comparative study of medieval childhood among Jewish and Muslim communities. Ronald C. Finucane, *The Rescue of the Innocents: Endangered Children in Medieval Miracles*, New York, St Martin's Press, 1997, op. cit., p. 168.

9 *Kindly Similitude: Marriage and Family in Piers Plowman*, Cambridge, D. S. Brewer, 1995, pp. 214, 191, 219, 217.

10 William Langland, *Piers Plowman, An Edition of the C-text*, Derek Pearsall, ed., Berkeley, University of California Press, 1982. All other references to Langland are to the B-text.

11 Tavormina, op. cit., pp. 195–6.

12 Tavormina, op. cit., p. 205.

Appendices

Appendix A

Documents Pertaining to Post-Plague Restrictions

1 *January 28, 1350*

To the Mayors and bailiffs of Sandwich. Order upon pain of forfeiture not to permit men at arms, pilgrims or any others of the realm to cross from that port without the king's special order, so that the king may not have cause to punish them for their negligences, and if they find any crossing without license henceforth they shall arrest them with their horses, armour, equipments, jewels, money and others [*sic*] goods and chattels found with them and the ships taking them with the masters and mariners thereof, and keep them safely until further order, certifying the king from time to time of the names of those arrested and of the value and nature of their goods, as no small portion of the people has perished in the present plague and the treasure of the realm is much exhausted, as the king has learned, and several people betake themselves to parts beyond with their money, and if this were permitted the realm would be so stripped both of men and treasure that grave danger might easily arise.

The like to the mayors and bailiffs of divers towns, as appears below …

> The sheriff of York.
> The sheriff of Lincoln.
> The sheriff of Norfolk and Suffolk …
> The bailiffs of Ipswich.
> The bailiffs of Harwich.
> The bailiffs of Dunwich.
> The bailiffs of Heth.
> The bailiffs of Oreford …[1]

2 *June 23, 1350*

To the sheriffs of London. Order, upon sight of these presents, to cause proclamation to be made that no earl, baron, knight, man at arms, pilgrim or any other, shall cross from the realm to parts beyond before the quinzaine of Michaelmas next, upon pain of forteiture, without the king's special order, in accordance with what has been determined before the king and his council, and if they find any doing the contrary after the proclamation, they shall take them with their equipment, and keep them in prison until the king has declared his pleasure.

[*Fœdera.*]

The like to the following, to wit:

The mayor and bailiffs of Sandwich and of ten other towns.

The bailiffs of Weymuth and of seven other towns.

The sheriff of Cambridge and Huntingdon and the sheriffs of fifteen other counties.[2]

3 *6 August 25 Edward III [1351]*[3]

Inquisition before Bartholomew de Burgherssh, constable of Dover castle and warden of the Cinq Ports.

The lady of Segrave crossed the channel contrary to the king's prohibition on 27 October 24 Edward III in a barge of William de Denum called *le Faucoun*, whereof Nicholas Lorecok was master, without the knowledge of the said William; she was met at night by Thomas Barbour, servant of Sir Walter de Mauny, by whom he was appointed to superintend the crossing; he broke his lantern with his foot so he could not exercise his office.[4]

4 *November 6, 1351*

To Bartholomew de Burgherssh, warden of the Cinque Ports and constable of Dover castle, or to him who supplies his place. Whereas on 28 January in the 24th year of the reign the king caused proclamation to be made in all ports of England that no man at arms, pilgrim or other person should cross from the realm to parts beyond without license, upon pain of forfeiture, and although several such men have crossed those parts without license, and the king several times ordered Bartholomew to certify him of the names of those who so crossed from the said 28 January, yet he has hitherto refused to do so: the king therefore orders him, upon pain of forfeiture, to take information of the names of those who have so crossed without license, contrary to the proclamation, and to certify the king thereupon in chancery with all possible speed.[5]

5 *May 10, 1369*

To John Page searcher of the king's forfeitures in the river Thames. Order to deliver to Joan wife of Thomas de Burton of London, by the mainprise of the said Joan, Thomas Frere and William de Burton of London, John Vautort and John Hautryve of Derbyshire, a sum of 43 *l.* 10 *s.* by him arrested in the said river at Graveshende; as on behalf of the said John humble petition is made to the king for dearrest and delivery of the said money and of herself, together with a ship of Flanders wherein it was found and the master thereof, shewing that to fulfil his vows her said husband departed from the city of London on a pilgrimage towards the Holy Land and other the thresholds of the saints, that on his journey he was in the parts over sea taken and imprisoned and put to ransom, and is yet there detained, that the said Joan desiring to deliver him sold all her lands, tenements and rents and her goods and chattels as well in the said city as elsewhere, receiving of the buyers the sum above mentioned, and knowing nought of the ordinance against taking money out of the realm without license, put herself with the money on board the said ship in the said river to sail to foreign parts for delivery of her husband, and that the searcher entered the said ship and making search found the said Joan with the said sum upon her, arrested as well the ship as the said Joan having upon her money to be taken out of the realm contrary to the ordinance, and the master and seamen of the ship, and is yet detaining them under arrest; and as well the said Joan as is the said Thomas Frere, William, John Vautort and John Hautryve, appearing in person in chancery, have mainperned to answer to the king for the said money, if it shall be determined that the same ought to pertain to the king.[6]

6 *February 10, 1376*

Commission to William Palyngham and William Palfreyman, reciting that, – whereas for urgent causes concerning the state and governance of the realm it has been ordained, with the assent of the council, that none shall cross the sea without the realm without the king's special license, and that in the case of all persons crossing from the realm diligent scrutiny shall be made that they take not with them gold or silver, jewels or letters of exchange, and that any bearer of such shall be sent before the king and council, (known merchants crossing in the exercise of their merchandise only excepted, who shall find security before bailiffs or keepers of the ports where they cross that they will use the money and letters which they take with them solely on their merchandise, on pain of forfeiture by the sender and imprisonment of the bearer), and that in all ports of the king's realm and power within seas and beyond there shall be diligent scrutiny that none coming from the court of Rome or other parts beyond seas bring within the realm letters patent, bulls, instruments, processes or other things prejudicial to the king or his subjects, and that none going with the king's license to the court of Rome or other foreign parts pass in any port until he have found security before the king in the Chancery not to attempt anything to the prejudice of the king or people, which ordinance has been proclaimed throughout the realm, – the king has appointed them to make such scrutiny in the town and port of Kyngeston and the adjacent arms of the seas and other waters and shores.[7]

7 *October 4, 1381*

Commission to John Lovecok of Rummeney, Henry Merley of Dover, William Brown of Sandwich and Philip Bode of Feversham to make due search in all ports in Kent for the observance of the ordinance against persons passing out of the realm without license, or exporting gold or silver in coin or bullion, jewels, or letters of exchange, unless they be well-known merchants, and of the statute (of provisors) of 27 Edward III against suing at the court of Rome or in a foreign realm.[8]

8 *June 15, 1389*

To the keepers of the passage in the port of London and the river Thames. Order under pain of forfeiture to suffer no lieges in that port and river to pass to any foreign parts save known merchants, any previous command of the king notwithstanding; as the pope has excommunicated all them of Spain who are the king's enemies and notorious schismatics, and all others who repair to them or have communication with them, and great number of king's lieges are minded to go on pilgrimage and for other causes to Santiago in Spain and other foreign parts, taking with them divers sums of money in the lump, in plate and in coin contrary to the king's order and prohibition.[9]

9 *March 8, 1391*

... [A]s in the statute lately published at Cantebrigge, among other things, order is made that no servant or labourer, man or woman, shall go forth from the hundred etc. where he dwells before the end of his term to serve or dwell elsewhere or under pretense of pilgrimage unless he carry a letter patent under the king's seal appointed for the purpose, containing the cause of such passage and the date of his return, if he ought to return ...[10]

10 *November 6, 1399*

Exemplification, at the request of John Gyles, mayor of Dover, and John Moryn, of letters patent dated 4 May, 4 Richard II, exemplifying an article (*French*) in an ordinance in Parliament, 9 Edward III, that no pilgrim pass out of the realm except at Dover.[11]

11 *September 10, 1400*

To the mayor and bailiffs of Lenne, and the keepers of the passage in that port. Order, for particular causes moving the king and council, to suffer all merchants, masters of ships and seamen of the king's friendship now in that port who will there to pass with their ships and merchandise to foreign parts, likewise all native merchants etc. and aliens also of the king's friendship who will there pass as aforesaid or will come to the realm, notwithstanding the king's former command forbidding them until further order to suffer any person native or alien of whatsoever estate or condition there to pass without special license of the king, known English merchants excepted, and forbidding them to suffer any aliens there touching to pass further to any parts of the realm. Proviso that answer be made to the king for customs etc. due upon any such merchandise, and that diligent search be made in that town and port from time to time that by colour of this command no spy shall there leave or enter the realm, and that no pilgrims or others of whatsoever estate or condition save the merchants, masters of ships and seamen aforesaid pass out without special license of the king and that those merchants etc. take with them no letters or aught else to the prejudice of the king or realm.[12]

12 *June 27, 1444*

[From the order publishing the truce made between Henry VI and Charles of France to last until 1 April 1446]

... [T]he subjects of either party [i.e. England and France] may during the truce come unarmed, abide, traffic except in goods suitable for war, and carry on all lawful occupations and business without fear, let, arrest or disturbance in the country of either party, paying the duties etc. appointed in places where they shall pass, save that nobles or men at arms may not enter castles, closed towns and strongholds without license of the lords or captains thereof or their lieutenants, with express declaration that those desiring to enter be few and unarmed, but true pilgrims may visit the ancient shrines of saints as pilgrims were used to do in companies great or small, and it shall be sufficient for them and for merchants and poor and humble men to ask leave of the porters to enter towns, castles, etc ...[13]

13 *July 12, 1473*
To the sheriffs of London. Order to cause proclamation to be made. (*English text follows.*) [*sic*] Forasmuch as this day many persons being strong of body to service in husbandry and other labours feign them to be sick and feeble and some...[*sic*] in going of pilgrimages and not of power to perform it without alms of the people, and some also feign to be clerks in universities using study and not of power to continue it without help of the people; by means of which feigning, divers fall into the said beggings in cities, boroughs and other places, and so living idly will not do service, but wander about from town to town in vagabondage, sowing seditious languages whereby the country people be put in great fear and jeopardy of their lives and losses of their goods, and many other inconveniences follow by occasion of the same, as murders, robberies and riots, mischievous to the disturbance of the people and contrary to the king's laws and peace. Our sovereign lord, intending the pacifying of the realm and restful governance of the same, according to his laws and statutes ordained in this behalf ministering also to his subjects without sparing of any person, of whatever estate, condition or degree he be, straightly chargeth and commandeth that no person able to labour and do service live not idly, but serve in husbandry and other businesses according to his laws; and that no person go in pilgrimage, not able to perform it without begging, unless he have letters testimonial under the great seal ordained for the same, testifying the causes of his going and the places whence he came and whither he shall go: and that no clerk of any university go begging for his sustenance, unless he have letters testimonial of the chancellor, witnessing that he is a clerk of poverty intending his learning not able to continue without relief of begging: and if any person do contrary hereunto, let him be taken and arrested by the sheriff, mayor, bailiff, constable, lord of the township, steward or any other governor of the shire, city, town or place where he is found and committed to ward, there to remain, until he have found surety to do service according to the law, and to be of good bearing against the king and his people: and if he can find no surety then he shall be committed to the king's next gaol, there to remain until the coming of the justice of gaol delivery, without bail or mainprise, and that every sheriff etc. put them in their uttermost devoir in arresting and punishing the said vagabonds, beggars and clerks as aforesaid, as they would avoid his great displeasure and the pains limited in the said statute; and that no gaoler or keeper of any gaol refuse to receive any such person committed to his ward, nor take any money at his coming into the prison or giving out of his bail or mainprise as they would avoid etc. Dated Westminster, 12 July.[14]

14 *February 8, 1493*

Mandate to the sheriff of Norfolk and Suffolk to publish the following proclamation:

'The kyng our soverayne lord is informed that full heynes murdres, and robries, thefte, decaye of husbondrye and othir enormyties and inconveniences daily increase within this his realme to the greate offense unto God, displeasour to his highnesse, hurt and impoverisshing vexacion and troble of his subgjettis by the mean of idelnesse and specially of vagabundes, beggers able to werk and by faitours; summe excusyng them self by colour of pylgrymages; summe excusyng them self by that thei were taken by the kynges enemyes upon the see summe by that thei be scholers of the on universite or the othir within this realme; summe that thei be heremytes and so beggyng by colour of feyned devocion and many other suspecious and vicious levynges thus used in this realme wherby if hasty remedye be not hadde the seid mischeves and other moo beth lyke to ensewe and encreace to the great noyaunce and hurt of his subgettis, for repressyng of the seid myschves and inconvenyences dyvers full resonable and notable statutes and lawes hath ben made as well in his tyme as in the dayes of his noble progenitours to the greate charge and coste of this his realme but the due effecte of them hath not ensued for lake of ther dewe execusion but forasmoche as the deth of man is to God above othir offenses singulerly displeasaunt and also to the kyng most detestable. For ther is nothyng erthely that he desireth more then that his subgettes may leve in suertie of ther bodyes accordyng to his lawes he will therfore that the statute made in his laste parliament save on which was ordeyned for hasty punysshement of murdres be put in execucion withoute favour or sparyng of eny persone for the welle and suertie of the lyves of his subgettes ... And for avoydyng of idelnesse by the meane of vagabundes, beggers, fautours and othir suspecte persons afor rehersed it is ordeyned by a statute made in the dayes of kyng Richard the Second that justices of peax, shiriffes, mayres, bayliffes, constables and othir governours of hundreds, citees, burghes and othir places within this realme to have pouer to examyn all vagabundes and faitours of ther mysbehavyng and evyll dedis and to compel them to find sufficient suertie of their good levyng and to answher to all defautes ayenst them to be allegged and if the same vagabundes fynd no such suertie then thei to be commytted to the next gaole ther to abyde, till the next commyng thethir of the justices of the gaole delyvere and the same justices of gaole delyvere then to do to them as shall seeme mooste convenyent acordyng to the lawe. But for as moch as the kynges grace moste entierly desireth amonges all erthely thinges the prosperite and restfullnesse of this his lande and his subgettes of the same to leve quietly and suerfully to the pleasour of God and accordyng to his lawes willyng and alwey of his pitee intendyng to reduce them therunto by softer meanes then by the extreme rygour therof consideryng also the great charges that shuld grow to his subgettes for bryngyng of the said vagabundes to the gaoles and the long abydyng of them therin wherby by lyklyhed many of them shuld lose ther lyves in moderyng of the seid statute his highnesse hath ordeyned that wher such mysdoers shuld by the seid examynacion be commytted to the comen gaole ther to remayne as is aboveseid that the shireffes, maires, bailiffs, high constables, petyconstables and all othir governours and officers of citees, burghes, townes, towneshippes, villages, and othir places, immediatly after and upon the heryng of this proclamacion make dewe serch and take or cause to be taken all such vagabundes, idell and suspecte persones levyng suspeciously and them so taken to sette in stokkes ther to remayne by the space of three dayes and three nyghtes and ther to have none othir sustinaunce but brede and water, and after the seid three dayes and three nyghtes, to be hadde oute and set at large and then to be sworn to avoyd the towne. And if eftsones he be taken in such defaute in the same towne or towneship, then to be sette in lykewise in the stokkes by the space of six dayes with lyke dyette as is aboverehersed. And if any person or persons gif othir mete or drynke to the said mysdoers beyng in stokkes in fourme aforeseid or the same prysoner faver in ther mysdoyng then thei to have lyke payne and imprisonament as is lymeted for the seid mysdoers. Also his highnesse chargeth and commaundeth that all manner of beggers not able to werke within six wekes next after this proclamacion made, goo rest and abyde in hys hundred wher he last dwelled or ther wher he is best knowen or borne ther to remayne and abyde withoute beggyng oute of the seid hundred upon payne to be punysshed as is aboveseid. And that no man be excused by that he is a clerke of the on universite or the othir withoute he shewe the letters of the chaunceler of the universite frome whens he seith he commyth nor non othir callyng hymself a soldeour, shipman or travalyngman without he brynge a letter frome his capiteynge or from the towne wher he landed and that he then to be sworn to goo to the streight highway into his contre. And over this it is ordeyned that if any mayer, shireff or othir officer aforerehersed execute not the premisses as is aboveseid of every vagabunde, heremyte or begger able to laboure, or clerke, pylgryme or shipman as ofte as eny such commyth in his sight, or that he hath therof knoewlegh within the towne wher he hath auctorite, rewle or governaunce, that as oft as any such of the seid mysdoers departeth unexamynd and unpunysshed as is abovesaid, for every mysdoer so departed he to loose 20 *d* ... And that the penaltie lymeted by this ordynans to be forfeicted by any officere or any othir persone for non punysshement of vagabundes and labourers and othir mysruled persons within every citee wher maire and aldermen be that the profite of every such penaltie be unto the alderman of every ward wher such forfeiture is hade and made to his owne use and profite. Also he chargeth and commaundeth that no shireff, mayre or othir officer afore reherced suffre any mannys servaunt to play at the dyce or at tenys under the paynes of the statutes ordeynded for the same. And as for men levyng suspeciously in any citee, burgh, towne according to the statute of Wynchestre do examyn all such persons so levyng and compell them that harboreth and loggeth any such to find suertie to answer for the defautes of them that thei so harborowe and all such as thei fynde lyvyng suspeciously to avoyd them the towne and not to tary ther over a day and nyght.' *Et hoc sub periculo incumbenti nullatenus omittas.*[15]

Appendix B

Letters of Protection and Power of Attorney

1 *April 23, 1309*
   Protection, for one year, for Alice, late the wife of Walter de Bello Campo, going on pilgrimage beyond seas.
   She also has letters nominating Nicholas de Aston and Peter de Wynnburne her attorneys for the same period.[16]

2 *October 25, 1309*
   Protection for one year, for Alice, late the wife of Roger le Bygod, earl of Norfolk, going on a pilgrimage to Santiago.[17]

3 *July 4, 1310*
   Robert son of Walter and Alice his wife, going to Jerusalem, have letters nominating William de Hanyngfield and Ralph de Hevenhale their attorneys for three years.[18]

4 *July 18, 1322*
   Margaret, late the wife of Gilbert de Knovill, going on pilgrimage to St Edmund's, Pontigny, has letters nominating Richard de Chissebich and Walter de Pynneho his [sic] attorneys for one year.[19]

5 *December 23, 1322*
   Mandate directed to sheriffs and other bailiffs for Queen Isabella, who is going on pilgrimage to divers places within the realm, to provide upon request carriage for her goods and harness and other necessaries for her household at her costs, until Michaelmas.[20]

6 *November 3, 1329*
   Protection, with clause *nolumus*, for two years, for Felicia late the wife of Roger de Somervill', going on pilgrimage to Santiago.
   The like for the following …

   Hawisia de Kaynes
   Alina late the wife of Edward Burnel,
   The abbess of Elnestowe …
   [all] for one year.[21]

7 *April 24, 1330*
   Protection, without clause, until the feast of the Purification, for Alina late the wife of Edward Burnel, going on pilgrimage to Santiago.[22]

8 *May 14, 1330*
   Protection, without clause, until Christmas, for Isolda, late the wife of John de Belhous, going on pilgrimage to Santiago.[23]

9 *February 3, 1331*
   Protection with clause *nolumus*, for one year, for … Isolda, late the wife of John de Belhous going on pilgrimage to Santiago, until the Feast of St Peter ad Vincula. Christina de Cassaulton.
   The prioress of Clerkenewell, for two years …[24]

10 *February 6, 1331*
Simple protection for one year for Alina late the wife of Edward Burnel going on pilgrimage to Santiago.[25]

11 *January 22, 1332*
Protection with clause *nolumus*, for one year, for Eleanor de Keynes going on pilgrimage beyond the seas.[26]

12 *January 28, 1332*
Reginald son of Herbert and Agnes his wife going on pilgrimage to Santiago have letters nominating William de Herlaston and William de Sancto Albano their attorneys in England until Midsummer.[27]

13 *February 12, 1332*
John de Monte Gomeri and Rose his wife, going on pilgrimage to Santiago, have letters nominating Robert de Hoo and William de Norwyk their attorneys in England until the feast of St Peter ad Vincula.[28]

14 *April 26, 1332*
Margery de Chaumpaigne, going beyond the seas in the company of Eleanor, the king's sister, has letters nominating John de Colby her attorney in England until the feast of St Peter ad Vincula.[29]

15 *December 15, 1332*
Matilda late the wife of Robert Banyard going on pilgrimage beyond the seas has letters nominating Richard de Depham and Henry de Garston her attorneys in England until Midsummer.[30]

16 *February 21, 1334*
Matilda late the wife of Robert Banyard, going on pilgrimage to Santiago, has letters nominating Roger de Norton and William de Alby her attorneys in England until Michaelmas.[31]

17 *August 20, 1335*
Matilda late the wife of Robert de Holand, going on pilgrimage to Santiago, has letters nominating Master John de Blebury and Gervase de Wilford her attorneys in England for one year.[32]

18 *March 12, 1336*
Matilda late the wife of Robert de Holand, going on pilgrimage to Santiago, has the like [letters] nominating Master John de Blebury and Gervase de Wilford in England for one year.[33]

19 *February 28, 1344*
Constance de Kyngeston, going on pilgrimage to Santiago, has letters nominating Henry de Eslyngton and John de la Mare as her attorneys in England until St Peter's Chains.[34]

20 *March 26, 1344*
Eleanor de Beaumont [the king's kinswoman], going on pilgrimage to Santiago, has letters nominating John le Blount of Sidyngton and Richard de Melbourn, clerk, as her attorneys in England until Michaelmas.[35]

21 *October 7, 1344*
Margaret, countess of Hereford and Essex, going to Santiago and other holy places of pilgrimage in foreign parts, has letters nominating Robert de Brightwell and William de Somerdeby, clerks, as her attorneys in England for one year …

She has other such letters in the name of Margaret late the wife of John de Bohun, earl of Hereford and Essex, for the same time.[36]

22 *March 22, 1348*
To the constable of Dover castle and to the warden of the Cinque Ports or to him who supplies his place in the port of Dover and to the mayor and bailiffs of Dover. Order to permit Elizabeth late the wife of Robert de Assheton, who is about to set out to the Holy Land on a pilgrimage, by the king's license, to cross from that port, with a chaplain and two yeomen, to the said ports.[37]

23 *April 12, 1350*
Mabel Fitz Waryn, going on pilgrimage beyond the seas, has letters nominating Richard de Wynesbury and John Fitz Waryn as her attorneys in England for one year.[38]

24 *May 30, 1350*
Safe-conduct, for one year, for Joan de Bar, countess of Surrey and Sussex, going on pilgrimage to visit the shrines of divers saints.[39]

25 *July 14, 1350*
To all the sheriffs, mayors, bailiffs, keepers of passages and inspectors whether in ports or without. Order to permit Eva de Seint Johan, who is about to set out on a pilgrimage to parts beyond the sea with fifteen persons in her company to stay there until Easter next, to cross with those persons with her reasonable expenses, provided that she do not take any *apportum* beyond her said expenses.[40]

26 *August 6, 1350*
License for Maud de Ferrers to go on pilgrimage from the port of Dover to parts beyond seas, with seven persons and seven horses and with her expenses in gold to the sum of 60 l. provided that she or any of her household in no wise make any apport beyond 60 l.[41]

27 *September 5, 1350*
Alice late the wife of Stephen de Waleys, going on pilgrimage beyond the seas, has letters nominating Thomas Fayrfax and John Deyvill as her attorneys for one year.[42]

28 *September 8, 1350*[43]
One hundred and seventy-seven others have like orders [to constable to Dover castle and warden of the Cinque Ports to permit people to cross on pilgrimage] at different dates to set out on a pilgrimage to Rome with yeomen, horses, etc …
    *reading" 'Agnes Gilmyns for Agnes Gulmyns …
    The following also have like orders…
    Ida lady of Nevill of Essex, with damsels and grooms to the number of twenty persons and twenty horses.[44]

29 *October 10, 1350*
Blanche late the wife of Thomas Wake of Lidel; [nominates] Walter de Carleton and Luke de Burgh [as her attorneys]. [She is going with many others on pilgrimage to Santiago for one year].[45]

30 *October 12, 1350*
Margery late the wife of William de Ros, going on pilgrimage to the city of Rome, has letters nominating Robert de Thorpe and Henry de Grene as her attorneys until Easter.[46]

31   *October 18, 1350*

To all the admirals, sheriffs, mayors, bailiffs, keepers of the passage in all the ports and maritime places of the realm, and others. Order to permit Reginald de Neuport to cross to parts beyond the sea as a pilgrim, for which the king has given him license, with a horse and his reasonable expenses in gold, without making any other *apportum*, notwithstanding any orders to the contrary.

The following have like writs to cross, to wit: ...

Beatrice Luterelle with a damsel, a chaplain, a yeoman and a groom.

Elizabeth late the wife of Bartholomew de Lysle with a chaplain, a damsel, two yeomen, three grooms and five horses ...

Joan de Nevill with one horse.

William de Shillyngton and Joan his wife.

Denise de Elsham and Adam de Farndon ...

Lucy de Hodelston of Lincoln, with a groom.[47]

32   *October 20, 1350*

[As in October 12, 1350, also on pilgrimage to Rome] Abbess of Berkyng, nominating Lionel de Bradenham and Adam de Waryn as above.[48]

33   *July 25, 1361*

To the mayor and bailiffs of Dertemuth or of Plumuth. Order to cause of sufficient ship, of those not arrested for the passage of Richard de Stafford seneschal of Gascony, to be delivered to Andrew Luterell and Elizabeth his wife for their passage and the passage of 24 persons, men and women, and 24 horses of their company, in either of the ports named where Andrew shall choose to cross the sea, any arrests of ships for the king's service (the passage of the said steward excepted) and any commands or commissions to the contrary notwithstanding; as the said Andrew and Elizabeth and their company are sailing for Santiago with the king's license.[49]

34   *May 2, 1363*

Katharine late the wife of Thomas de Berkele the elder, going on pilgrimage beyond the seas, has letters nominating William de Chiltenham and William Westhale as her attorneys in England for one year.[50]

35   *March 28, 1365*

Joan de Northgrave, going on pilgrimage beyond the seas with the king's license, has letters nominating Walter Motoun and Thomas Baillif 'of the Ferne' as her attorneys in England for 2 years.[51]

36   *October 13, 1366*

Margaret de Ravenesholme, going on pilgrimage by the king's license, has letters nominating John Clyvele and John de Wylingham, citizens of London, as her attorneys in England for 1 year.[52]

37   *November 28, 1367*

[License to cross beyond the seas for] William Lench and Cecily, his wife, from the port of Dover on a pilgrimage to the city of Rome, with 2 yeomen, 4 hackneys, each under the price of 40 s., a letter of exchange of Silvester Nicholas of Lombardy for 40 l., and 20 l. for their expenses.

Alice Chandeller, from the same port to the city of Rome, with a yeoman, 2 hackneys, as above, a letter of exchange with the same Silvester of 12 l., and 20 marks for her expenses.

Adam Stable and Katharine, his wife, as above, with 2 yeomen, 3 hackneys, as above, a letter of the same Silvester for 50 l., and 20 l. for their expenses.[53]

38 *March 14, 1403*
License for Agnes Bardolf, lady of Wormegay, late the wife of Thomas Mortymer, 'chivaler,' to go on pilgrimage to the cities of Rome and Cologne and other foreign parts from any port of the realm with twelve men and twelve horses in her company and her goods and harness, and to pay 300 l. for her expenses to merchants of Genoa or other persons in the realm, who will pay to her letters of exchange to their fellows in foreign parts.[54]

Appendix C

Papal Letters

1 *10 John XXII[55] – March 1326*
To [Master Hugh de Engolisma, archdeacon of Canterbury, papal nuncio]. Faculty to grant dispensations to persons, who, having vowed to visit Rome and Santiago, are unable by reason of age, sickness, or wars, to do so.[56]

2 *12 John XXII – February 1328*
To Margaret wife of Edmund de Wodestok, son of the late King Edward ... Indult that her confessor shall give her penance and absolution, and commute her vows, except those of pilgrimage to Rome and Santiago.[57]

3 *14 John XXII – 13 November 1329*
To [Bertrand Cariti and Raymund de Quercu, papal nuncios in Scotland].
Granting them faculty to terminate the vows of those who purposed to visit Rome or Santiago, and are hindered by age or sickness, into a subsidy against the heretics in Italy.[58]

4 *14 John XXII – 3 April 1330*
To Matilda de Bionie, of the diocese of London, who, on her way to visit the Holy Sepulchre, Santiago, and Assisi, was, after leaving Valence, upset out of a boat on the Rhone, when some of her fellow-pilgrims were drowned, and her money lost so that she could not prosecute her pilgrimage. Dispensation to enter some convent instead of fulfilling her purpose.[59]

5 *2 Benedict XII – 7 August 1336*
To queen Philippa. Indult that her confessor may commute vows which she cannot conveniently observe, those of pilgrimage to the Holy Land, Rome, and Santiago, and of continence and chastity excepted.[60]

6 *2 Clement VI – 11 November 1343*
To the bishop of London. Mandate to allow [Elisabeth de Burgo, lady of Clare] to commute her vow of pilgrimage to the Holy Land and to Santiago de Compostella for other pious works. He is to forward to Santiago the oblation which she would have given.[61]

7 *2 Clement VI – 1343*
Elizabeth de Burgo lady de Clara, kinswoman of the queen. That she may choose a confessor, who shall transmute the vow she made in her husband's lifetime to visit the Holy Land and Santiago di Compostella, which, being forty, she cannot hope to fulfill, to some other works of piety, and to absolve her.
   Granted. Avignon, 11 Kal. Nov.[62]

8 *3 Clement VI – 5 May 1345*
To Raimond Pelegrini, canon of London, papal nuncio. Faculty to dispense those of England who are unable to fulfil their vows to visit Rome, Santiago, or the Holy Land, on condition of their giving the cost of their journey to the war against the enemies of the catholic faith and the defence of the faithful in the east.[63]

9 *February 1, 1347*
License for Elizabeth de Burgo to found a house of Friars Minors in Walsyngham.[64]

10 *3 Innocent VI – 1355*
Joan de Barro Ducis (Bar le Duc), countess of Warenne…Whereas she, while at sea between England and France, vowed not to return to England until she visited Santiago, and afterwards on hearing of her husband's death returned to look after his property in England without fulfilling her vow, she prays for dispensation to put off the fulfillment of it for three years.
   Granted for a year and a half, or the vow may be commuted for a work of piety by the Great Penitentiary, who may absolve her and enjoin a salutary penance.
   Avignon, 16. Kal. April.[65]

11 *7 Innocent VI – 8 January 1359*
To the bishop of London. Mandate, on petition of king Edward, to approve and publish the absolution given to his mother, queen Isabella, since deceased, by her confessor, for non-fulfillment of her vow to visit the Holy Sepulchre.[66]

12 *2 Urban V – 12 December 1363*
Relaxation, during ten years, of a year and forty days of enjoined penance to penitents who on the principal feasts of the year visit the chapel of St Mary the Virgin, in the poor hospital of Canterbury, commonly called 'Estbruge', founded by St Thomas the Martyr, for the poor, for persons going to Rome, for others coming to Canterbury and needing shelter, and for lying-in women.[67]

13 *2 Boniface IX – 14 October 1391*
To the bishop of London. Mandate to commute into other works of piety the vow of Margaret, wife of George Frwngg, knight, dwelling in London, who when wife of the late Thomas de Naunton, knight, vowed at his command and with his consent to visit Santiago de Compostella, but who on account of her age and the number of her children, and because the said George does not consent, is unable to fulfill her vow. The bishop is to impose a salutary penance, and cause her to assign for the repair of the churches of Rome, to the collector deputed in the Roman court for the purpose by the pope, a sum equal to the expenses of the journey and the offerings which she would have made to the church of Santiago.[68]

14 *2 Boniface IX – 14 October 1391*

To the bishop of London. Mandate to commute into other works of piety the vows of pilgrimage of William Cressewyc and Alice his wife, citizens of London, who have both attained their fiftieth year, and who vowed to visit, William many years ago the Holy Sepulchre, and Alice, then unmarried, the church of SS. Peter and Paul, Rome. Although William was absolved from his vow by the late Simon, bishop of Palestrina, then cardinal priest of St Sixtus, legate in those parts, and gave certain sums for the repair of the churches of Canterbury and London, and although they, towards the fulfillment of their vow, sent at their own expense two men, one to Jerusalem and the other to Rome; and although both were afterwards absolved by Pileus, bishop of Tusculum, then cardinal priest of St Praxed's, nuncio in those parts, with authority to so absolve, who imposed on them a certain sum as a subsidy for the Roman church, they desire to tranquillise their consciences. They are to assign for the repair of the church of Rome, to the collector deputed in the Roman court for the purpose by the pope, a sum equal to the expenses of their respective journeys and offerings.[69]

15 *2 Boniface IX – 6 May 1392*

To Thomas Bradeley, Augustinian friar of St Mary's hospital, *de Alto Passu* without Bischupesgate, London, Thomas atte Swan, layman, Elizabeth wife of Henry Herburi, donsel, and Margaret wife of John Gramsande, layman, of the dioceses of Exeter, Canterbury, and Worcester. Indult that their confessors may grant them, on the usual conditions, without coming to Rome, the indulgence of the jubilee of the year 1390. They are to visit churches in England on fifteen days, during two months after receipt of these presents.[70]

16 *2 Boniface IX – 3 June 1392*

To Nicholas, bishop of Dunkeld. Indult to grant that twenty-four persons of the realm of England at his choice, of either sex, may gain the indulgence of the jubilee, as above, Reg. Lat. i. f. 149. They are to visit on seven days, as above *ibid*. The present indult is to hold good for three months after his arrival in the said realm.[71] ['of either sex' is a not infrequent wording]

17 *3 Boniface IX – 6 June 1392*

To John de Werk, mayor, John Merser, Thomas Papedy, Richard [de] Rotherford, Robert de Prendirgest, and Richard de York, laymen, Joan wife of John de Werk, Margaret wife of John Merser, Agnes wife of Thomas [Papedy], Margaret wife of Richard de Rotherford, and Elizabeth de Werk, of the town of Berwyk in the diocese of St Andrews. Indult that their confessors may grant them, being penitent, the indulgence of the jubilee, commuting the toil and cost of the journey into other works of piety. They are to send to the basilicas and churches of Rome the oblations which they would have offered, and to visit on fifteen days within two months from the receipt of these presents churches appointed by their confessors.[72]

18 *5 Nicholas V – 1 July 1451*

[To Sibyl, noblewoman, relict of Roger Boys, nobleman, knight, of the diocese of Norwich]. Indult that the confessor of her choice may absolve her from all her sins, even in cases reserved to the apostolic see, once in life, and also (seeing that she, who is about eighty years old, vowed to visit the Shrines of SS. Peter and

Paul, and that on account of a certain hindrance and old age she cannot do so, and has sent at her expense a certain religious and a servant to visit the said shrines) may absolve her from the said vow, enjoining penance.[73]

19 *7 Nicholas V – 1453*

To John le Scrop, nobleman, baron, to the diocese of York and Elizabeth his wife, noblewoman. Indult to them and each of them to choose their confessor, secular or religious, who may absolve them from all sentences of excommunication etc., and from perjury, and enjoin penance; and commute their vows, past and future, and their debts to persons of whom they have no knowledge, into other works of piety, vows of pilgrimage to the Holy Land, Rome and Compostela, continence and chastity alone except. Should such persons come to their knowledge they shall nevertheless make them satisfaction.[74]

20 *1 Pius II – 12 February 1458*

To Edmund Grai, lord de Ruthyn, nobleman, and Katherine his wife, noblewoman, of the diocese of Lincoln. Indult that they may choose as their confessor any fit priest, secular or regular, who … [*sic*] enjoin penance *as above*, f. 42d; may commute into other works of piety their vows of pilgrimage and abstinence and any others, except vows of pilgrimage to the Lord's Sepulchre, SS. Peter and Paul's [Rome] and St James in Compostella, and vows of religion, and may absolve them from all sentences of excommunication etc; and that the said confessor or other of their choice may grant them … [*sic*] commute such fast into other works of piety … To Edmund Hampden, lord of the place of Dudyngton, nobleman, and Anne his wife, noblewoman, of the diocese of Lincoln. The like …[75]

21 *2 Paul II – 3 May 1466*

To the bishop of London. Mandate, as below. The recent petition of Agnes Cauod, nun of the priory of St Mary *de Gratia*, O.S.A., in the diocese of Dublin, contained that she lately left the said priory, with license of her ordinary, came to the Roman court as a pilgrim, and visited the shrines of SS. Peter and Paul, Rome; and that she subsequently transferred herself from the said priory to that of Koveney, O.S.B., in the diocese of Lincoln, and there took the habit of the order of St Benedict, and made her profession, wherefore she fears lest by the statutes etc. of the said priory of St Mary and of the order of St Augustine, etc., she has incurred sentence of excommunication. At the said petition of Agnes, who alleges that on account of her singular devotion to the said order of St Benedict she desires to remain in the said priory of Koveney, the nuns of which live under a stricter rule, the pope hereby orders the above bishop, if he finds the facts to be as stated, to absolve Agnes from such sentence, enjoining a salutary penance, etc., and to grant that she may remain in the said priory of Koveney for life.[76]

22 *4 Paul II – October 3, 1467*

To Margaret queen of England …

Indult, at her petition (to the effect that, when living in England she, constrained by very many sufferings and tribulations, made divers and almost innumerable vows, impossible of fulfillment by her on account of her weak health, for example many fastings, the observance of which vows very often involves fasting four or five times a week and several pilgrimages to divers places unsafe for her, or rather inaccessible for her without manifest bodily peril, wherefore, as also because she is deprived of her moveable goods, she cannot conveniently fulfil, as is becoming and as she desires, the aforesaid and many other vows taken by her) to choose a fit secular or regular priest as her confessor who, after having heard her confession, may grant her absolution, once only, for her crimes, excesses and sins and perjuries and transgressions of any vows, and also from all sentences of excommunication etc., even in cases reserved to the apostolic see, except offence against ecclesiastical liberty, violation of interdict imposed by the said see, crimes of heresy, any offence of disobedience or rebellion or conspiracy against the person or estate of the Roman pontiff or the apostolic see, etc., and, in general, in the cases contained in the usual bull of Holy Thursday, and in other cases not reserved to the said see absolution as often as opportune, enjoin salutary penance and commute into other works of piety all her vows, past and future, which she is or shall be unable conveniently to observe, except only the vow of Crusade, and moreover that the said confessor or other of her choice may grant to her, being penitent and having confessed, plenary remission of all her sins, once in life and once in the hour of death …[77]

Notes

1 *Calendar of the Close Rolls, Edward III, 1349–1354*, prepared under the superintendence of the Deputy Keeper of the Records, London, Mackie and Co., His Majesty's Stationery Office, 1906, p. 206.
2 Ibid., p. 233.
3 25 Edward III refers to the 25th year of the reign of Edward III.
4 Harley Rodney and J. B. W. Chapman, eds, *Calendar of Inquisitions Miscellaneous 1348–1377*, Vol. 3, London, His Majesty's Stationery Office, 1937, p. 21.
5 *Calendar of the Close Rolls, Edward III, 1349–1354*, op. cit., p. 399.
6 *Calendar of Close Rolls, Edward III, 1369–1374*, prepared under the superintendence of the Deputy Keeper of the Records, London, Mackie and Co., His Majesty's Stationery Office, 1911, pp. 27–8. Edward III orders her money returned to her on May 22 of that year, p. 28.
7 *Calendar of the Patent Rolls, Edward III, 1374–1377*, prepared under the superintendence of the Deputy Keeper of the Records, London, Mackie and Co., His Majesty's Stationery Office, 1916, p. 312.
8 *Calendar of the Patent Rolls, Richard II, 1381–1385*, prepared under the superintendence of the Deputy Keeper of the Records, London, Her Majesty's Stationery Office, 1897, p. 80.
9 *Calendar of the Close Rolls, Richard II, 1385–1389*, prepared under the superintendence of the Deputy Keeper of the Records, London, Mackie and Co., His Majesty's Stationery Office, 1921, p. 592.
10 *Calendar of the Close Rolls, Richard II, 1389–1392*, prepared under the superintendence of the Deputy Keeper of the Records, London, Mackie and Co., His Majesty's Stationery Office, 1921, pp. 255–6.
11 *Calendar of the Patent Rolls, Henry IV, 1399–1401*, prepared under the superintendence of the Deputy Keeper of the Records, London, Mackie and Co., His Majesty's Stationery Office, 1903, p. 68.

12 *Calendar of the Close Rolls, Henry IV, 1399–1402*, prepared under the superintendence of the Deputy Keeper of the Records, London, His Majesty's Stationery Office, 1927, p. 170.

13 *Calendar of the Close Rolls, Henry VI, 1441–1447*, prepared under the superintendence of the Deputy Keeper of the Records, Ed. W. H. B. Bird, London, Mackie and Co., His Majesty's Stationery Office, 1937, pp. 232–4.

14 *Calendar of the Close Rolls, Edward IV, 1468–1476*, prepared under the superintendence of the Deputy Keeper of the Records, London, Mackie and Co., Her Majesty's Stationery Office, 1953, pp. 298–9.

15 *Calendar of the Patent Rolls, Henry VII, 1485–1494*, prepared under the superintendence of the Deputy Keeper of the Records, London, Mackie and Co., His Majesty's Stationery Office, 1914, pp. 434–7.

16 *Calendar of the Patent Rolls, Edward II, 1307–1313*, prepared under the superintendence of the Deputy Keeper of the Records, London, Mackie and Co., His Majesty's Stationery Office, 1894, p. 122.

17 Ibid., p. 195.

18 Ibid., p. 233.

19 *Calendar of the Patent Rolls, Edward II, 1321–1324*, prepared under the superintendence of the Deputy Keeper of the Records, London, Mackie and Co., His Majesty's Stationery Office, 1904, p. 181.

20 Ibid., p. 227.

21 *Calendar of the Patent Rolls, Edward III, 1327–1330*, prepared under the superintendence of the Deputy Keeper of the Records, London, Mackie and Co.,Her Majesty's Stationery Office, 1891, pp. 454–5.

22 Ibid., p. 514.

23 Ibid., p. 523.

24 *Calendar of the Patent Rolls, Edward III, 1330–1334*, prepared under the superintendence of the Deputy Keeper of the Records, London, Mackie and Co., Her Majesty's Stationery Office, 1893, p. 70.

25 Ibid., p. 69.

26 Ibid., p. 232.

27 Ibid., p. 247.

28 Ibid., p. 252.

29 Ibid., p. 275.

30 Ibid., p. 379.

31 Ibid., p. 513.

32 *Calendar of the Patent Rolls, Edward III, 1334–1338*, prepared under the superintendence of the Deputy Keeper of the Records, London, Mackie and Co., Her Majesty's Stationery Office, 1895, p. 163.

33 Ibid., p. 235.

34 *Calendar of the Patent Rolls, Edward III, 1343–1345*, prepared under the superintendence of the Deputy Keeper of the Records, London, Mackie and Co., His Majesty's Stationery Office, 1902, p. 209.

35 Ibid., p. 224.

36 Ibid., p. 350.

37 *Calendar of the Close Rolls, Edward III, 1346–1349*, op. cit., p. 501.

38 *Calendar of the Patent Rolls, Edward III, 1348–1350*, op. cit., p. 489.

39 Ibid., p. 514.

40 *Calendar of the Close Rolls, Edward III, 1349–1354*, op. cit., p. 230.

41 *Calendar of the Patent Rolls, Edward III, 1348–1350*, op. cit., p. 556.

42 Ibid., p. 571.

43 This information prefaced by 'To Bartholomew de Burgherssh, constable of Dover castle and warden of the Cinque Ports, or to him who supplies his place in the port of Dover. Order to permit William fitz Waryn, with six yeomen and seven horses, to cross from

that port on a pilgrimage to the city of Rome, with his expenses in gold, without any other *apportum.*'

44 *Calendar of the Close Rolls, Edward III, 1349–1354*, op. cit., pp. 267–8.

45 *Calendar of the Patent Rolls, Edward III, 1348–1350*, op. cit., p. 572.

46 Ibid., p. 581.

47 *Calendar of the Close Rolls, Edward III, 1349–1354*, op. cit., pp. 271–2.

48 *Calendar of the Patent Rolls, Edward III, 1348–1350*, op. cit., p. 581.

49 *Calendar of Close Rolls, Edward III, 1360–1364*, prepared under the superintendence of the Deputy Keeper of the Records, London, Mackie and Co., His Majesty's Stationery Office, 1909, p. 197.

50 *Calendar of the Patent Rolls, Edward III, 1361–1364*, prepared under the superintendence of the Deputy Keeper of the Records, London, His Majesty's Sationery Office, 1912, p. 335.

51 *Calendar of the Patent Rolls, Edward III, 1364–1367*, prepared under the superintendence of the Deputy Keeper of the Records, London, His Majesty's Stationery Office, 1912, p. 100.

52 Ibid., p. 320.

53 *Calendar of the Patent Rolls, Edward III, 1367–1370*, prepared under the superintendence of the Deputy Keeper of the Records, London, Mackie and Co., His Majesty's Stationery Office, 1913, p. 71.

54 *Calendar of the Patent Rolls, Henry IV, 1401–1405*, prepared under the superintendence of the Deputy Keeper of the Records, London, Mackie and Co., His Majesty's Stationery Office, 1905, p. 214. 'Pardon to Warin fitz Fouk le Cook of Addelyngton, co. Chester for the death of Thomas Mortymer' [May 27, 1401] (*Calendar of the Patent Rolls, Henry IV, 1399–1401*, op. cit., p. 444).

55 10 John XXII refers to the 10th year of the papacy of Pope John XXII.

56 W. H. Bliss, ed., *Calendar of Entries in the Papal Registers Relating to Great Britain and Ireland 1305–1342*, London, Eyre and Spottiswoode, 1895, p. 474.

57 Ibid., p. 278.

58 Ibid., p. 494.

59 Ibid., p. 318; Constance Mary Storrs, *Jacobean Pilgrims From England to St James of Compostella from the Early Twelfth to the Late Fifteenth Century*, Santiago de Compostela, Xunta de Galicia, 1994, p. 61.

60 Bliss 1895, op. cit., p. 531.

61 W. H. Bliss and C. Johnson, eds, *Calendar of Entries in the Papal Registers Relating to Great Britain and Ireland 1342–1362*, Vol. III, London, Eyre and Spottiswoode, 1897, 112.

62 W. H. Bliss, ed., *Papal Petitions to the Pope 1342–1419*, Vol. I, London, Eyre and Spottiswoode, 1896, pp. 22–3.

63 Bliss 1897, op. cit., p. 17.

64 *Calendar of the Patent Rolls, Edward III, 1345–48*, Prepared under the superintendence of the Deputy Keeper of the Records, London, His Majesty's Stationery Office, 1903, p. 255.

65 Bliss 1896, op. cit., p. 287.

66 Bliss 1897, op. cit., p. 605.

67 *Calendar of Entries in the Papal Registers Relating to Great Britain and Ireland 1362–1404*, W. H. Bliss and J. A. Tremlow, eds, London Eyre and Spottiswoode, 1902, p. 36.

68 Ibid., pp. 388–9.

69 Ibid., p. 389.

70 Ibid., p. 379.

71 Ibid., p. 379.

72 Ibid., p. 325.

73 *Calendar of Entries in the Papal Registers Relating to Great Britain and Ireland 1447–1455*, J. A. Tremlow, ed., Hereford, The Hereford Times Limited, 1915, p. 525.

74 Ibid., p. 123.
75 *Calendar of Entries in the Papal Registers Relating to Great Britain and Ireland 1455–1464*, J. A. Tremlow, ed., London, His Majesty's Stationery Office, 1921, pp. 520–1.
76 *Calendar of Entries in the Papal Registers Relating to Great Britain and Ireland 1458–1471*, J. A. Tremlow, ed., London, His Majesty's Stationery Office, 1933, p. 541.
77 Ibid., pp. 273–4.

Works cited

Manuscript sources

Bodleian Library
    Bodley. 264.266v
    Douce 300.F.1, 7v, 24v
    Douce 374.F.86
    Laud Misc. 740, 19v
British Museum
    Add. 18, 632
    Cotton Tib. A vii, f. 40
    Royal 2 B VII f. 393 v.
    Royal 18 D II f. 148
Public Record Office
    PRO E 101/92/2m.12, 13.
    PRO E 101/92/12m.10d-11d.

Printed primary sources

Adams, Norma and Charles Donahue Jr., eds, *Select Cases From the Ecclesiastical Courts of the Province of Canterbury c. 1200–1301*, London, Selden Society, 1981.

Adler, Marcus Nathan, trans., *The Itinerary of Benjamin of Tudela: Travels in the Middle Ages*, Malibu, Joseph Simon Pangloss Press, 1987.

Aldington, Richard, trans., *The Fifteen Joys of Marriage*, London, George Routledge and Sons Ltd, 1925.

Anderson, Alan Orr, trans., *Early Sources of Scottish History A.D. 500 to 1286*, Vol. 2, Edinburgh, Oliver and Boyd, 1922.

Aristotle, *The Generation of Animals*, A. L. Peck, trans., Cambridge, Harvard University Press, 1979.

Atkinson, E. G., ed., *Calendar of Inquisitions Post Mortem and Other Analogous Documents Preserved in the Public Record Office*, Vol. IX, London, The Hereford Times Limited, His Majesty's Stationery Office, 1916.

Banks, Mary M., ed., *An Alphabet of Tales: An English 15th Century Translation of the Alphabetum Narrationum*, 2 Vols, London, EETS, Kegan Paul, 1905.

Barratt, Alexandra, *Women's Writing in Middle English*, London, Longman, 1992.

Bayard, Tania, trans. and ed., *A Medieval Home Companion: Housekeeping in the Fourteenth Century*, New York, HarperPerennial, 1991.

Bede, *Ecclesiastical History of the English People*, Leo Sherley-Price, trans., London, Penguin, 1990.

Benson, Larry D., ed., *The Riverside Chaucer*, New York, Houghton Mifflin, 1987.

Blamires, Alcuin, ed., *Woman Defamed and Woman Defended: An Anthology of Medieval Texts*, Oxford, Clarendon Press, 1992.

Bliss, W. H., ed., *Calendar of Entries in the Papal Registers Relating to Great Britain and Ireland, 1305–1342*, London, Eyre and Spottiswoode, 1895.

— and C. Johnson, eds, *Calendar of Entries in the Papal Registers Relating to Great Britain and Ireland 1342–1362*, Vol. III, London, Eyre and Spottiswoode, 1897.

— and J. A. Tremlow, eds, *Calendar of Entries in the Papal Registers Relating to Great Britain and Ireland 1362–1404*, London, Eyre and Spottiswoode, 1902.

—, ed., *Papal Petitions to the Pope 1342–1419*, Vol. I, London, Eyre and Spottiswoode, 1896.

Blumenfeld-Kosinski, Renate, trans. and ed., *The Writings of Margaret of Oingt*, Newburyport, MA, Focus Information Group, Inc., 1990.

Bödtker, A. Trampe, ed., *The Middle-English Versions of Partonope of Blois*, London, Kegan Paul, 1912.

Bond, Gerald A., ed., *The Poetry of William VI, Count of Poitiers, IX Duke of Aquitaine*, New York, Garland, 1982.

Bradley, Henry, ed., *Caxton's Dialogues in French and English*, London, Kegan, Paul Trench, Trübner & Co. Ltd, 1900.

Brereton, Georgine E., and Janet M. Ferrier, *Le Menagier de Paris*, Oxford, Oxford University Press, 1981.

Brewer, E. Cobham, *A Dictionary of Miracles*, London, Chatto and Windus, 1884.

Calendar of Close Rolls, prepared under the superintendence of the Deputy Keeper of the Records, London, Mackie and Co. (His Majesty's Stationery Office).

—, *Edward III, 1346–1349*, 1905.

—, *Edward III, 1349–1354*, 1906.

—, *Edward III, 1360–1364*, 1909.

—, *Edward III, 1369–1374*, 1911.

—, *Richard II, 1377–1381*, 1914.

—, *Richard II, 1385–1389*, 1921.

—, *Richard II, 1389–1392*, 1922.

—, *Henry IV, 1399–1402*, 1927.

—, *Henry VI, 1441–1447*, W. H. B. Bird, ed., 1937.

—, *Edward IV, 1468–1476*, 1953.

Calendar of Inquisitions Miscellaneous 1348–1377, Vol. 3, London, His Majesty's Stationery Office, 1937. (Her Majesty's Stationery Office)

Calendar of the Patent Rolls, prepared under the superintendence of the Deputy Keeper of the Records, London, Her/His Majesty's Stationery Office.

—, *Edward II, 1307–1313*, 1894.

—, *Edward II, 1321–1324*, 1904.

—, *Edward III, 1327–1330*, 1891.

—, *Edward III, 1330–1334*, 1893.

—, *Edward III, 1334–1338*, 1895.

—, *Edward III, 1343–1345*, 1902.

—, *Edward III, 1345–1348*, 1903.

—, *Edward III, 1348–1350*, 1905.

—, *Edward III, 1350–1354*, 1909.

—, *Edward III, 1358–1361*, 1911.

—, *Edward III, 1361–1364*, 1912.

—, *Edward III, 1364–1367*, 1912.

—, *Edward III, 1367–1370*, 1913.

—, *Edward III, 1374–1377*, 1916.

—, *Richard II, 1381–1385*, 1897.

—, *Richard II, 1388–1392*, 1902.

—, *Richard II, 1391–1396*, 1905.

—, *Henry IV, 1399–1401*, 1903.

—, *Henry IV, 1401–1405*, 1905.

—, *Henry VII, 1485–1494*, 1914.

Champion, Pierre, ed., *Les Cent Nouvelles Nouvelles*, 2 Vols, Paris, E. Droz, 1928.

Chapman, J. B. W., *et al.*, eds, *Calendar of Inquisitions Post Mortem and Other Analogous Documents Preserved in the Public Record Office*, Vol. XIII, London, Her Majesty's Stationery Office, 1954.

—, eds, *Calendar of Inquisitions Post Mortem and Other Analogous Documents Preserved in the Public Record Office*, Vol. XIV, London, Her Majesty's Stationery Office, 1952.

Clark, Andrew, ed., *Lincoln Diocese Documents 1450–1544*, EETS, London, Kegan Paul, Trench, Trübner & Co. Ltd, 1914.

Colledge, Edmund and James Walsh, trans., *Julian of Norwich Showings*, New York, Paulist Press, 1978.

Constable, G., ed., *The Letters of Peter the Venerable*, 2 Vols, Cambridge, MA, Harvard University Press, 1967.

Cook, Albert Stanburrough, ed., *A Literary Middle English Reader*, Boston, Ginn and Company, 1915.

Crow, Joan, ed., *Les Quinze Joyes de Mariage*, Oxford, Blackwell, 1969.

Davis, J., ed., *The Ancient Rites, and Monuments of the Monastical and Cathedral Church of Durham*, London, W. Hensman, 1672.

Dawes, M. C. B., *et al.*, eds, *Calendar of Inquisitions Post Mortem and Other Analogous Documents Preserved in the Public Record Office*, Vol. XV, London, Her Majesty's Stationery Office, 1970.

Delany, Sheila, trans., *A Legend of Holy Women: Osbern Bokeham Legends of Holy Women*, Notre Dame, University of Notre Dame Press, 1992.

D'Evelyn, Charlotte and Anna J. Mill, eds, *The South English Legendary*, Vol. I, London, EETS, 1956.

Ellis, Roger, ed., *The Liber Celestis of St Bridget of Sweden*, Vol. 1, Oxford, EETS/Oxford University Press, 1987.

Emerton, Ephraim, trans., *The Letters of Saint Boniface*, New York, Octagon Books, 1973.

Erbe, Theodor, ed., *Mirk's Festial: A Collection of Homilies by Johannes Mirkus*, London, Kegan Paul, EETS, 1905.

Excerpta Historica, or Illustrations of English History, London, Samuel Bentley, 1831.

Fowler, J. T., ed., *Extracts from the Account Rolls of the Abbey of Durham*, 3 Vols, Durham, Andrews & Co., 1899.

Furnivall, Frederick J., ed., *The Fifty Earliest English Wills in the Court of Probate, London; A.D. 1387–1439; with a Priest's of 1454*, London, Trübner & Co./Oxford, Oxford University Press, 1882/1964.

—, ed., *Political, Religious, and Love Poems*, London, K. Paul, Trench, Trübner & Co./Oxford, Oxford University Press, 1903/1965.

—, ed., *Queene Elizabethes Achademy*, London, N. Trübner & Co., 1869.

Gairdner, James, ed., *The Paston Letters*, 5 Vols, London, Chatto and Windus, 1904.

Gessler, Jean, ed., *Deux Manuels de Conversation imprimés en Angleterre au XVe siècle*, Bruxelles, Édition de la Librairie Encyclopédique, 1941.

—, *Le Livre des Mestiers* , Bruges, Le Consortium des Maîtres imprimeurs brugeois, 1931.

Jacob, Ernest F., ed., *The Register of Henry Chichele, Archbishop of Canterbury, 1414–1443*, Vol. 2, Oxford, Oxford University Press, 1937.

Jessopp, A. and M. R. James, eds, *The Life and Miracles of St William of Norwich by Thomas of Monmouth*, Cambridge, Cambridge University Press, 1896.

King, E. J., *The Rule Statutes and Customs of the Hospitallers 1099–1310*, London, Methuen, 1934.

Kingsford, Charles Lethbridge, ed., *The Stonor Letters and Papers 1290–1483*, Vols I and II, London, Offices of the [Camden] Society, 1919.

Langland, William, *Piers Plowman: An Edition of the C-Text*, Derek Pearsall, ed., Berkeley, University of California Press, 1982.

—, *The Vision of Piers Plowman (B-Text)*, A. V. C. Schmidt, ed., London, J. M. Dent, 1995.

Leadam, I. S. and J. F. Baldwin, eds, *Select Cases Before the King's Council 1243–1482*, Cambridge, The Harvard University Press, 1918.

Lemay, Helen Rodnite, *Women's Secrets: A Translation of Pseudo-Albertus Magnus's De Secretis Mulierum with Commentaries*, Albany, State University of New York Press, 1992.

Lethbridge, Charles, ed., *The Stonor Letters and Papers 1290–1483*, Vols I and II, London, Offices of the [Camden] Society, 1919.

The Library of the Palestine Pilgrims' Text Society, Vol. I, Repr. New York, AMS Press, 1971.

Loomis, Roger Sherman and Rudolph Willard, eds, *Medieval English Verse and Prose*, New York, Appleton-Century-Crofts, Inc., 1948.

Lucas, Peter J., ed., *John Capgrave's Abbreuiacion of Cronicles*, London, Oxford University Press/EETS, 1983.

Luke, Harry C., trans. and ed., *A Spanish Franciscan: Narrative of a Journey to the Holy Land*, London, Palestine Exploration Fund's Office, 1927.

Luria, Maxwell S. and Richard L. Hoffman, eds, *Middle English Lyrics*, New York, W. W. Norton & Company, 1974.

Lyte, H. C. Maxwell, *Dunster and Its Lord 1066–1881*, Exeter, William Pollard, 1882.

MacCracken, Henry N., ed., *The Minor Poems of John Lydgate*, Vol. I, Oxford, Oxford University Press, 1911/1962.

—, ed., for EETS by Oxford University Press, 1934/1961.

Magnusson, Magnus and Hermann Pálsson, trans., *The Vinland Sagas: The Norse Discovery of America*, Harmondsworth, Penguin, 1985.

Matthews, William, ed., *Later Medieval English Prose*, New York, Appleton-Century-Crofts, 1963.

McNeill, John T. and Helena M. Gamer, eds and trans., *Medieval Handbooks of Penance*, New York, Octagon Books, 1965.

Meech, Sanford Brown and Hope Emily Allen, eds, *The Book of Margery Kempe*, London, Oxford University Press/EETS, 1961.

Metcalfe, W. M., W. V. Harcourt, W. C. Bolland, eds, *Year Books of Edward II: The Eyre of Kent, 6 & 7 Edward II, 1313–1314*, London, Bernard Quaritch, 1910.

Michaud, Joseph F., *Bibliothèque des Croisades*, Vol. III, Paris, A. J. Ducollet, 1829.

Miller, Robert P., *Chaucer: Sources and Backgrounds*, New York, Oxford University Press, 1977.

Morris, Christopher, ed., *The Journeys of Celia Fiennes*, New York, Chanticleer Press, 1947.

Nichols, Francis Morgan, ed. and trans., *The Marvels of Rome: Mirabilia Urbis Romae*, New York, Italica Press, 1986.

Nicolas, Nicholas Harris, *Privy Purse Expenses of Elizabeth of York: Wardrobe Accounts of Edward the Fourth*, London, William Pickering, 1830/repr., New York, Barnes & Noble, 1972.

Oates, J. C. T. and L. C. Harmer, eds, *Vocabulary in French and English: A Facsimile of Caxton's Edition c. 1480*, Cambridge, Cambridge University Press, 1964.

Paden, William D., trans. and ed., *The Medieval Pastourelle*, Vols I and II, New York, Garland, 1987.

Panofsky, Erwin, trans. and ed., *Abbot Suger on the Abbey Church of St-Denis and its Art Treasures*, 2nd Edn, Gerda Panofsky-Soergel, ed., Princeton, Princeton University Press, 1979.

Pichon, Baron Jérôme, *Le Ménagier de Paris: Traité de morale et d'économie domestique composé vers 1393 par un bourgeois parisien*, 2 Vols, 1846 (repr., Geneva, Slatkin, 1966).

Pizan, Christine de, *A Medieval Woman's Mirror of Honor*, Charity Cannon Willard, trans., Madeleine Pelner Cosman, ed., New York, Persea Books, 1989.

Pratt, Josiah, ed., *The Acts and Monuments of John Foxe*, 4th ed., London, The Religious Tract Society, 1887.

Putnam, Bertha Haven, ed., *Proceedings Before the Justices of the Peace in the Fourteenth and Fifteenth Centuries Edward III to Richard III*, London, Spottiswoode, Ballantyne & Co Ltd, 1938.

Rickert, Edith, compiler, *Chaucer's World*, Clair C. Olson and Martin M. Crow, eds, New York, Columbia University Press, 1948.

Robertson, James Craigie, ed., *Materials for the History of Thomas Becket*, Vol. I, London, Longman & Co., 1875.

Rodney, Harley and J. B. W. Chapman, eds, *Calendar of Inquisitions Miscellaneous 1348–1377*, Vol. 3, London, His Majesty's Stationery Office, 1937.

Roulx, J. Delaville Le, *Cartulaire Général de l'ordre des Hospitalliers de S. Jean de Jérusalem (1100–1310)*, Paris, Ernest Leroux, 1894.

Ruiz, Juan, *The Book of Good Love*, Rigo Mignani and Mario A. Di Cesare, trans., Albany, State University of New York Press, 1970.

Sacchetti, Franco, *I Sermoni Evangelici: Le Lettere*, ed. O. Gigli, Florence, 1857.

Sargent, Michael G., ed., *Nicholas Love's 'Mirror of the Blessed Life of Jesus Christ'*, New York, Garland, 1992.

Sayles, G. O., ed., *Select Cases in the Court of King's Bench under Richard II, Henry IV and Henry V*, Selden Society, Vol. VII, London, Bernard Quaritch, 1971.

Serjeantson, Mary, ed., *Legendys of Hooly Wummen by Osbern Bokeham*, London, Oxford University Press/EETS, 1938.

Sinclair, K. V., ed., *The Hospitallers' Riwle*, London, Anglo-Norman Text Society, 1984.

Smith, Toulmin and Lucy Toulmin Smith, eds, *English Gilds*, London, Oxford University Press, 1924.

Stewart, Aubrey, trans., *Theoderich: Guide to the Holy Land*, New York, Italica Press, 1986.

Taylor, Richard, *Index Monasticus*, London, Richard and Arthur Taylor, 1821.

Thompson, Craig R., trans., *The Colloquies of Erasmus*, Chicago, The University of Chicago Press, 1965.

Toulmin Smith, Lucy, ed., *A Common-Place Book of the Fifteenth Century*, London, Trübner and Co., 1886.

Tremlow, J. A., ed., *Calendar of Entries in the Papal Registers Relating to Great Britain and Ireland, 1447–1455*, Hereford, The Hereford Times Ltd, 1915.

—, ed., *Calendar of Entries in the Papal Registers Relating to Great Britain and Ireland, 1455–1464*, London, His Majesty's Stationery Office, 1921.

Tremlow, J. A., ed., *Calendar of Entries in the Papal Registers Relating to Great Britain and Ireland, 1458–1471*, London, His Majesty's Stationery Office, 1933.

Van Caenegem, R. C., ed., *English Lawsuits from William I to Richard I*, Vols I and II, London, Selden Society, 1990.

Voragine, Jacobus de, *The Golden Legend: Readings on the Saints,* William Granger Ryan, trans., Vol. I, Princeton, NJ, Princeton University Press, 1993.

Ward, Jennifer C., trans. and ed., *Women of the English Nobility and Gentry 1066–1500*, Manchester, Manchester University Press, 1995.

Waterton, Edmund, *Pietas Mariana Britannica*, London, St Joseph's Catholic Library, 1879.

Wheatley, Henry B., ed., *Reliques of Ancient English Poetry*, Thomas Percy, original ed., Vol. 2, New York, Dover Publishing, 1966.

Wilkinson, John, trans. and ed., *Egeria's Travels*, London, SPCK, 1971.

Williams, Clare, trans., *Thomas Platter's Travels in England 1599*, London, Jonathan Cape, 1937.

Windeatt, B. A., trans., *The Book of Margery Kempe*, Harmondsworth, Penguin Books, 1985.

Wood, Mary Anne Everett, ed., *Letters of Royal and Illustrious Ladies of Great Britain*, 3 Vols, London, Henry Colburn, 1846.

Woolgar, C. M., *Household Accounts From Medieval Households*, Parts 1 and 2, Oxford, Oxford University Press, 1992/3.

Wright, Thomas, ed., *The Book of the Knight of La Tour-Landry*, New York, Greenwood Press, 1906 EETS/1969.

Wright, T., ed., *Letters Relating to the Suppression of the Monasteries*, London, Printed for the Camden Society by J. B. Nicholson and Son, 1843.

Secondary sources

Ady, Julia M., *Pilgrims' Way from Winchester to Canterbury*, reprint of 1893, New York, AMS Press, 1974.

Alexander, Jonathan and Paul Binski, eds, *Age of Chivalry: Art in Plantagenet England 1200–1400*, London, Weidenfeld and Nicolson, 1987.

Allen, John, 'Englishmen in Rome and the Hospice 1362–1474', *The English Hospice in Rome, The Venerabile* 21, 1962, pp. 43–81.

Artress, Lauren, *Walking a Sacred Path: Rediscovering the Labyrinth as a Spiritual Tool*, Riverhead Books, New York, 1995.

Aston, Margaret, 'Segregation in Church', in W. J. Sheils and D. Wood, eds, *Women in the Church*, Oxford, Basil Blackwell, 1990, pp. 237–294.

Atkinson, Clarissa, Constance H. Buchanan and Margaret R. Miles, eds, *Immaculate and Powerful: The Female in Sacred Image and Social Reality*, Boston, Beacon Press, 1985.

Atkinson, Clarissa, *The Oldest Vocation: Christian Motherhood in the Middle Ages*, Ithaca, Cornell University Press, 1991.

Bachelard, Gaston, *The Poetics of Space*, Maria Jolas, trans., foreword by Etienne Gilson, Boston, Beacon Press, 1964.

Badir, Patricia, 'Playing Space: History, the Body, and Records of Early English Drama', *Exemplaria* IX, 1997, pp. 255–80.

Bechtold, Joan, 'St Birgitta: The Disjunction Between Women and Ecclesiastical Male Power' in Julia B. Holloway, *et al.*, eds, *Equally in God's Image: Women in the Middle Ages*, New York, Peter Lang, 1992, pp. 88–102.

Beckwith, Sarah, *Christ's Body: Identity, Culture and Society in Late Medieval Writings*, London, Routledge, 1993.

Bellamy, John G., *Crime and Public Order in England in the Later Middle Ages*, London, Routledge & Kegan Paul, 1973.

Belloc, Hilaire, *The Old Road*, London, Archibald Constable and Company, 1904.

Bennett, George, ed., *The Kent Bibliography: A Finding List of Kent Material in the Public Libraries of the County and of the Adjouning London Boroughs*, London, Library Association, 1977.

Binns, Alison, *Dedications of Monastic Houses in England and Wales 1066–1216*, Woodbridge, Suffolk, The Boydell Press, 1989.

Boenig, Robert, *Chaucer and the Mystics: The Canterbury Tales and the Genre of Devotional Prose*, Lewisburg, Bucknell University Press, 1995.

Botfield, Beriah, *Manners and Household Expenses in the 13th and 15th Centuries*, London, William Nicol, 1841.

Bourdieu, Pierre, *Outline of a Theory of Practice*, Richard Nice, trans., Cambridge, Cambridge University Press, 1977.

Brown, Peter, *The Cult of the Saints: Its Rise and Function in Latin Christianity*, Chicago, University of Chicago Press, 1981.

—, '"Parfit Glorious Pilgrimage", Canterbury '90', *The Chaucer Newsletter* 12, 1990, pp. 1–2.

Brown, Sarah, *Stained Glass in Canterbury Cathedral*, Cathedral Gifts Ltd, 1991.

Burger, Glenn, 'Kissing the Pardoner', *Publications of the Modern Language Association* 107, 1992, pp. 1143–56.

Bynum, Carolyn Walker, *Fragmentation and Redemption: Essays on Gender and the Human Body in Medieval Religion*, New York, Zone Books, 1991.

—, *Holy Feast and Holy Fast*, Berkeley, University of California Press, 1987.

—, *Jesus as Mother: Studies in the Spirituality of the High Middle Ages*, Berkeley, University of California Press, 1982.

Camille, Michael, *Image on the Edge: The Margins of Medieval Art*, London, Reaktion Books, 1992.

—, 'Seeing and Reading: Some Visual Implications of Medieval Literacy and Illiteracy', *Art History* 8, 1985, pp. 26–49.

Campbell, James, ed., *The Anglo-Saxons*, London, Penguin Books, 1991.

Campbell, Mary B., *The Witness and the Other World: Exotic European Travel Writing, 400–1600*, Ithaca, Cornell University Press, 1988.

Casson, Lionel, *Travel in the Ancient World*, Baltimore, The Johns Hopkins University Press, 1994.

Certeau, Michel de, *The Practice of Everyday Life*, Steven F. Rendall, trans., Berkeley, University of California Press, 1984.

Charles, Alan, *Exploring the Pilgrims' Way: Winchester to Canterbury*, Newbury, Berkshire, Countryside Books, 1992.

Clay, Rotha Mary, *The Medieval Hospitals of England*, London, Frank Cass & Co, Ltd, 1966.

Crewe, Sarah, *Stained Glass in England 1180–1540*, London, Her Majesty's Stationery Office, 1987.

Joan Crow, 'A Little Known Manuscript of the *Quinze Joyes de Mariage*', *Studies in Medieval French*, E. A. Frances, ed., Oxford, Clarendon Press, 1961, pp. 121–49.

Damico, Helen and Alexandra Hennessey Olsen, eds, *New Readings on Women in Old English Literature*, Bloomington, Indiana University Press, 1990.

Davidson, Linda K. and Maryjane Dunn-Wood, *Pilgrimage in the Middle Ages: A Research Guide*, New York, Garland, 1993.

Davies, Horton and Marie-Hélène, *Holy Days and Holidays: The Medieval Pilgrimage to Compostela*, Lewisburg, Bucknell University Press, 1982.

Davis, Natalie Zemon, *Society and Culture in Early Modern France*, Stanford, Stanford University Press, 1975.

—, and Randolph Starn, 'Introduction', *Representations* 26, 1989, pp. 1–6.

Delany, Sheila, *Impolitic Bodies: Poetry, Saints, and Society in Fifteenth-Century England: The Work of Osbern Bokenham*, New York, Oxford University Press, 1998.

Deleuze, Gilles and Félix Guattari, *A Thousand Plateaus: Capitalism and Schizophrenia*, Brian Massumi, trans., Minneapolis, University of Minnesota Press, 1987.

Dickinson, J. C., *The Shrine of Our Lady of Walsingham*, Cambridge, Cambridge University Press, 1956.

Dimendberg, Edward, 'Henri Lefebvre on Abstract Space', in Andrew Light and J. M. Smith, eds, *Philosophy and Geography II: The Production of Public Space*, Lanham, MD, Rowman & Littlefield Publishers, 1998, pp. 17–47.

Dinshaw, Carolyn, *Chaucer's Sexual Poetics*, Madison, The University of Wisconsin Press, 1989.

Dobson, R. B., *The Peasants' Revolt of 1381*, London, Macmillan, 1970.

Doob, Penelope Reed, *The Idea of the Labyrinth from Classical Antiquity through the Middle Ages*, Ithaca, Cornell University Press, 1990.

Dronke, Peter, *Women Writers of the Middle Ages*, Cambridge, Cambridge University Press, 1984.

Dubisch, Jill, *In a Different Place: Pilgrimage, Gender, and Politics at a Greek Island Shrine*, Princeton, Princeton University Press, 1995.

Duby, Georges, ed., *A History of Private Life, Vol. II: Revelations of the Medieval World*, Arthur Goldhammer, trans., Cambridge, MA, Belknap Press, 1988.

Duffy, Eamon, 'Holy Maydens, Holy Wyfes: The Cult of Women Saints in Fifteenth- and Sixteenth-Century England', in W. J. Sheils and D. Wood, eds, *Women in the Church*, Oxford, Basil Blackwell, 1990, pp. 175–96.

—, *The Stripping of the Altars: Traditional Religion in England c. 1400–c. 1580*, New Haven, Yale University Press, 1992.

Dupront, Alphonse, *Du Sacré: Croisades et pèlerinages: Images et langage*, Paris, Gallimard, 1987.

During, Simon, ed., *The Cultural Studies Reader*, London, Routledge, 1993.

Eade, John and Michael J. Sallnow, *Contesting the Sacred: The Anthropology of Christian Pilgrimage*, London, Routledge, 1991.

Farmer, David Hugh, *The Oxford Dictionary of Saints*, 3rd Edn, Oxford, Oxford University Press, 1992.

Fein, Susanna Greer, David Raybin and Peter C. Braeger, eds, *Rebels and Rivals: The Contestive Spirit in The Canterbury Tales*, Kalamazoo, MI, Medieval Institute Publications, 1991.

Finucane, Ronald C., *Miracles and Pilgrims: Popular Beliefs in Medieval England*, London, Dent, 1977.

—, *The Rescue of the Innocents: Endangered Children in Medieval Miracles*, New York, St Martin's Press, 1997.

—, *Soldiers of the Faith: Crusaders and Moslems at War*, New York, St Martin's Press, 1983.

—, 'The Use and Abuse of Medieval Miracles', *History* 60, 1975, pp. 1–10.

Florival, M. de, 'Un Pèlerinage au XIIe Siècle: Marguerite de Jérusalem et Thomas de Froidmont', *Bulletin de la Société Académique de Laon* 2, 1887.

Flynn, Richard, 'The Intersection of Children's Literature and Childhood Studies', *Children's Literature Association Quarterly* 22/3, 1997, pp. 143–5.

Fowler, David C., *The Life and Times of John Trevisa, Medieval Scholar*, Seattle, University of Washington Press, 1995.

Frances, E. A., ed., *Studies in Medieval French*, Oxford, Clarendon Press, 1961.

Frank, Robert Worth, Jr., 'Pilgrimage and Sacral Power', in B. N. Sargent-Baur, ed., *Journeys Toward God: Pilgrimage and Crusade*, Kalamazoo, MI, Medieval Institute Publications, 1992, pp. 31–43.

Geary, Patrick J, *Furta Sacra: Thefts of Relics in the Central Middle Ages*, Princeton, Princeton University Press, 1978.

—, 'Sacred Commodities: The Circulation of Medieval Relics', in *The Social Life of Things, Commodities in Cultural Perspective*, Arjun Appadurai, ed., Cambridge, Cambridge University Press, 1986, pp. 169–91.

Gibson, Gail McMurray, 'St Margery: *The Book of Margery Kempe*', in Holloway, et al., eds, *Equally in God's Image: Women in the Middle Ages*, New York, Peter Lang, 1990, pp. 144–63.

—, *The Theater of Devotion: East Anglian Drama and Society in the Late Middle Ages*, Chicago, The University of Chicago Press, 1989.

Gilchrist, Roberta, *Gender and Material Culture: The Archaeology of Religious Women*, London, Routledge, 1994.

— and Marilyn Oliva, *Religious Women in Medieval East Anglia*, Norwich, Centre of East Anglian Studies, 1993.

Giuseppi, M. S., ed., *Guide to the Contents of the PRO*, Vol. I, London, Her Majesty's Stationery Office, 1963.

Glover, Terrot Reaveley, *Life and Letters in the Fourth Century*, New York, G. E. Stechert & Co., 1901/1924.

Gordon, Eleanora C., 'Accidents Among Medieval Children As Seen From the Miracles of Six English Saints and Martyrs', *Medical History* 35, 1991, pp. 145–63.

Habermas, Rebekka, 'Weibliche Erfahrungswelten: Frauen in der Welt des Wunders', in B. Lundt, ed., *Auf der Such noch der Frau im Mittlatter: Fragen, Quellen, Antworten*, München, Wilhelm Fink Verlag, 1991, pp. 65–80.

Hahn, Cynthia, 'Loca Sancta Souvenirs: Sealing the Pilgrim's Experience', in R. Ousterhout, ed., *The Blessings of Pilgrimage*, Urbana, University of Illinois Press, 1990, pp. 85–96.

—, 'Seeing and Believing: The Construction of Sanctity in Early-Medieval Saints' Shrines', *Speculum* 72, 1997, pp. 1079–106.

Hallissy, Margaret, *Clean Maids, True Wives, Steadfast Widows: Chaucer's Women and Medieval Codes of Conduct*, Westport, CT, Greenwood Press, 1993.

Harrod, Henry, 'Extracts from Early Wills in the Norwich Registries', *Norfolk Archaeology* 4, 1855, pp. 317–39.

Hart, Richard, 'The Shrines and Pilgrimages of the County of Norfolk', *Norfolk Archaeology* 6, 1864, pp. 277–94.

Harvey, David, *The Condition of Postmodernity*, Cambridge, MA, Blackwell, 1989.

Harvey, Nancy Lenz, *Elizabeth of York: The Mother of Henry VIII*, New York, Macmillan Publishing Co Inc., 1973.

Hay, George, 'Pilgrims and the Hospice', *The English Hospice in Rome*, *The Venerabile* 21, 1962, pp. 99–144.

Heffernan, Thomas, J., *Sacred Biography: Saints and Their Biographers in the Middle Ages*, Oxford, Oxford University Press, 1988.

Hell, Vera and Hellmut, *The Great Pilgrimage of the Middle Ages: The Road to St James of Compostela*, London, Barie and Rockliff, 1964/1979.

Higgins, Paul Lambourne, *Pilgrimages: A Guide to the Holy Places of Europe for Today's Traveller*, Englewood Cliffs, Prentice-Hall Inc., 1984.

Hill, D. Ingram, *The New Bell's Cathedral Guides Canterbury Cathedral*, London, Bell & Hyman Ltd, 1986.

Hilton, Rodney, *Class Conflict and the Crisis of Feudalism: Essays in Medieval Social History*, London, The Hambledon Press, 1985.

Holloway, Julia B., Constance S. Wright and Joan Bechtold, eds, *Equally in God's Image: Women in the Middle Ages*, New York, Peter Lang, 1990.

Holloway, Julia B., *Pilgrim and the Book: A Study of Dante, Langland and Chaucer*, 2nd Edn, New York, Peter Lang, 1992.

—, trans., *Saint Bride and Her Book*, Newburyport, MA, Focus Texts, 1992.

Howard, Donald R., *Writers and Pilgrims: Medieval Pilgrimage Narratives and their Posterity*, Berkeley, University of California Press, 1980.

Hudson, Anne, *The Premature Reformation: Wycliffite Texts and Lollard History*, Oxford, Clarendon Press, 1988.

'Insignes et Souvenirs de Pèlerins et Autres "Menues Choseites" de Plomb Trouvées dans la Seine', *Le Petit Journal des Grandes Expositions*, Hors-série, Musée national du Moyen Âge, Mai/Septembre 1997.

James, M. R., *Suffolk and Norfolk*, London, J. M. Dent & Sons Ltd, 1930.

James, M. R. and E. W. Tristram, *The Wall Paintings in Eton College Chapel and in the Lady Chapel of Winchester Cathedral*, Oxford, Oxford University Press, 1929.

Jonassen, Frederick B., 'The Inn, the Cathedral, and the Pilgrimage of *The Canterbury Tales*' in S. G. Fein, et al., eds, *Rebels and Rivals: The Contestive Spirit in The Canterbury Tales*, Kalamazoo, MI, Medieval Institute Publications, 1991, pp. 1–35.

Jusserand, J. J. *English Wayfaring Life in the Middle Ages (Fourteenth Century)*, Lucy Toulmin Smith, trans., 4th Edn, New York, G. P. Putnam's Sons, 1950.

Kendall, Alan, *Medieval Pilgrims*, New York, G. P. Putnam's Sons, 1970.

Kieckhefer, Richard, *Unquiet Souls: Fourteenth-Century Saints and Their Religious Milieu*, Chicago, The University of Chicago Press, 1984.

Kimmelman, Michael, 'No Substitute for the Real Thing', *The New York Times, Sunday* Arts and Leisure, February 22, 1998, p. 41.

Kleinberg, Aviad M., *Prophets in Their Own Country: Living Saints and the Making of Sainthood in the Later Middle Ages*, Chicago, The University of Chicago Press, 1992.

Köster, Kurt, *Ausgrabungen in Schleswig: Pilgerzeichen und Pilgermuscheln von Mittelalterlichen Santiagostraßen*, Neumünster, Karl Wachholtz Verlag, 1983.

Kriss-Rettenbeck, Lenz and Gerda Möhler, eds, *Wallfahrt Kennt Keine Grenzen*, Zürich, München, Verlag Schnell & Steiner, 1984.

Krötzl, Christian, 'Parent-Child Relations in Medieval Scandinavia According to Scandinavian Miracle Collections', *Scandinavian Journal of History* 14, 1989, pp. 21–37.

Labarge, Margaret Wade, *A Small Sound of the Trumpet*, Boston, Beacon Press, 1986.

Lefebvre, Henri, *The Production of Space*, Donald Nicholson-Smith, trans., Oxford, Blackwell, 1991.

Le Goff, Jacques, *Time, Work, and Culture in the Middle Ages*, Arthur Goldhammer, trans., Chicago, The University of Chicago Press, 1980.

Leon, Harry J., 'A Medieval Nun's Diary', *Classical Journal* 59, 1963, pp. 121–7.

Lewis, Bernard, ed. and trans., *Islam from the Prophet Muhammad to the Capture of Constantinople*, Vols I and II, New York, Oxford University University Press, 1987.

Leyser, Henrietta, *Medieval Women: A Social History of Women in England 450–1500*, New York, St Martin's Press, 1995.

Light, Andrew and Jonathan M. Smith, eds, *Philosophy and Geography II: The Production of Public Space*, Lanham, MD, Rowman & Littlefield Publishers, 1998.

Littlehales, Henry, ed., *Some Notes on the Road from London to Canterbury in the Middle Ages*, London, N. Trübner & Co., 1989.

Lochrie, Karma, *Margery Kempe and Translations of the Flesh*, Philadelphia, University of Pennsylvania Press, 1991.

Lundt, Bea, ed., *Auf der Suche nach der Frau im Mittelalter: Fragen, Quellen, Antworten*, München, Wilhelm Fink Verlag, 1991.

Luttrell, Anthony, 'Englishwomen as Pilgrims to Jerusalem: Isolda Parewastell, 1365' in J. B. Holloway, *et al.*, eds, *Equally in God's Image: Women in the Middle Ages*, New York, Peter Lang, 1990, pp. 184–97.

Lyte, H. C. Maxwell, *Dunster and Its Lord 1066–1881*, Exeter, William Pollard, 1882.

MacLehose, William F., 'Nurturing Danger: High Medieval Medicine and the Problem(s) of the Child', in *Medieval Mothering*, John Carmi Parsons and Bonnie Wheeler, eds, New York, Garland, 1996, pp. 3–24.

Magoun, Francis P., '*Hymselven Lik a Pilgrym to Desgise*: *Troilus* V, 1577', *Modern Language Notes* 59, 1944, pp. 176–8.

Mahoney, Dhira B., 'Margery Kempe's Tears and the Power over Language', in S. J. McEntire, ed., *Margery Kempe: A Book of Essays*, New York, Garland, 1992, pp. 37–50.

Mann, Jill, *Chaucer and Medieval Estates Satire: The Literature of Social Classes and the General Prologue to the Canterbury Tales*, Cambridge, Cambridge University Press, 1973.

Marks, Claude, *Pilgrims, Heretics and Lovers*, New York, Macmillan, 1975.

Marks, Elaine and Isabelle de Courtivron, eds, *New French Feminisms*, New York, Schocken Books, 1980.

Martin, Laurence and Sylvia, *England: An Uncommon Guide*, New York, McGraw-Hill Book Company Inc., 1963.

Mayr-Harting, H., 'Functions of a Twelfth-Century Shrine: The Miracles of St Frideswide', in H. Mayr-Harting and R. I. Moore, eds, *Studies in Medieval History Presented to R. H. C. Davis*, 1985, pp. 193–206.

McAvoy, Liz Herbert, 'Motherhood: *The Book of Margery Kempe*', *Medieval Feminist Newsletter* 24, 1997, pp. 23–26.

McCall, Andrew, *The Medieval Underworld*, London, Hamish Hamilton, 1979.

McEntire, Sandra J., ed., *Margery Kempe: A Book of Essays*, New York, Garland, 1992.

McKenney, Ruth and Richard Bransten, *Here's England*, New York, Harper & Row, 1955.

McSheffrey, Shannon, *Gender and Heresy: Women and Men in Lollard Communities 1420–1530*, Philadelphia, University of Pennsylvania Press, 1995.

Melczer, William, *The Pilgrims' Guide to Santiago de Compostela*, New York, Italica Press, 1993.

Mernissi, Fatima, 'Women, Saints, and Sanctuaries', *Signs* 3, 1977, pp. 101–12.

Metcalfe, W. M., *Pinkerton's Lives of the Scottish Saints*, 2 Vols, Paisley, Alexander Gardner, 1889.

Miles, Margaret, 'Pilgrimage as Metaphor in a Nuclear Age', *Theology Today* 45, 1988, pp. 166–79.

Mills, Patti Ann, *Spiritual Correction in the Medieval Church Courts of Canterbury*, Dissertation, University of Rochester, Ann Arbor, MI, UMI, 1980.

Moore, Henrietta L., *Space, Text and Gender: An Anthropological Study of the Marakwet of Kenya*, Cambridge, Cambridge University Press, 1986.

Morrison, Susan S., 'Introduction: Medieval Children's Literature', *Children's Literature Association Quarterly* 23, 1998, pp. 2–6.

Myers, A. R., *England in the Late Middle Ages*, Harmondsworth, Penguin, 1963.

Nichols, Stephen G., 'The Interaction of Life and Literature in the *Peregrinationes ad loca sancta* and the *chansons de geste*', *Speculum* 44, 1969, pp. 51–77.

Nora, Pierre, 'Between Memory and History: *Les Lieux de Mémoire*', Marc Roudebush, trans., *Representations* 26, 1989, pp. 7–25.

—, *Les Lieux de Mémoire*, Paris, Editions Gallimar, 1984.

Obelkevich, J., ed., *Religion and the People*, Chapel Hill, NC, University of North Carolina Press, 1979.

Ousterhout, Robert, ed., *The Blessings of Pilgrimage*, Urbana, University of Illinois Press, 1990.

Overing, Gillian R. and Marijane Osborn, *Landscape of Desire: Partial Stories of the Medieval Scandinavian World*, Minneapolis, University of Minnesota Press, 1994.

Owst, G. R., *Literature and Pulpit in Medieval England*, Oxford, Basil Blackwell, 1966.

—, *Preaching in Medieval England: An Introduction to Sermon Manuscripts of the Period c. 1350– 1450*, Cambridge, Cambridge University Press, 1926.

Parsons, John Carmi and Bonnie Wheeler, eds, *Medieval Mothering*, New York, Garland, 1996.

Patterson, Lee, *Chaucer and the Subject of History*, Madison, The University of Wisconsin Press, 1991.

— ed., *Literary Practice and Social Change in Britain, 1380–1530*, Berkeley, University of California Press, 1990.

Pope, Barbara Corrado, 'Immaculate and Powerful, The Marian Revival in the Nineteenth Century', in C. Atkinson, et al., eds, *Immaculate and Powerful: The Female in Sacred Image and Social Reality*, Boston, Beacon Press, 1985, pp. 173–200.

Power, Eileen, trans., *The Goodman of Paris*, London, Routledge, 1928.

— and M. M. Postan, ed., *Medieval Women*, Cambridge, Cambridge University Press, 1975.

Raff, Thomas, ed., *Wallfahrt Kennt Keine Grenzen (Katalog der Ausstellung im Bayerischen Nationalmuseum, München, 1984)*, München, C. Wolf & Sohn, 1984.

Renaud, J. G. N., ed., *Rotterdam Papers: A Contribution to Medieval Archaeology*, Rotterdam, W. Stempher and Zoon C. V. Deventer, 1968.

Rosenwein, Barbara H., *Negotiating Space: Power, Restraint, and Privileges of Immunity in Early Medieval Europe*, Ithaca, Cornell University Press, 1999.

Ross, Ellen, 'Diversities of Divine Presence: Women's Geography in the Christian Tradition', in J. Scott and P. Simpson-Housley, eds, *Sacred Places and Profane Spaces: Essays in the Geographies of Judaism, Christianity, and Islam*, New York, Greenwood Press, 1991, pp. 93–114.

Rossiaud, Jacques, *Medieval Prostitution*, Lydia G. Cochrane, trans., Oxford, Basil Blackwell, 1988.

Rothkrug, Lionel, *Religious Practices and Collective Perceptions: Hidden Homologies in the Renaissance and Reformation*, Waterloo, Ont., Dept. of History, University of Waterloo, 1980.

Sargent, Michael G., ed., *Nicholas Love's 'Mirror of the Blessed Life of Jesus Christ'*, New York, Garland, 1992.

Sargent-Baur, Barbara N., ed., *Journeys Toward God: Pilgrimage and Crusade*, Kalamazoo, MI, Medieval Institute Publications, 1992.

Scott, Jamie and Paul Simpson-Housley, eds, *Sacred Places and Profane Spaces: Essays in the Geographies of Judaism, Christianity, and Islam*, New York, Greenwood Press, 1991.

Sered, Susan Starr, 'Rachel's Tomb and the Milk Grotto of the Virgin Mary: Two Women's Shrines in Bethlehem', *Journal of Feminist Studies in Religion* 2, 1986, pp. 7–22.

Shahar, Shulamith, *Childhood in the Middle Ages*, Chaya Galai, trans., Routledge, London, 1990.

Sheils, W. J. and Diana Wood, eds, *Women in the Church*, Oxford, Basil Blackwell, 1990.

Sigal, Pierre-André, 'La grossesse, l'accouchement et l'attitude envers l'enfant mort-né à la fin du moyen âge d'après les récits de miracles', in *Santé, médicine et assistance au moyen-age: 110e Congrès national des Sociétés savantes, Montpellier, 1985*, Paris, 1987, pp. 23–41.

Simek, Rudolf, Jónas Kristjánsson and Hans Bekker-Nielsen, eds, *Sagnaskemmtun: Studies in Honour of Hermann Pálsson*, Wien, Hermann Böhlaus Nachf, 1986.

Simons, Eric N., *Henry VII: The First Tudor King*, New York, Barnes & Noble Inc., 1968.

Sivan, Hagith, 'Holy Land Pilgrimage and Western Audiences: Some Reflections on Egeria and Her Circle', *Classical Quarterly* 38, 1988, pp. 528–35.

—, 'Who Was Egeria? Piety and Pilgrimage in the Age of Gratian', *Harvard Theological Review* 81.1, 1988, pp. 59–72.

Smith, Neil, 'Antinomies of Space and Nature', in A. Light and J. M. Smith, eds, *Philosophy and Geography II: The Production of Public Space*, Lanham, MD, Rowman & Littlefield Publishers, 1998, pp. 49–69.

Soergel, Philip M., Review of Eamon Duffy's *The Stripping of the Altars*, *Speculum* 69, 1994, pp. 766–8.

Soja, Edward, 'History, Geography, Modernity', in S. During, ed., *The Cultural Studies Reader*, London, Routledge, 1993, pp. 135–50.

Spain, Daphne, *Gendered Spaces*, Chapel Hill, The University of North Carolina Press, 1992.

Speed, Peter, ed., *Those Who Prayed: An Anthology of Medieval Sources*, New York, Italica Press, 1997. ·

Spitzer, Leo, 'The Epic Style of the Pilgrim Aetheria', *Comparative Literature* 1, 1949, pp. 225–58.

Staley, Lynn, *Margery Kempe's Dissenting Fictions*, University Park, PA, The Pennsylvania State University Press, 1994.

Stallybrass, Peter and Allon White, *The Politics and Poetics of Transgression*, Ithaca, Cornell University Press, 1986.

Stenton, F. M., 'The Road System of Medieval England', *The Economic History Review*, VII, 1936, pp. 1–21.

Storrs, Constance Mary, *Jacobean Pilgrims From England to St. James of Compostella From the Early Twelfth to the Late Fifteenth Century*, Santiago de Compostela, Xunta de Galicia, 1994.

Strohm, Paul, *Social Chaucer*, Cambridge, Harvard University Press, 1989.

Sumption, Jonathan, *Pilgrimage: An Image of Mediaeval Religion*, Totowa, NJ, Rowman and Littlefield, 1975.

Swanson, R. N., *Religion and Devotion in Europe, c. 1215– c. 1515*, Cambridge, Cambridge University Press, 1995.

Talbot, C. H., ed. and trans., *The Anglo-Saxon Missionaries in Germany*, London, Sheed and Ward, 1954.

Tanner, Norman P., *The Church in Late Medieval Norwich*, Toronto, Pontifical Institute of Medieval Studies, 1984.

—, ed., *Heresy Trials in the Diocese of Norwich, 1428–31*, London, Butler & Tanner Ltd, 1977.

Tavormina, M. Teresa, *Kindly Similitude: Marriage and Family in Piers Plowman*, Cambridge, D. S. Brewer, 1995.

Taylor, G. R. Stirling, *The Story of Canterbury*, London, J. M. Dent & Sons, Ltd, 1912.

Temperley, Gladys, *Henry VII*, Westport, CT, Greenwood Press, 1914/1971 repr.

Tétreault, Mary Ann, 'Formal Politics, Meta-Space, and Construction of Civil Life', in A. Light and J. M. Smith, eds, *Philosophy and Geography II: The Production of Public Space*, Lanham, MD, Rowman & Littlefield Publishers, 1988, pp. 81–97.

Toy, John, ed., *A Guide and Index to the Windows of York Minster*, York, Dean & Chapter of York, 1985.

Trinkaus, Charles and Heiko A. Oberman, eds, *The Pursuit of Holiness in Late Medieval and Renaissance Religion*, Studies in Medieval and Reformation Thought, No. 10, Leiden, E. J. Brill, 1974.

Tuan, Yi-Fu, *Space and Place: The Perspective of Experience*, Minneapolis, MN, University of Minnesota Press, 1977.

—, *Topophilia: A Study of Environmental Perception, Attitudes, and Values*, Englewood Cliffs, NJ, Prentice-Hall, 1974.

Turner, Victor and Edith Turner, *Image and Pilgrimage in Christian Culture*, Oxford, Basil Blackwell, 1978.

Uitz, Erika, *Die Frau in der Mittelalterlichen Stadt*, Leipzig, Edition Leipzig, 1988.

Vallance, Aymer, *Greater English Church Screens*, London, B. T. Batsford, 1947.

Vauchez, André, *Sainthood in the Later Middle Ages*, Jean Birrell, trans., Cambridge, Cambridge University Press, 1997.

Vikan, Gary, 'Pilgrims in Magi's Clothing: The Impact of Mimesis on Early Byzantine Pilgrimage Art', in R. Ousterhout, ed., *The Blessings of Pilgrimage*, Urbana, University of Illinois Press, 1990, pp. 97–107.

Virgoe, Roger, ed., *Private Life in the Fifteenth Century: Illustrated Letters of the Paston Family*, New York, Weidenfeld & Nicolson, 1989.

Wallace, David, 'Pilgrim Signs and the Ellesmere Chaucer', *The Chaucer Newsletter* 11, 1989, pp. 1–3.

Ward, Jennifer C., *English Noblewomen in the Later Middle Ages*, London, Longman, 1992.

Warner, Marina, *Alone of All Her Sex: The Myth and Cult of the Virgin Mary*, New York, Alfred A. Knopf, 1976.

Watt, Francis, *Canterbury Pilgrims and Their Ways*, New York, Dodd, Mead and Co., 1917.

Weber, Clifford, 'Egeria's Norman Homeland', *Harvard Studies in Classical Philology* 92, 1989, pp. 437–56.

Whatmore, Leonard E., *Highway to Walsingham*, Walsingham, The Pilgrim Bureau, 1973.

Whiting, B. J., 'Troilus and Pilgrims in Wartime', *Modern Language Notes* 60, 1945, pp. 47–9.

Wiesner-Hanks, Merry and Melissa J. Martens, compilers, *Early Women's Literature: A Provisional Check List of Works in the Newberry Library Written By or About Women and Published Before 1700*, Chicago, The Newberry Library, 1993.

Wilkinson, John, Joyce Hill and W. F. Ryan, *Jerusalem Pilgrimage 1099–1185*, London, The Hakluyt Society, 1988.

Williamson, W. W., 'Saints on Norfolk Rood-Screens and Pulpits', *Norfolk Archaeology* 31, 1955–7, pp. 299–346.

Wilson, Katharina M., ed., *Medieval Women Writers*, Athens, GA, The University of Georgia Press, 1984.

— and Elizabeth M. Makowski, *Wykked Wyves and the Woes of Marriage: Misogamous Literature from Juvenal to Chaucer*, Albany, State University of New York Press, 1990.

Wright, Christopher John, *A Guide to the Pilgrims' Way and North Downs*, London, Constable & Co. Ltd, 1977.

Wunderli, Peter, ed., *Reisen in reale und mythische Ferne: Reiseliteratur in Mittelalter und Renaissance*, Düsseldorf, Droste, 1993.

Zacher, Christian K., *Curiosity and Pilgrimage: The Literature of Discovery in Fourteenth-Century England*, Baltimore, The Johns Hopkins University Press, 1976.

Zika, Charles, 'Hosts, Processions and Pilgrimages: Controlling the Sacred in Fifteenth-Century Germany', *Past and Present* 118, 1988, pp. 25–64.

Index